"*Born on the Edge of Race and Gender* is far more than the traditional transgender memoir, as it places Willy Wilkinson's stories of childhood gender nonconformity and adulthood transition within the context of intersecting identities, and his several decades-long commitment to public health and policy advocacy for transgender communities. Smart, illuminating, passionate, and often humorous, it is a wonderful read for anyone interested in transgender activism, intersectionality, and social justice more generally."

—**JULIA SERANO**, author of *Whipping Girl: A Transsexual Woman on Sexism and the Scapegoating of Femininity*, and *Excluded: Making Feminist and Queer Movements More Inclusive*

"Willy Wilkinson's *Born on the Edge of Race and Gender* is an important addition to the ever-growing body of trans narratives in American literature. Willy's nakedly honest stories about resilience, disability, racism, parenting, surgical complications, and more provide a refreshingly intersectional and nuanced perspective on life as a full, complex transgender person."

—**MASEN DAVIS**, Codirector of Global Action for Trans Equality

"It's incredibly useful—even life-changing—whenever an experienced community health worker like Willy Wilkinson records the years of on-the-ground knowledge they've developed. It's even more so when it comes to communities, like trans people and people of color, whose health disparities remain underexplored, particularly by workers who are of the people. But it's truly a gift when that person also has the soul of a creative writer, as Wilkinson does. His professional expertise on the individual tolls of intersecting oppressions is deep, making *Born on the Edge of Race and Gender* useful to other health workers and future medical historians. However, the book's even more enduring impact comes from a balancing of this informative impulse with a willingness to relate how transphobia, homophobia, and racism play out in his own life and across his own body in deft, emotional recollections that lead readers to more intimately grasp the urgency of the trans-inclusive health care reform he calls for. This is how change is made."

—**MITCH KELLAWAY**, Advocate.com reporter and coeditor of *Manning Up: Transsexual Men on Finding Brotherhood, Family & Themselves*

BORN
ON
THE
EDGE
OF
RACE
AND
GENDER

Published 2015
Printed in the United States of America
ISBN: 978-0-9970123-0-9
E-ISBN: 978-0-9970123-1-6
Library of Congress Control Number: 2015956879

Cover and interior design by Tabitha Lahr

Hapa Papa Press
PO Box 27401, Oakland, CA 94602
www.willywilkinson.com

The author has changed some names, places, and recognizable details to protect the privacy of individuals mentioned in the book.

An earlier version of "Freedom to Love: Where Same-Sex and Interracial Marriage Convene" (in the chapter entitled "Winter of Love") appeared in the *San Francisco Chronicle* on March 5, 2004, and March 12, 2004. Reprinted with permission.

An earlier version of "Reveling in Our Authenticity" appeared in *Trans Bodies, Trans Selves*, Laura Erickson-Schroth, editor. Oxford University Press, 2014. Reprinted with permission.

An earlier version of "Sculptor" appeared in *Manning Up: Transsexual Men on Finding Brotherhood, Family & Themselves*, Zander Keig and Mitch Kellaway, editors. Transgress Press, 2014. Reprinted with permission.

"Scorched" first appeared in *The Very Inside: An Anthology of Writing by Asian and Pacific Islander Lesbian and Bisexual Women*, Sharon Lim-Hing, editor. Sister Vision Press, 1994.

"So Far" and "Turn of the Head" were performed in the film *Against a Trans Narrative*, Jules Rosskam, director, 2008.

BORN ON THE EDGE OF RACE AND GENDER

A VOICE FOR CULTURAL COMPETENCY

WILLY WILKINSON

HPP

Hapa Papa Press

CONTENTS

PART 3: ROUGH AROUND THE EDGES

PART 4: EXPANDING THE EDGES

PART 5: SCULPTING THE EDGES

PART 6: THE EDGE OF LIBERATION

PART 7: THE CUTTING EDGE

FOREWORD

Born on the Edge of Race and Gender is an extraordinary work by one of the most fearless and dynamic voices of our time—a multilayered masterpiece that may well be the most accessible, lively, and honest account yet of life as a transgender man. For those who have encountered Willy Wilkinson's hauntingly complex and personal explorations of race and gender before, whether in print or through spoken word, this book will not disappoint. For those meeting him for the first time, prepare to be dazzled, shaken, and amazed. This is not only a major contribution to the literature on transgender and intersectional advocacy but a powerful—and liberating—work of art.

This book is also an important corrective to the erasure of transgender people of color from many histories of the trans movement. Wilkinson gives voice to an important narrative that is not often heard—that of transgender and gender-nonconforming people of color who have played major roles in our history and movement, but whose lives and stories have been relegated to the margins.

After years of living in the shadows of the gay rights movement, the transgender movement is coming into its own and gaining unprecedented visibility and momentum. Wilkinson is uniquely well positioned to illuminate this moment, and he does so with compelling originality by using the power of storytelling to highlight many of our movement's most pressing—and often controversial—issues. Other transgender authors have shared their personal stories, and books such as *Transgender Rights* have explored the legal and political history of the transgender movement, but none has melded and transformed these two genres as Wilkinson does here, drawing on more than five decades of personal experience to contextualize the legislative and policy battles of our day.

The range of issues Wilkinson covers is impressive: the importance of bathroom and locker-room access for trans people; creating LGBTQ-affirming schools and supporting the children of trans parents; health care for trans people, including detailed information on the challenges of accessing transition-related care through Medicare and the medical, social, and psychological realities of phalloplasty; civil rights legislation based on sexual orientation and gender identity; mental health issues and suicide; hate crimes and murder; the ways in which transgender men of color are profiled and targeted; the importance of using appropriate names and pronouns; ambiguity and the complexity of not fitting neatly into categories or community membership rules; the intersections between mixed heritage, disability, and transgender experience; and the importance of family acceptance for LGBTQ youth and adults.

Far more than just a memoir, this book is also a treasure trove of intersectional research, wisdom, and practical knowledge, distilled by one of the nation's foremost experts on public health and other issues affecting transgender people, and one of the most experienced, hands-on cultural competency trainers in our movement. In every chapter, as Wilkinson shares his own stories and life experience, he also explores the most up-to-date research and best practices on particular topics, drawn from a vast array of sources and practical knowledge and seamlessly integrated into his compelling personal narratives.

For example, Wilkinson juxtaposes his struggles as a gender-nonconforming child growing up in California in the 1960s and '70s, when public awareness of transgender people was virtually nil, with the recent emergence of groundbreaking new laws protecting transgender youth. Enacted in 2013, AB 1266, California's School Success and Opportunity Act, is the first state law that expressly empowers transgender students to use restrooms and locker rooms, and to play on sports teams, that match their gender identity. Wilkinson traces a direct line between the constant harassment and ridicule he faced at school as a child and the sea change these new policies represent—and that his own advocacy helped to bring about. Today, AB 1266 and many similar local policies across the country are requiring schools not only to protect transgender youth but to treat them with respect.

In response, many of the same conservative groups that previously targeted lesbians and gay men are now setting their sights on transgender people. Across the country, bathrooms have become a new fault line in the struggle to win basic equality for transgender people. By demonizing transgender people as dangerous predators who threaten the safety and privacy of others, these groups are actively campaigning to repeal anti-discrimination protections or even to make it a crime for a transgender person to use a public restroom or sex-segregated facility.

Wilkinson brings humanity—and truth—to this issue. Far from posing a threat to other people, he shows that transgender people experience enormous vulnerability in sex-segregated spaces and seek only to keep their own privacy and dignity intact. For example, in describing his daily struggles to protect his own privacy in a men's locker room, Wilkinson perfectly—and hilariously—captures the anxiety of many nonsurgical transgender men in such spaces: "like a stealth trans Houdini positioned an arm's length from danger, I get my junk-packed underwear and swim trunks on and off in a blink, carefully covering myself with a casually placed towel and pretending I'm not stressed every time." These stories validate transgender men and humanize our fears, making us feel less freakish and alone, while helping others understand our vulnerabilities and see through attempts to portray us as monstrous villains.

Wilkinson's experiences of living on the boundaries of race and gender also shed new light on partnering and parenting—and on the complexity of family law issues for transgender people. Like many other transgender men of his generation, Wilkinson identified as a lesbian before coming out as transgender. Unlike many others, he chose not to medically transition or to identify within a gender binary for many years. He writes powerfully about his joy at being able to marry his wife in 2004, when San Francisco Mayor Gavin Newsom began issuing marriage licenses to same-sex couples—as well as his ambivalence about being misrepresented in news stories at the time as a "lesbian." As the child of interracial parents who were able to marry only after the California Supreme Court struck down the state's law barring interracial marriage in 1948, Wilkinson also offers an important counterpoint to those who have dismissed the marriage equality movement as irrelevant to transgender people. His analysis of the ways in which marriage equality has benefited the transgender movement and paved the way for greater trans visibility is refreshingly original and makes a significant contribution to that debate.

Similarly, not since Jamison Green's *Becoming a Visible Man* has anyone written so compellingly about how social and legal contexts affect our families and the experience of being a transgender parent. Wilkinson's descriptions of his children, snuggling their transgender stuffed animals and growing up without a shred of insecurity about the legal stability of their family, speak volumes about how much has changed even in the decade since Green wrote about his devastating lack of legal protections as a nonbiological transgender father. Today, as Wilkinson powerfully shows, it is possible for children to grow up not only with a secure legal relationship to their transgender parent but with social acceptance as well, in an atmosphere of openness toward and even celebration of diverse families. While that possibility is still only a dream in many places, Wilkinson's portrayal of his family's reality is revolutionary and helps us see the future we must all work to create.

Wilkinson also breaks new ground in his relentless honesty about his experiences—both good and bad—of medically transitioning and undergoing genital reconstructive surgery. As is true throughout the book, Wilkinson's experience tracks significant developments in transgender law. He is able to access medical treatment and surgery only because of long-sought breakthroughs in health care law, including the enactment in the last few years of the first-ever state laws barring discrimination against transgender people in private health insurance plans, the first-ever litigation successfully challenging the exclusion of sex-reassignment surgeries under Medicare in 2014, and the inclusion of antidiscrimination protections for transgender people in the Affordable Care Act regulations in 2015. Wilkinson brilliantly shows both the profound personal impact and the current limitations of these advances. Even as these new legal protections enable him to obtain lifesaving care that would have been completely out of reach in the past, he still must struggle with remaining aspects of discrimination, particularly in the Medicare system, that continue to leave transgender patients at serious medical and financial risk.

Personally, Wilkinson shares his exhilaration at medically transitioning and the profound impact, in particular, of obtaining a phalloplasty. He is brutally honest about the physical pain and serious medical complications this surgery has caused, as well as about the positive and sometimes unexpected ways in which it has transformed his sense of himself and his place in the world. In particular, Wilkinson's description of how phalloplasty affected his marriage is among the book's most enlightening and empowering moments.

This is an intensely open and generous book—one that bravely shines a light on experiences that are far too rarely, and in some cases almost never, discussed. It is also a book of great moral clarity and inspiration. The challenges transgender people face are urgent and require enormous education and resources. And yet, too often, our attempts to enlist greater understanding and support fail because we are too angry, too dogmatic, or simply too hurt to communicate effectively. In contrast, the voice that emerges from these pages is mature, patient, humble, kind—yet always clear about the terrible harms caused by discrimination and unexamined privilege, and about the need for greater accountability. Like that of every true artist and leader, Wilkinson's work is ultimately a provocation to our own integrity and passion for justice and change. By the power of his own example, he calls on us to resist the temptation of single-lens approaches and to recognize the intersecting complexities of our heritages, identities, bodies, and lives. At this critical time in the transgender and larger social justice movements, when so much progress seems possible, we especially need Wilkinson's voice—its optimism about our ability to reach and understand one another, and its call for us to claim our power and resilience.

—Shannon Price Minter, Esq.
   Coeditor, *Transgender Rights*
   President Obama's Commission on White House Fellowships

GETTING THERE

GETTING THERE

In August 1988, on the heels of the summer Olympics and the Tour de France, I saddled up my deep-red, eighteen-speed bicycle, stretched my legs, and rode from Boston to San Francisco. I longed for the soul-stirring stillness of wide-open spaces and the bristling fire and pure joy of adventure. I needed a good ride.

I found little tree-canopied back roads, and cows that startled and ran from me as I rode by. I tasted the full-bellied satisfaction of a hearty camp-stove meal following a daylong grind. I flew down mountains at forty miles per hour in thirty-degree weather with a swift, cool breeze on my cheeks and ice running through my core.

It wasn't about the number of miles, or the number of days, or the enormous quantities of food I consumed. It wasn't about the number of fixed flat tires, bad directions given by the car-driving public, or ignorant comments from random men trying to pretend they knew something about bicycles. It wasn't about my trusty steed.

It was the good old-fashioned folks who took my biking buddy Checka and me in and fed us. It was fresh-grown, roadside corn, sold through the honor system. It was sleeping wherever we could get away with it. It was the realization that this country, the United States, is bigger than I ever imagined and that my perspective was narrowly bicoastal.

Most of all, it was the grueling, triumphant ascents. It was sinewy thigh muscle mixed with a lifetime of determination. It was booking up steep mountain grades, not just for the fleeting downhill speed run but for the love of the climb.

Checka had called me out of the blue six months earlier, from Boston. "I've always had a dream of riding across the country," she began. "You want to do it?" I was a sucker for adventure. At home in San Francisco, I said yes immediately, without hesitation. For the next six months I trained, gathered my gear, and ate a tiny lunch every day so I could save a few bucks from my meager earnings.

I flew to Boston, and we began our ambitious expedition. The first few days we were sore, grateful for rain on day three so we could take a day off to rest our painful legs. But after a week on the bike, we were comfortable riding eighty miles a day. In the beginning we played it safe, sleeping at hostels and campsites. But as time went on and money thinned out, we found ways to get free lodging at churches; in barns, backyards, and living rooms; in open fields and behind buildings. Though there were times when we were treated with great suspicion, most of the time our light-skin privilege and Checka's finesse with deeply religious Christians helped us get what we needed.

"I can't imagine that you'd have husbands who would let you do this," one pinched church lady said with a Southern drawl. Like many others, she wanted to know what we, as two women, were doing "alone" on the road. Checka responded, "We're not alone. We're with each other."

Checka was a big, strong, tawny-skinned dyke[1] whose indigenous roots became more pronounced the farther we rode into the sun. With her long, muscular legs, she left me in the dust on the rolling hills but struggled with the uphill climbs. As I sucked down a pint of chocolate milk at the summit, she'd arrive breathless, saying, "I just want to *be there* already." True, there was nothing like being where we were meant to be that night, spreading out our gear at a makeshift campsite in a starry field or abandoned barn.

But somehow, the sweet rewards of nightfall in a warm sleeping bag never diminished my love for the getting there, the process.

And like that epic bicycle ride across the United States so long ago, this book is about the ascents and descents, the times I got lost, and the people who fed me along the way. At its heart, it's a story of one mixed

Asian American transgender life, where ambiguity and complexity are a given and finding one's voice is a triumphant rewrite of old scars. At the same time, it's a reflection on dirt roads built where none existed and those we are now paving together.

Whether we're taking steps to live authentically or finding acceptance of ourselves and others, developing cultural competency or changing systems and institutions, it's a journey. Whatever the process, it doesn't usually happen quickly and can't be forced. But therein lies the wisdom.

Because, really, it's all about the getting there.

YOU KNOW WHAT TIME IT IS

"*Condones, condones,*" I announced, as I strode the pungent, piss-stained streets of San Francisco's Tenderloin district. "*Quién quiere condones?*" I asked the Central American dudes selling weed. "*Calientes del horno!*" I offered, in a singsong Mexican accent, which brought a smile to their weathered faces. Condoms, fresh from the oven.

It was 1988, not long after I returned to San Francisco by bicycle from Boston, my thick thigh muscles busting through my jeans. The HIV/AIDS epidemic was raging, and I was distributing bleach and condoms on the streets of the TL, talking about HIV prevention with dope fiends, sex workers, homeless folks, and everybody else who was out there. People were hustling, tweaking, hitting bottom. I listened to them talk about their lives and helped them get connected to services.

My attitude was not one of looking down on them, nor was it based on shared experience, exactly, but I had struggled enough on the edge of survival to know about pain. Not that my pain was the same pain as that of the straight, middle-aged African American dude nodding on a park bench, or the Puerto Rican sister getting the shit beaten out of her by her old man, or the Vietnamese immigrant massage-parlor worker desperate for English skills and a man to help her out of that trap.

But I discovered that it didn't really matter. On the street, people didn't categorize or place value on others demographically the way I had experienced in other communities. If you were genuine and came from the heart, that's what mattered. I was asking them to find inspiration to stay alive in the midst of slow death. Sneak the condom on the trick.

Make the effort to use bleach, even if you don't have a reason. And in the midst of a suicide mission, who does?

So I gave them a reason. I didn't follow anybody into the back alleys or wherever they did their business. I just gave them the tools. A one-ounce bottle of bleach to clean their rig. Lubricated or Kiss of Mint condoms. *Freshen your breath at the same time, honey.* I didn't care what they did, as long as they played it safe. When they couldn't find a reason, like their children, or their lover, or their mother, or the simple joy of living, I gave them one. *Do it for me, babe. Stay alive, friend. I need you here.*

My work as a community health outreach worker was about being neighborly, offering nonjudgmental information and resources. Chit-chatting with the Caucasian trans woman who had been working the street since early morning, chasing a habit. Hanging out at the bar that Asian trans women sex workers frequented at night, many after presenting as male during the day. Connecting with the African American guy who'd posture his sexual prowess around his friends, then get me alone to ask his burning questions about HIV transmission.

But it was also about touching souls, stopping the spin for a minute and asking folks to imagine something beyond the mix. *The pulse of the street deafens while yours quickens to the chase. In the quiet of your soul lies a place that wants to stay alive. Don't think for a minute that this shit ain't real.*

You know what time it is.

My colleagues and I often used that phrase on the street to emphasize that it was time, of course, to get with the program, take steps to prevent HIV infection. But the phrase has also been used in reference to transgender people getting "clocked," read as trans. Sometimes the phrase has a neutral connotation, a matter-of-fact tone. Yet cisgender (nontransgender) people and even other transgender people have used it with a certain bravado, congratulating themselves for their ability to unlock the mystery, solve the puzzle, and unveil or gloat about a trans person's "true" birth sex. The phrase rewards a correct assessment, while those who don't perceive a person's trans status are often denigrated or shamed for being less astute. Sometimes the phrase is used to gossip about the revelation: *You know what time it is,* conferred with pointing fingers and a knowing raised eyebrow.

Time can be a complicated thing for many trans people. Many of us have people from our pasts who resist or have difficulty updating our names, pronouns, and gendered expressions. Some may perceive us as dismissing, ignoring, or erasing the past, whether or not that's true for us. And a lot of us *do* want to bury our past and move on. *It was hard enough to get here and be seen for who I am. Why look back?*

In 2015, I'm the microdude you might side-eye in the grocery store checkout line with five gallons of milk, leaning in to inquire, "Are they on sale?" I have three car seats and a potty chair in the back of my vehicle. I spend my time raising my kids, in coordination with Georgia, the woman I've created family with over the past twenty years. I help my nine-year-old with his math homework, play catch with my six-year-old daughter, and teach my three-year-old son the importance of *not* throwing poop in the bathtub, especially when someone's in it. I want to be witnessed in present tense, to be referred to with male pronouns and terms, as the man I am now. But everything I am today is profoundly shaped by my past—five decades navigating a racially nonconforming, gender-transgressive, disabled body, sculpted by the legacy of Asian female subjugation, transphobia, homophobia, and racism that has impacted my life since the womb.

I am called upon to tell my story. *You know what time it is.*

*   *   *

In April 2014, I had the opportunity to attend the Transgender Leadership Summit in Southern California, sponsored by Transgender Law Center. At the opening plenary, then-executive director Masen Davis asked people who had been "doing this work" for more than ten years to stand up and say how long it had been. My rock-star sister Cecilia Chung said twenty-one years. Then Masen turned to me. "Willy?" I hesitated, as I wondered what he meant by "this work." Did he mean work with the transgender community? I thought back to my work with trans sex workers in 1988, so I said twenty-six years. Then I thought about how I started organizing Asian lesbians in 1983, and how some of us were trans and gender nonconforming then but just didn't have the language for it.

That would be thirty-one years. Apparently I'm an old-ass mofo *and* an Asian who can't do the math. Later, someone asked me how long it had been, said I hardly looked old enough, and I responded, "Well, thank you. I'm clinging desperately to my youth."

I have had access to an antiaging formula that few men would try: estrogen. *You know what time it is.*

*   *   *

My people on my mother's side journeyed by boat from famine-stricken China to a small apartment directly above the heat of a restaurant kitchen in rural Hawaii. My father's family traveled by Mormon caravan to Utah, then to the dirt-poor, Depression-era hills of Oakland, where carefully pinched coins paid the milkman.

I was born in the early '60s in a San Francisco suburb, the fourth child of a Chinese mother and a Caucasian father. I was assigned female at birth, though I knew from before I could speak that I was male. When I changed my name to Willy at age nine, in the early '70s, there was no public awareness of transgender issues, no educational resources for my family and community, and no systemic support in my Bay Area public school. Harassed by my peers for being Chinese and silenced by my family for my racially ambiguous appearance, gender nonconformity, and femaleness, I knew early on that I was on my own.

When I turned eighteen, it was not an option to come out as trans. In the early '80s, there was no visible transgender community, and the existence of female-to-male transgender individuals was not acknowledged in any arena. Though I had never seen myself as female, I found resonance with the lesbian community—fierce women who defied gender expectations and pushed the boundaries of social constraints. I realized that I had to be female in order to be a lesbian. So I came out first as a woman, then as a lesbian, and then as a lesbian of color. I embraced a community that celebrated the lives and concerns of women at a time when women were struggling to get respect.

I wanted to know lesbians who might understand my cultural framework, so I organized Asian lesbians for self-reflection, visibility, and empowerment. I was energized by the bold ideas, righteous anger, and articulation of the lesbian of color movement of the '80s, though my racially mixed appearance and male name led some people to question my membership in the community. I found other mixed people who had also experienced unwelcome exclusion because of their racially layered features.

I was terrified to speak, but I wasn't afraid to write. I addressed racism in the lesbian community, homophobia in the Asian community, and difficulty reconciling a lesbian identity with the cultural expectations of our families and communities, and the stereotypes that larger society perpetuated. I wrote about the politics of Asian lesbianism in a world that prescribed that we be quietly accommodating or embody a submissive, exotic erotica fantasy. I explored the challenges of individual and collective empowerment while working through years of oppressive societal and cultural messages. As coeditor of *Phoenix Rising*,[2] the Asian and Pacific Islander (API) lesbian newsletter, I invited the perspectives of a broad range of API ethnicities and identities. I asked my community to confront its own prejudices and rules of membership.

And then shit hit me over the head. A large light fixture fell on me in a restroom and gave me a concussion, which knocked me down and put me in bed with what I came to understand as a disabling chronic illness. I was sick for days that became weeks that became months that became years that became decades. I lived in the underbelly of invisible disability, appearing healthy but bone skinny and grasping for mental clarity. I navigated the unwelcoming system of public benefits, got treated like crap by the various entities that policed me, and was perpetually broke-ass, always looking for the next opportunity to hustle a buck. I wanted nothing more than to enlighten, beautify, and change the world, but my self-esteem was stuck on the bottom of some Medi-Cal worker's shoe.

When the transgender movement exploded in the mid-'90s in San Francisco, I came out again, this time as transgender. Strongly identified with women but internally driven by maleness, I identified as third gender and felt that my gender was inextricably linked to my mixed heritage. The community was culturally very different from the lesbian of color community that had been my home for so many years. But what the trans movement lacked in soulful music and home-cooked food, it made up for in the way it ignited my senses and stirred my discomfort with in-

equality. Little by little, I went against the silencing of my cultural training. I began to speak up, articulate, and advocate for the rights of trans
people to be treated as full human beings. I organized the first support
groups for API transmasculine folks, and people of color on the female-
to-male spectrum. I started the first HIV prevention program for trans
men who have sex with other men and participated in groundbreaking
trans research.[3] In 2004, I launched the Health Care Access Project at
Transgender Law Center, the first program in the nation to provide transgender cultural competency training for health providers, educate community members about their rights in health care settings, and advocate
for comprehensive access to care.

In the late '90s, when I began conducting cultural competency trainings for community health providers on the range of lesbian, gay, bisexual,
transgender, and queer (LGBTQ) issues, there was very little understanding about transgender people. As I educated medical, mental health, and
substance use disorder providers about complex gender identity, long before the concept of the binary gender system or nonbinary gender identities came into use, people looked at me quizzically as they tried to wrap
their minds around a broad spectrum of possibilities.

Today, many people are still confused about nonbinary gender expressions, but we have come such a long way in the discussion of gender
identity. Minds are expanding to embrace complex life experience and
demographics. Intersectional identities are recognized and celebrated.
My race, too, is nonbinary. My health status, my class experience—all
nonbinary. I believe that we as a society now have the capacity to comprehend these complexities.

But our work extends beyond sharing and understanding these personal stories; we need to take action. Our lives are on the line.

Now that same-sex couples can put a ring on it, the bathroom has
become a lightning rod for opponents of LGBTQ rights. With proposed
legislation in several states preventing trans people from using the restroom in accordance with their gender identity, trans folks can't even pee
in peace. Trans kids are being prevented from an education that honors
them for who they are. Four decades after I changed my name to Willy, I
often wonder what it would have been like if my school had had a policy

that required my teachers and peers to respect me for who I was. And yet, decades later, trans kids are still being disrespected. In the absence of trans-affirming school policies, and even in some areas where those policies are in place, trans kids are not being referred to by the name they identify with, are required to use the restroom that doesn't fit their gender identity, and sometimes are unable to graduate because they are denied physical education classes in their appropriate gender. Trans kids are under attack *now*. We need to advocate for the rights of trans children to get an education like everybody else, and for trans folks to be able to use the restroom.[4] These are basic human rights. *You know what time it is.*

Despite's California's tremendous gains in health care access for trans people, and the discrimination protections of the Affordable Care Act, I got a hard lesson when I sought access to transition-related care. Discrimination against trans people in health insurance and health care settings still goes unchecked because the health care needs of trans people are not considered equal to everybody else's. The system that perpetuates trans exclusions in health insurance is outrageous health care discrimination like no other. Many trans people can't get coverage for care related to their gender transition, or for gender-specific care that insurance companies believe to be incongruent with the gender on their medical record. Even seemingly unrelated health care needs, such as a liver condition or a *broken bone*, are often not covered because insurance companies claim that these health conditions are related to hormone use.[5] Transition-related surgery and even basic primary care are out of reach for most trans people in the United States and around the world. Comprehensive, federal access to care for trans people is long overdue in the United States. We need nondiscriminatory health insurance and culturally competent and medically competent health services. *You know what time it is.*

When an Asian trans brother killed himself, I got an excruciatingly painful lesson in the impact of suicide in our community. Christopher Lee was a pioneering filmmaker, cofounder of the first North American transgender film festival, and the best man at my wedding. He was marginally housed, living with mental health and physical disabilities, and had difficulty accessing a trans-competent, inpatient mental health facility in the San Francisco Bay Area. In the United States, 41 percent of trans people have attempted suicide in their lifetime. That's nine times the 4.6 percent rate of lifetime attempts among the overall US population.[6]

In December 2014, we lost seventeen-year-old Leelah Alcorn in Cleveland, Ohio, who was subjected to Christian conversion therapy and who pleaded in her suicide note, "Fix society. Please." In March 2015, we lost eighteen-year-old Blake Brockington, the African American activist who in 2014 became the first trans homecoming king in Charlotte, North Carolina, despite incessant bullying. When he aged out of the foster care system that had supported him after his family rejected him, he became homeless. In late 2014 and the first quarter of 2015, we lost trans youth to suicide every one or two weeks, many of whom were teenagers and leaders.[7] On September 28, 2015, less than twenty-four hours after transfeminine Canadian Ryley Courchene took her life, sixteen-year-old Skylar Lee, a brilliant Korean American transmasculine leader, was the seventeenth reported transgender suicide in North America that year.[8] Just eleven days before, Skylar published a well-received article that encouraged an intersectional approach to racial justice and queer liberation: "It is not justice if we ignore the interconnected oppression of those we share community with."[9] The heartbreak of multiple suicide losses is overwhelming. We need to put an end to the cultural, socioeconomic, and institutional conditions that drive trans people to suicide. *You know what time it is.*

In 2014, eighteen-year-old Michael Brown was shot and killed in Ferguson, Missouri, Eric Garner was choked and killed in Staten Island, New York City, and twelve-year-old Tamir Rice was shot and killed in Cleveland, Ohio. These egregious killings shone a spotlight on the long legacy of police violence directed toward unarmed African American men and boys. As we protest the injustice of police brutality by representatives of law enforcement who are often not held accountable, we must also pay attention to the police harassment that torments LGBTQ people of color, especially trans people of color. In 2013, Cece McDonald was incarcerated for defending herself against racist, transphobic violence that targeted her as a black trans woman. Trans women of color are routinely jacked up for "walking while trans," as in the case of Monica Jones, an African American trans woman who was arrested in Phoenix, Arizona, in

2013 for "manifesting prostitution" simply because she accepted a ride from undercover cops. Express your outrage at the injustice, and advocate for systemic change. *You know what time it is.*

When Taja Gabrielle de Jesus was stabbed in San Francisco on February 1, 2015, she became the fifth trans woman of color to be murdered in the United States in the first four weeks of 2015, and the fourth trans woman of color murdered in California in the previous four months.[10] In response to her brutal murder, the Trans* Activists for Justice and Accountability Coalition (TAJA) demanded safe, affordable housing in San Francisco, a city disrupted by massive gentrification, and that funding be redirected from jails to trans community support programs, particularly those focusing on reentry support and antiviolence work. By mid-October, *twenty-one* trans women, primarily trans women of color, were murdered in the United States in 2015—a number that exceeds trans murders in 2014.[11] You wouldn't know it by looking at what the mainstream media reports, but it is a *state of emergency* for trans women of color. The overwhelming grief in my trans community is palpable, the structural inequalities rampant. As Jen Richards wrote, "The progress of the trans movement, the dignity of LGBT rights, the very heart of a progressive culture that prides itself on individual liberty and self-determination, should be measured by how it responds to this crisis."[12] The LGBTQ rights movement has allocated relatively little funding and resources to this critical emergency. Let's put a laser focus on this epidemic of violence and take determined steps to end it. *You know what time it is.*

LGBTQ people in the United States are discriminated against in every arena: employment, housing, health care, education, public accommodations, lending, and jury duty. The passage of the Religious Freedom Restoration Act (RFRA) in Indiana in March 2015 brought to light the fact that the federal RFRA has been on the books since 1993, and twenty states have similar laws that legislate the right to discriminate against LGBTQ people under the guise of "religious freedom." Yet the Indiana law goes much further: it legislates that businesses are protected against civil suits brought by individuals, not only the government, providing a broad license to discriminate.[13] It showcases the bigotry of a resentful Christian right-wing faction that is desperately attacking the liberties of LGBTQ people. And the assaults keep coming. We need federal, comprehensive nondiscrimination protections based on sexual orientation and gender identity. Let's move forward now on civil rights legislation so that LGBTQ Americans can finally be full citizens with basic human rights. *You know what time it is.*

We can no longer put our heads in the sand; diversity is here to stay. Community health organizations, businesses, educational institutions, and many other entities are not going to stop needing to address cultural competency issues. Get the tools, develop an action plan, and create LGBTQ-affirming services and systems. Talk to your family members; train your staff; educate your community; develop an in-depth understanding of the multiple layers of oppression that LGBTQ people of color experience. Learn how to show respect; develop competency; update policies, procedures, and systems. Give generously to organizations that advocate for LGBTQ rights, and those that provide support services for marginalized LGBTQ people. *You know what time it is.*

People are dying, falling through the cracks, struggling to survive. We need a cultural, institutional, and legislative shift.

You know what time it is.

MEMOIR AS A CULTURAL COMPETENCY TOOL

I stumbled sleepily out of bed in the pitch dark, hurrying to pick up my two-year-old from his crib. It was 5:00 a.m., and he was crying from a bad dream. I was called upon to hold and soothe him and give him a Band-Aid so he felt secure that his hurt had been properly addressed. Mama is usually the go-to person for this sort of thing when the kids get scared or skin their knee. I'm sloppy seconds. But this time, my little guy requested me.

As I rubbed his back, his tense body began to relax. When I put him back in his crib, I told him I loved him. He responded enthusiastically, in his high little baby voice, "I love you *too*, Dada!" I smiled and thought about getting ready for the long drive and the daylong training I was conducting that day. It occurred to me that this was what it was all about—being there for someone in that tender place.

If you've ever held a crying child in the night, supported a friend who was hurting, helped a client in need, or stood with a colleague who felt unsupported, you know the well of compassion that you have inside.

Over the years, I've worked with tens of thousands of community health providers, educators, business professionals, social justice workers, and others to help them develop their cultural competency on LGBTQ issues and create LGBTQ-affirming systems in their respective settings. I love the engagement, the exploration of thought and inquiry. I welcome questions at all knowledge levels. I learn something every time.

One of the most profound things I have learned is that the world is full of people who are tremendous allies to LGBTQ individuals and families. I feel exceptionally privileged to do this work because, unlike so many people in LGBTQ communities, particularly transgender people, who especially struggle for acceptance, fair treatment, and access, I get to experience on a regular basis the ways in which people who are not part of this community are eager to do the right thing. They may not get the language perfectly. The way they communicate may reflect a larger societal perspective that does not normalize our experience or view us as fully equal, like referring to people who aren't LGBTQ as "regular people" or "normal people." But their hearts are in the right place and their minds are following.

I see community health providers who are moved by the daily struggles of the people they serve, educators who are touched by the journeys of their students, and business professionals whose hearts are changed by the lessons learned from their colleagues. Even if they've never contemplated LGBTQ issues, people of every skin tone, religious background, and walk of life join the conversation, whether they're hospital administrators or receptionists, university officials or service workers. I observe how their own experiences with challenge and adversity, within their belief systems and the cultural fabric of their lives, have given them the tools to have empathy for people who don't look or act like them.

With every event, I have the opportunity to watch this magical glow emanate from the faces of my training participants as they come into awareness of the complex identities, challenging life circumstances, lack of health care access, and legal issues that LGBTQ people face. As they wrap their minds around nontraditional gender identities, they learn to speak new languages, incorporate customs that are different from their own, and develop systems to ensure consistency. In essence, they are expanding their cultural awareness and learning to integrate their knowledge and skills into their interactions with LGBTQ people. And as the speaker who facilitates this process, I feel profoundly privileged to bear witness to their transformations.

As a writer and as a qualitative researcher, I have always loved hearing people's stories. I'm curious about the perspectives of everyone in the room. When I first began training people on LGBTQ issues, it made sense to invite my audiences to brainstorm about language they had heard in reference to LGBTQ people, to ask their burning questions, and to engage in problem solving on LGBTQ-related challenges in their setting. Drawing from how I myself respond best in learning environments, I developed an interactive, engaging style that is best described as old-school "popular education." It elicits participants' questions, comments, and expertise to create a dynamic learning environment in which participants are part of the educational process, rather than just receptacles for information. And honestly, I don't feel that it's my place to be didactic about such complex and variable community concepts and issues. I prefer to spark their emotional and intellectual engagement through discussion, interactive exercises, and storytelling. I enjoy facilitating a process where people engage in meaningful dialogue, evaluate areas of concern, identify priorities, and take action. Ultimately, they leave feeling energized and better equipped to provide LGBTQ-affirming services in their workplaces and educational settings.

As a trainer, I view my role as that of someone who paints a broad picture of a population, because it's not about me; I'm just one person in this colorful, vibrant community. It's my job to illustrate the larger issues that impact a diverse group of people. Time after time, I recognize that it is the personal stories that touch people most profoundly. When I show film clips of LGBTQ people—with their multilayered experiences of race, ethnicity, disability, and class, with or without family acceptance—in interactions with their family members, or trying to get a job, or poetically describing the intense fear of being targeted on the street, people connect on an emotional level. As the films play, I hear participants sigh and signify. When the lights go on, I see the tears in their eyes and the ideas churning in their heads. These images move training participants in ways that statistics and best practices never will.

For this reason, I am compelled to tell my personal story within a larger cultural competency, public health, and policy advocacy framework.

*   *   *

Cultural competency refers to the ability to understand, communicate with, and effectively interact with diverse populations and can be measured by awareness, attitude, knowledge, skills, behaviors, policies, procedures, and organizational systems. I have written this poetic, journalistic memoir in an effort to contribute to the field of cultural competency, particularly transgender cultural competency within an intersectional framework. At the same time, this book illustrates Asian American issues and touches on issues that impact communities of color. It addresses lesbian and larger LGBTQ issues. It highlights invisible disability and celebrates the burgeoning intersectional disability justice movement. And it explores mixed-heritage oppression, the issues of mixed-race people, particularly *visibly* mixed people, an area that is not often recognized as an important cultural competency concern.

Use this book to develop understanding of cultural frameworks, systematic discrimination, and the practical institutional and legislative solutions that can help create equal access for the transgender, gender-nonconforming, and larger LGBTQ communities. Use the tools at the end to assess your organization, educational institution, or business. Identify areas of concern, develop an action plan, and create change.

We've witnessed how the power of storytelling has elevated social movements. The more we tell our stories and listen to the stories of others, the better equipped we will be to transform the world.

CLOSE
TO
THE
EDGE

SCORCHED [14]

heat of august in arizona or utah or something
bryce canyon a big white overgrowth
jagged and rough
not like the smooth black burning car seat
of our air conditioned dodge dart
i am sticking to the vinyl not made for little legs in shorts
head over the edge
the edge of the front seat
like a puppy panting, tongue out
searching for that blast
of artificial cool
in my face
mom and dad and guidebooks
and me
where is everybody
no sisters no brothers no lines
marking back seat territory
they are gone
they grew up
and too cool for this
i am alone

alone in this thick white heat
heavy over darkened asphalt

another diner USA
and mom's got another waitress flustered
over her request for soyu sauce
after they tear up the kitchen finding only worcestershire
which doesn't come close and sure ain't chinese
she realizes she happens to have a small bottle in her purse
just checking
just making sure
a few more folks
can dance
for us
i am holding on
hanging onto the overshellacked table
dying for something standard
regular and all-American
a treat only gotten
in special circumstances
cheeseburger, the child's plate
root beer, carbonated and foreign, its taste overdone
i am hanging on
hanging onto another red-checked tablecloth
plastic menu/smile
i wanna know
i wanna know
does this waitress
do these people
what do they think
what does it look like
do I look like anybody
do they wonder
do they think
i'm adopted?

FOUR MINUTES TO MIDNIGHT

I was born at four minutes to midnight one balmy September night in the Year of the Tiger. Close to the edge. My Chinese mother took one look at the soft down of my brand-new, seven-pound body, birthed from the cocoon of her flesh, and registered a shock of auburn. "That's not my baby!" she exclaimed in disbelief. "That baby has red hair. All my babies have black hair. That's not my baby!" And so it began: surprise, assessment, and disappointment. My looks weren't my only surprise, though.

One month before I was born, my father told my mother that they were going for ice cream. Eight months pregnant in the August heat and always an ice cream enthusiast, she left the house wearing a brightly colored, loose-fitting muumuu, her standard garb. They arrived shortly thereafter at a residence, which was filled with my mother's tittering female friends and coworkers, Caucasian women with bouffants and carefully pressed dresses, eagerly awaiting her surprise baby shower. Among the other games they played that day was one in which my mother was asked to pull a long black hair from her head and thread it through her wedding ring.

"Swing it!" her friends encouraged. "Go ahead!" As she held the hair, the women eagerly watched the direction of the pendulous ring, a popular predictor of birth sex in the days before ultrasounds were available. Swinging up and down, rather than left to right, the ring indicated the gender very clearly. The women cheered and congratulated her on her achievement, another baby boy. Later, in the still of night, after everyone had gone to sleep and the house was dark, I gave her a swift kick to let her know that they were right.

When I emerged into the world, my parents were surprised to discover that I was not the boy they were expecting, or so they thought. Once I was on the outside, I began my fourth trimester, a bundle of reflexes and images, compactable and foldable like a plucked chicken. It was 1962. Parents didn't worry about all this child-centered nonsense of healthy environments, listening to children, and nontraditional identity development. A few months later, my mom went back to work as a first-grade teacher, returning hurriedly every day at noon to nurse me, toting cartons of cigarettes purchased for my chain-smoking caregiver, who insisted on keeping the doors and windows closed. Though my parents briefly considered the impact of secondhand smoke on their newborn, Mrs. Gerken charged only thirty cents an hour and, according to my mother, "she was a good babysitter."

My memories of my first years in smoky lockdown are dreamlike and visually hazy, like the ever-present smoke cloud itself. Splashing in the sink at the end of the narrow kitchen, I watched as the muted light from the window behind me offered small patches of illumination in an otherwise dark tomb. The warmth of the water, the firm sides of the sink, and the embrace of my smoking babysitter made me feel safe as I looked out on the cluttered counters from the height of my perch.

My parents had been ambivalent when they discovered that my mother was pregnant with me, a surprise child following three kids: my brother, age ten, and my sisters, ages eight and six. "We had already given away all the baby clothes," my mother recounted, describing the stress she felt about my impending arrival. They wondered how they would raise another kid when they thought they were done with having babies. But my sisters, Sunya and Su-Lin, were excited to care for me, so they spent many hours changing me and brushing my hair.

Whether it was my sisters, my parents, or my babysitter, people were always trying to put me in dresses and get me to play with dolls. I couldn't understand why. From as early as I can remember, I hated that stuff. One day, Sunya was trying to put me in a dress. I squirmed. I resisted. I pushed her. I grabbed the dress and threw it across the room, then tossed a doll at her, as I often did, the strength of my determined physicality my only language in my preverbal toddlerhood.

*   *   *

I am hapa, a Hawaiian term that derives from the term *hapa haole*, which means "half white." The term *hapa haole* was originally used to describe people who were Hawaiian and Caucasian, but after the influx of Chinese, Japanese, Korean, and Filipino people as guest workers in Hawaii in the nineteenth and twentieth centuries, it became commonly used to describe people who were mixed Asian and white. Currently, particularly on the West Coast, the term *hapa* is used to describe a broad spectrum of mixed API individuals.

My mother's family name, Chang, is the third-most-common surname in mainland China. There are two branches of families who go by this name; our people are referred to as the Tummy Button Changs.

According to family legend, as told by my mother, the first Chang who bore my mother's family surname was an old man who owned a large parcel of land in southern China. One day he went walking through his land and was invited to stay for dinner by a family along the way. The man of the house offered him one of his three daughters for marriage. As the man observed the daughters preparing dinner, one wrapped a piece of ginger in her shirt and pulled it up to her mouth to bite it, exposing her belly button. When this old dude got a glimpse of her belly, apparently he saw a childbearing future. He announced, "I'll take the ginger crusher." For this reason, our family name is called the Tummy Button Changs.

Many generations later, my mother's father journeyed to Sandalwood Mountain, as Hawaii was called, at the age of fourteen to "pick up the gold off the streets." One of his sisters was sold into slavery to pay for his journey. He started as a dishwasher and worked his way up until he had a restaurant. Despite going bankrupt three times, he was able to maintain his restaurant and regularly send his sister money. He learned that she had married another slave, but, sadly, he eventually lost touch with her and never knew her fate.

My mother's mother was born in Hawaii, though she spoke only Cantonese. Her feet were not bound, because foot binding had disabled her older sister, who had an ongoing infection, experienced chronic, debilitating pain, cried all the time, and couldn't walk. My grandmother escaped foot binding because it was her job to carry her older sister to the bathroom and wherever else she needed to go. The way my mother conveyed the story, the reason my great-aunt suffered so much was that they waited until she was eight to bind her feet, rather than mutilating them at age four. Since her feet were larger, they had to brutally break her feet in half and bend them underneath. I learned that, in actuality, the foot-binding process was conducted between the ages of four and nine and was the same process regardless of the age of the girl. This barbaric ritual was usually performed by an elder female family member who was not the girl's mother, since the mother might sympathize with the girl's tremendous pain and not be able to keep the bindings tight.

Since the ideal size of the foot was three inches, the toes were curled under and pressed forcefully into the sole, which broke them. Then the foot was pulled in line with the leg and the arch was forcefully broken. Bandages were wound tightly to press the sole of the foot into the heel. The bandages were frequently unbound in order to beat the sole of the foot to make the broken bones more flexible and rebind them more tightly. The toes remained broken for years and usually had ongoing infections. Since there was limited circulation in the foot, the toes would sometimes rot and fall off, which was considered a good thing. Thus, girls with toes that were fleshier had pieces of broken glass or tile bound into the feet in order to deliberately introduce infection. Not surprisingly, many experienced disease related to infection, and some died of septic shock.[15]

*   *   *

The brother of Sun Yat-sen, the Chinese revolutionary and founding father of the Republic of China, came to Hawaii to look for a wife. He considered my grandmother because she was skilled at sewing and cooking but passed on her because her feet weren't bound. Though they emanated the foul odor of rotting flesh, "lotus feet" were considered intensely erotic and symbolized a higher-class status. Those who could walk did so very precariously, with a swaying gait. Foot binding limited mobility, rendering women at home and dependent on their families, and made it difficult to participate in social life, politics, and the larger world.[16]

Don't even get me started about how the ginger crusher was mere chattel who didn't have a choice when she was married off to an old man, or the horrifying, dehumanizing cruelty that my great-aunts each suffered at the hands of their families. I feel thoroughly nauseated when I think of the intense pain girls and women with bound feet went through. I find it deeply unsettling to fathom a ritual in which older female family members initiate young girls into a lifetime of extreme pain and disability while telling them they are becoming beautiful and attaining a higher social status.

The experience of foot binding is only two generations before me. While cultural mores haven't been nearly as extreme for me as a third-generation, American-born, female-bodied individual, the subjugation of women that has been endemic to Chinese culture for eons was passed down to me and made an indelible imprint on my psyche.

*   *   *

On my father's side, my two great-great-grandfathers, Orson Pratt and Erastus Snow, were part of Brigham Young's caravan that crossed the plains in search of a place for a Mormon settlement. While Brigham Young was sick, Pratt and Snow used the "ride and tie" method to arrive in the Salt Lake Valley three days before Brigham Young's party on July 21, 1847.[17] With one horse between them, one walked while the other rode ahead, leaving the horse tied and setting out on foot, so that the other person could ride once they reached the horse. When they arrived in the valley, they declared, "Hosanna! This is the place!"

Both were members of the quorum of the Twelve Apostles of the Church of Jesus Christ of Latter-Day Saints. Snow was a leading colonizer in the southwest and eastern US states, as well as in Scandinavia. Pratt was a writer, historian, and philosopher who made scientific observations during the expedition west, coinvented a wooden odometer, and later preached about the doctrine of plural marriage. Orson Pratt laid out Salt Lake City with wide streets so that one could turn a horse and carriage around without having to back up.

My father's mother was the youngest of ten children. She read voraciously, played cowboys and Indians, and grew up in a culture that centered white people as the norm. She fell in love with my grandfather, whose sweet whistle and jaunty levity announced him as he walked down the street to visit her. Together they left Utah and the Mormon church and moved to California in the 1920s. During World War II, she joined the new class of working women, becoming a proud Rosie the Riveter who worked at the shipyards in Richmond, California. An aspiring writer, she proudly published an article about this experience in the September 1943 issue of *Harper's* magazine, entitled "From Housewife to Shipfitter."

*   *   *

My mother grew up in the rural town of Wahiawa on the Hawaiian island of Oahu, the youngest and only girl in a family with four older brothers, who ridiculed her relentlessly and beat her up on a regular basis. She walked barefoot through pineapple fields to get to school, where she skipped two grades and read every book in the school library before discovering the public library. After school she chopped vegetables and served food in her family's Chinese restaurant. Few people went out for Chinese food in the pre–World War II era, but her family's business boomed once they got their liquor license, and the soldiers from nearby Schofield Barracks stepped out on payday. The family lived in the two-room apartment above the restaurant, where my mother slept over the blaring jukebox and the chaos of drunken soldiers. When she had to go anywhere, she walked down the middle of the street, staying clear of the soldiers as best she could. Most were gentlemen, but she had experienced harassment and the threat of sexual violence, which she escaped thanks to the kung fu skills her brothers had taught her. She studied hard and pushed against cultural barriers to become the first girl in her entire extended family to go to college.

My father is English, Irish, and Scottish, from the rugged country of Depression-era Oakland, when everyone in the hills was poor. The oldest of three and the only boy, he was the son of an accountant and a homemaker. He explored the local terrain, hungrily finding golden-delicious apple trees, picking and eating every part of the fruit and chewing on the stem and seeds. My father's family pinched every dollar and coin, grew what they could in the garden, and raised chickens with limited success. In order to level the sloping hillside so they could garden, he sweated through lengthy sessions jointly wielding a well-worn handsaw with his father, carefully pulling metal to wood back and forth, sawdust flying, to chop down eucalyptus trees. During World War II, my father was drafted into the US Army. When he returned from military service, he attended college at UC Berkeley, which was free except for a $37.50 administration fee.

My parents met in Berkeley in 1949, when my father was a student at UC Berkeley. Dressed in her usual slender satin Chinese dress and beehive hairstyle, my mother arrived at his low-rent men's co-op several blocks west of campus, a dinner guest of another resident. It was a Tuesday, my father's night to cook. With no cooking smells emanating from the kitchen, a few roommates were starting to pop in to assess his progress, which was somewhere between complete lack of preparation and panic. He asked my mother if she knew how to make stew. With soy sauce, ginger, garlic, red wine, stew meat, vegetables, and a hurried trip to the corner store, together they created their first of many satisfying meals, her presence toasted with the remaining wine.

My father took her to the beach at night on one of their first dates, where he gathered wood, made a campfire, and, to her delight, pulled a frying pan out of his backpack. He served her freshly prepared pork chops and red wine, which she found delectable and charming.

Their interracial union was controversial at the time, as California had just repealed the antimiscegenation law in 1948, though antimiscegenation law wouldn't change on a federal level until 1967. When my mom called her mother to tell her, "Someone wants to marry me," her mother didn't disapprove that he was *haole* but simply asked if he met the qualifications of a good husband—kindhearted and able to provide. "Oh, yes," my mother assured her, neglecting to mention that he was a starving student. But, thanks to the GI Bill, they were able to put a down payment on a house for $1. The mortgage was $75 a month.

*   *   *

When I was a year and a half, I bent over on the front lawn of our house, assuming the toddler "downward dog" stance, and peered into a dark hole. "Do you see China?" my mother and siblings asked. "If you look hard enough, you can see China." They encouraged me to keep at it. I looked and looked but never did find China. I wondered why they had all seen it, and if I was the only one who couldn't.

At three, I wandered into my thirteen-year-old brother, Steve's, room, the new room they had converted from the garage. He was entertaining some friends. "Hey, show us your hairy chest!" Steve commanded. Dutifully, I raised my shirt over my face. Everyone had a good laugh.

By that time I had earned the nickname Squirrelly because stuff from my brother's room had a way of disappearing and reappearing in the room I shared with my sister Su-Lin. He got all the good stuff—a baseball, a cap, a big leather mitt, cars, and trains. I never got cars or trains, no matter how much I asked for them.

I was playing on the floor at my mother's feet, listening to the shrieks of laughter as she told her friends about me as if I wasn't right next to her. "And I said, 'That's not my baby! That baby has red hair. All my babies have black hair. That's not my baby!'" She pointed at me, then said, "They got lighter down the line. This one is shark bait!" More laughter. I didn't know what that meant, exactly, but it made me feel like my skin wasn't strong enough or good enough.

One morning I walked into my parents' small, cluttered room. My mother lay asleep on the bed, wearing a long nightgown and a hairnet. I pulled her eyes open. Her eyes moved around; she mumbled something, then went back to sleep. I turned and walked into the bathroom. My nostrils flared at the pungent mold and bright pink tile. There, on the toilet, sat my mother's hair on someone else's Styrofoam head. This was new information. I wondered why my mother's hair wasn't really the hair I thought it was. "Mom, why is your hair on this thing?" I asked her when she woke up. She muttered something that sounded like, "Don't talk about that!" Was her hair wrong like mine was? How come I wasn't supposed to talk about it?

By age four, I knew how to tie my shoes and how to use chopsticks. I loved my dark blue vest and brown pants because they were the most

boyish clothes I had and I could be a cowboy. I had made a stuffed animal I named Horse, a crudely stitched, comfortingly soft flannel creature
filled with old nylons, its shape the side view of a horse, with two legs,
not four. I sewed it all by myself and slept with it every night. That
and my hand-me-down, dingy white cotton bedspread with little, pokey
bumps all over, which I loved to fiddle with while drifting off to sleep to
the vibrations of my brother's band playing loud rock music in the living
room. My dad kept telling them, "Keep it down!" but I loved the music.
Who cared if it was late? That's when I practiced counting.

One night I lay in bed in the dark room with my two-dimensional
horse and counted all the way to a hundred in Cantonese. Then I did it
in English. "Ninety-eight, ninety-nine, tendy, tendy-one . . ." I ran out to
ask my father what was after "tendy."

I could always rely on my father for measured, thoughtful answers
to my questions about the world around me. My mother loved to walk
around saying, "Your father is the Great White Hope. I am just the humble concubine. I shuffle my feet behind the first wife." I had no idea what
a concubine was, nor what she meant about shuffling her feet behind the
first wife, but I knew it wasn't as good as being the Great White Hope.
That was definitely good.

One day I asked him, "Are all the people on money white men?" My
dad paused as he always did, taking a minute to gather his thoughts, and
responded, "Yes. They're all former presidents of the United States."

I thought about this information and my place in the world. I was a
boy inside. My father was the Great White Hope, and my mother was a
humble concubine. All the people on the money were white men. I was
four years old and ready to make my first major life decision. I decided
that I wanted to be white and male, and that I would work very hard to
become that. That was the only way to become president, and the best
way to get money and for people to think you were good. I was going to
be white and male.

ALLERGIC TO CHILDREN

I was shivering in a majestic redwood grove at a kiddie birthday party for a spirited, red-haired five-year-old in my daughter's preschool class. His down-to-earth moms had rented a picnic area nestled in the brisk, natural air-conditioning of mature redwoods. I looked up to gaze at the beautiful maze of interlocking tree branches blanketing a blue sky, then reached for another greasy potato chip.

Outside the grove, the parking lot was sunny and twenty degrees warmer, with an elaborate play structure nearby. Surely it was time to shed this down coat and take the kids to the play structure. It was almost May, and I still had no idea who most of the people were, though presumably they were parents at my daughter's preschool. I knew the names of a few of the moms and kids, but I was largely out of the loop. Georgia had done most of the drop-offs and pickups that year, while I'd stayed home to read to our baby and put him down for his nap.

I looked over at my older son, who was busy wielding an enormous ten-foot stick. "Don't swing that near people," I cautioned. At least he was bonding with the four- and five-year-olds as they excitedly built a fort with the sticks they found. I was relieved I didn't have to listen to him moping that he was bored, begging to go home.

The brief conversations I had with the guys were limited to jokes about the meager food offerings. The women talked about the usual parenting topics: bedtime and screen time and sibling rivalry. I was bored out of my skull. With three kids, I'm at a kiddie birthday party almost every weekend, tossed into an intimate social situation with people I hardly know, wondering if I can find a single point of connection beyond parenthood. The recognition that I might have to work very hard to find a compelling topic of shared interest with these folks made me feel isolated and frustrated.

A few of the moms and kids gravitated to a small patch of sun that supplied a little warmth in this grandiose icebox. One woman asked me where I grew up. "On the peninsula," I replied.

"Me too. Where on the peninsula?" she asked.

"San Mateo," I responded.

Her too. What high school did I go to? Like Google Maps zooming in closer with every snapshot, we found ourselves describing the locations of our parents' homes, within a couple blocks of each other.

When I described where we lived, she said, "Wait, what's your family name?" When I told her, she said, "Mrs. Wilkinson is your mom?" I lit up. People who'd had my mom in first grade were always popping up, and their memories of this wacky teacher during their shy, formative years always made them smile. "She was my favorite teacher of all time. She made everyone feel comfortable. She was so loving. I remember when I saw her driving once and I said, 'That's not a camel!' She'd told us that she rode to school on a camel."

I laughed, thinking of all the tall tales my mom told her first-graders. That she lived in a tree house. Sometimes it was an igloo, or a mud hole, or a submarine. Her mode of transportation changed from year to year—a banana slug, a camel, a hippopotamus. That's why she was always late. The camel always got lost.

"One time," the woman continued, "she was putting water in the fish tank and I asked her what she was doing. She said she was giving the fish some water to drink. I thought that was so funny."

My mom painted grand pictures of her cartoon life, with her four kids jumping into her kangaroo pouch at the end of the day. When new students arrived in first grade, still adjusting to the school experience, she engaged them by calling them by the wrong name. "Magillicutty? Abercrombie? Josephine?" "My name is Sarah," a little girl would respond in a whisper. My mom had a way of warming the little buggers right up. Once they were ready to talk and came at her with questions, she'd back off, saying, "I'm allergic to children!"

Every morning she would hammer out songs on the school's aging, out-of-tune piano while the class mumbled the words off-key. She could play anything by heart and didn't need to look at the keys. She kept her gaze on the kids to be sure no one was getting into trouble. When the notes stumbled over themselves, she said, "The piano makes mistakes." In the minds of six-year-olds, it all made sense.

Which is why my experience as a child was entrenched in a decidedly odd sense of reality that slowly disentangled itself over time.

Names announce us and tell our stories. The name I was given at birth was not right for me, so I chose my destiny by renaming myself at a young age.

It was the day after Thanksgiving, and I was watching TV in the living room with my siblings. We had spent the holiday at my grandparents', my father's parents, where they donned tall, buckled pilgrim hats that they'd crafted out of black and white construction paper. Kids ran around and under the table, and the adults enjoyed wine and cocktails. As usual, my mom brought Peking duck and chow mein to go along with the turkey, mashed potatoes, cranberry sauce, and pumpkin pie that my other relatives contributed. My father's mother complained that Thanksgiving was "getting too ethnic."

So my mother responded by standing in the middle of the living room the next day and announcing, as she often did, "Your father is the Great White Hope. I am just his humble concubine shuffling four steps behind him." I went back to watching *The Courtship of Eddie's Father* on our heavy black-and-white TV. The show was about a white guy, a widower played by Bill Bixby; his seven-year-old son, Eddie; and their accommodating Japanese housekeeper, played by Miyoshi Umeki, who won an Oscar in 1957 for *Sayonara*. For some reason that was never really explained, Mrs. Livingston, the Japanese housekeeper, had a *haole* last name, just like we did. She seemed to really care about the guy and his son, spoke with an eager-to-please accent, and did everything for them. I was seven, just like Eddie on the show. I wondered, *If he has this Japanese lady doing everything for him, how come I have to make my own lunch?* And our threadbare orange couch and nasty gray carpet didn't look anything like their house.

"Goo' mohnin', Meestah Eddie's fathah," Mrs. Livingston said demurely, bowing. She bowed a lot. I knew about bowing. You had to clasp your hands and bow when old Chinese people and relatives came around. "T'ank you vely much, Meestah Eddie's fathah." She shuffled off to happily provide for the needs of the widower and his son.

I knew about the "mister" thing, too. My mom's mother referred to my dad as Meestah Bop. He was Bob to everybody else, but to her he was Meestah Bop. And the family-relationship thing, too. Mrs. Livingston never called the guy by his name. It was all about his relationship to his son, just as my mother's family members' names, in line with Chinese tradition, were Son Number One, Aunt Number Two.

And then there was all the cultural misunderstanding. Even though Mrs. Livingston had a college degree, she was kind of slow on the uptake. She was dependable and philosophical but mostly a silly, confused foreigner who was struggling to understand the ways of this American family. My mother was confused a lot, too. "What do you mean, 'too ethnic'? Are the pilgrim hats too ethnic?" she asked my grandmother innocently.

Apart from the reflection of our family, however twisted, that I found in this show, I loved that Eddie's best friend was a young Jodie Foster, as dykey as ever. As his little tomboy buddy, she was way more butch than pampered, lily-livered Eddie, who could barely wipe his own nose.

* * *

My mother was named May-Blossom, according to her mother's distinct wish for a Chinese-sounding English name, though she has been known mostly as Blossom throughout her life. My mom wanted the same for me, so she named me after a popular Chinese actress, whose name easily anglicized into a common '60s girl name.

I hated how it defined me as a girl. People thought they knew something about me because my name identified me as a girl, and because there were two other girls in my class with the same name. It was supposed to be Chinese if it were said with a Chinese accent and intonation, up and down, like a song I couldn't dance to. The rhythm wasn't right. The soul of who I was wasn't there, not in this name.

By the time I was six, I felt distant and disassociated from this name. The person with that name sparked surprise and discomfort and was inconvenient. The person with that name got their dinner food snatched by Mom, piece by piece, if they turned their head for a moment or didn't show enough focused interest, much like my mom's four older brothers had done to her because she was the "lowly girl child" and didn't need to eat as much food. The person with that name had a lot of questions.

*   *   *

At the age of nine, I was actively looking for a boy's name. In elementary school, we had a physical education teacher who called all of my siblings Wilkie, after our family name. Mr. Schogland used a wheelchair because he had had polio, so he enlisted eager volunteers to demonstrate whatever moves we were supposed to do. "Keep it up, Wilkie!" he called over to me, as I hit the pavement with a set of push-ups. I liked that he called me Wilkie. It made me feel connected to my siblings who came before me, and motivated me to push harder. Mr. Schogland was a well-loved PE teacher. He was confident and decisive and made everybody want to run or do calisthenics. And he was cool. At lunchtime he spun records so we could dance to songs like the ones in Sunya's stack of 45s: "Signed, Sealed, Delivered I'm Yours," by Stevie Wonder, or "ABC" by the Jackson 5.

I contemplated changing my name for months before I told my mother that I was looking for a boy's name. The day I told her, I was massaging her after school, like I always did. I enjoyed massaging her. It was a Chinese tradition that had been passed down in her family, and it made her happy. Sometimes she massaged me, too. She had taught me to walk on her back when I was eleven months old, a couple of months after I learned to walk on the ground. On weekend mornings she'd call my sisters and me into her bedroom to walk on her back and massage her "aches and pains" while she lay facedown, immobile, exhausted from the week.

That particular afternoon, when my mom and I were alone, as my toes pressed incrementally down the sides of her spine, she asked me why

I wanted to change my name. I told her that I wanted a name that was a boy's name because I was a boy. The room enveloped me with its silence.

I was done with that girl name that had never been right. I told everybody that my name was Willy now, that I was no longer that other name. Most people refused to call me Willy, but my fourth-grade teacher did sometimes, with a slow Southern flair that made it feel extra special. It was such a relief.

My sister Su-Lin, who was in high school, understood that my name was Willy. My brother and his girlfriend got it. My relatives on my father's side didn't have a problem with it. But my Chinese cousins thought it was all a big joke, like my "shark bait" skin. Most people didn't understand that I was serious. This wasn't some nickname that I was going to forget about when I was done with it, like some forgotten toy. This was my new name. I really did not want to hear that other name, but people insisted on using it anyway.

*   *   *

In sixth grade I got in trouble when I put a bunch of banana slugs in a boy's locker over the weekend. It was a wet winter Saturday, and the slugs had come out in full force in my backyard. I used two sticks as chopsticks to gather about twenty of them in a plastic bag, then took them to school to release in this kid's locker. I did it for my friend because she wanted to get him back for "liking" her. By Monday, the slugs had crapped and made slug scum trails all over his binder, books, and locker. I thought it was hilarious, and so did my friends, but my humanities teacher, who usually called me Willy, made a point of announcing to the class how pissed she was at me by using my girl name.

The boy responded by giving my friend a card with a dead frog glued onto red construction paper, with a speech balloon that said, "I love you." I thought it was really cool—like, *What a find: a dead frog!*—but she thought it was gross.

A few of my friends asked me, "Willy, when are you going to get a sex change?" I wore my Charlie Brown sweater and hunting hat every day. My mom named my sweater that not because it had anything to do with Charlie Brown, but because I never took it off. I had bought it at a thrift store for fifty cents right before sixth grade started. Even though I changed the shirt I wore under it every day, no one ever saw that. It started to look kind of ragtag. In the beginning of the school year, the sweater was a clean white acrylic blend, with a blue-and-red design across the chest, but by the end of the year it was pilled and dingy gray.

My hunting hat was red and black corduroy, with a big bill and earflaps. I made a cut on the lining inside the top of the hat and stitched Velcro so it could close. I hid money in it, like Tatum O'Neal in *Paper Moon*. I loved that hat and didn't take it off for a couple of years.

One weekend, out with my parents, we ran into a pleasant coworker of my father's.

"Oh, this must be one of your sons," she acknowledged warmly. "Uhh . . . yes," stammered my father, "this is my son," then identified me by my girl name for comic effect. As soon as the coworker was out of earshot, my exasperated mother angrily commented, "I thought we had three daughters!"

At school there were four female aides who worked with our history and humanities teachers. They all wore so much perfume that I was overcome with intense sneezing fits and couldn't breathe half the time. One time the history teacher leaned back on his high stool and made a broad gesture to clasp his hands over his neatly crossed legs. His shag haircut and long, reddish-brown mustache pointed to his wide black collar and black polyester slacks. He made a point of addressing me by my girl name, like he always did, then asked, "Didn't I see David Hazelwood wearing those same pants?" He grinned mischievously, pointing to my faded brown cords with light blue patches on the knees. A bunch of kids laughed.

That's how things were throughout my K–12 experience—a few supportive teachers and friends, and a whole lot of taunting and resistance. Most of my teachers, like a lot of my peers, emphasized my girl name repeatedly, loudly, and extra long. In high school, there was one male Spanish teacher who wore pink shirts and socks, gave me lots of A-pluses with smiley faces, and never had difficulty calling me Willy. But my haughty high school English teacher, who taught us to critically analyze literature and for whom I produced carefully thought-out and well-structured essays that earned me school-wide English awards, addressed me very emphatically by my girl name throughout high school. Even three decades later, at my thirtieth high school reunion, he made a point of putting me in my place by dramatically referring to me by my girl name.

But back in sixth grade, there was one art teacher whom I'll never forget, a soft-spoken, gray-haired woman who eyed the ceramic bowls and line drawings I created with warmth and appreciation. She consistently called me Willy. She never questioned me for being me. Never did I feel as if she couldn't see me, or as if she needed to insist that I was someone other than who I said I was. Later, I learned that she lived with another teacher at the school, a woman, for many years. She shines in my childhood memories because she was a teacher who looked at me with the same appreciation that she had for art. Rather than seeing a flaw that needed reshaping, she saw the beauty and art form in human diversity. It's my memory of her, and the way her heart was in the right place, that makes the profound liberation of legislation like AB 1266, California's School Success and Opportunity Act, which took effect decades later, in 2014, resonate with me.

*   *   *

AB 1266, the School Success and Opportunity Act, was signed into California law by Governor Jerry Brown in 2013 to provide transgender students the right to access public school settings in accordance with their gender identity and expression. While there were no systems in place to educate my family or support me in the public school system back in the '70s, there is now. The first of its kind anywhere in the country, AB 1266 requires staff at public schools in California to address trans and gender-nonconforming students by the appropriate name and pronoun, provide access to gender-specific settings, such as restrooms and sports teams, update records to reflect name and gender, and ensure the safety and well-being of trans students.

The opposition tried to gather enough signatures in 2014 to impose a referendum by spreading the misconception that this bill was going to give boys license to torment young girls in the bathroom. School administrators in San Francisco and Los Angeles and parts in between spoke out about how they have been implementing these trans-affirming policies for years without incident. Fortunately, the opposition didn't succeed, and now trans kids in California public schools have legal backup to be respected for who they are.

Laws like AB 1266 give trans and gender-nonconforming students the respect, relief, and systemic support that I couldn't get as a young trans kid growing up in the Bay Area in the early '70s. I fully support the efforts to implement this law in California and the ongoing efforts to pass similar legislation in other states around the United States.

It's for people like Pat Cordova-Goff, who transitioned in high school while her family struggled with homelessness. After being excluded from sports because of her trans status, she became one of the first transgender athletes to benefit from this legislation when she made the girls' varsity softball team, an accomplishment she worked very hard to achieve. She founded her Los Angeles County school's Gay-Straight Alliance and, at just seventeen, gave a well-articulated keynote speech at the Transgender Leadership Summit in Southern California in 2014.

AB 1266 is for people like Ashton, who wasn't allowed to use the student restroom at his Central California school and was required to wait for someone to unlock a staff bathroom, which always made him late to class. Because of his gender identity, he wasn't allowed to participate in physical education classes, which he needed to graduate.

This critical legislation protects students like Jewles Gutierrez, who was penalized when she fought back against the bullies who had tormented her repeatedly. Her Bay Area school ultimately used a restorative justice model to address the conflicts that arose in association with her trans status. Jewles was one of the grand marshals at the 2014 San Francisco Pride Parade.

AB 1266 is for my daughter's dear preschool friend, a sweet Mexican-Nicaraguan American boy who rocks cat ears and pink sparkly outfits and prefers to wear his hair long. And it's for his parents. Despite coming from a traditional cultural framework and having never thought about gender identity before the issue presented itself in their child, these beautiful people have supported their child every step of the way. When he rejects boys' clothes, they take him to the girls' department. When he wants to be a fairy princess for Halloween, they make it possible for him to be who he is. Parent to parent, I admire the pure grace with which they show their unconditional love.

The passage of this legislation sparked increased attacks on trans youth of color, so a coalition of organizations—including the Transgender Law Center, Gay-Straight Alliance Network, and American Civil Liberties Union, among others—have built a network of organizations to ensure that the education work relating to this legislation has a racial justice lens. So many of our young people, including these individuals I've mentioned, are bravely fighting for their right to be themselves on their own terms. These trans youth of color show the strength, leadership, and resilience of our future—young people who are naming themselves and standing up to systems that have a responsibility to protect them.

*   *   *

As a trans kid who dared to be myself at a time when personal choice for a female-born individual was not often honored, and when there was no understanding of trans identities, I experienced a certain out-of-control helplessness, a violating, unpredictable humiliation that was a constant in my life. I spent my childhood years pushing in every way I could to assert my new name and to bury the old. Too many people pushed back, and way too many people taunted me with the old name. Family members put me in my place for having the audacity to name myself and to present my masculine self. Too many teachers, school officials, peers, and community members resisted. Over the years, men assured me that I had no right to claim a masculine name, and women questioned my loyalties.

In 1998, Georgia and I got married. At the engagement party, the few non-LGBTQ people—family members and high school friends—found each other. And there, in their whispering, snickering corner, they disclosed to my new in-laws what my name used to be. There was a duty to inform, apparently.

There are trans people who will readily, and without reservation, share what their old name used to be; I am not one of them. I don't want to be asked about it; I don't want it dug up; I don't want anyone announcing it. People who knew me back in the day get no special status for having this knowledge; there is no bravado in parading this insider information for the curious objectification of others.

My old name was hurled at me to punctuate every masculine moment, every spark of individuality, independence, and creativity. "Mom, I figured out what I want to major in," I announced excitedly, after contemplating mathematics and psychology in my first year in college. I had found an interdisciplinary major that gave me an opportunity to exercise social analysis. "I'm majoring in women's studies, with a minor in biology. I'm taking this Introduction to Feminism class."

"Feminism? Does that mean being feminine?" she responded, eyeing me sideways, with her signature coy pseudoinnocence, and using my girl name for emphasis.

*   *   *

Fifteen years after I changed my name, when I was twenty-four, my mother finally got with it. Not consistently, but she finally came to an understanding that this was my name. After all, I was changing it legally. The name Willy was not going away.

In the '80s, a name change was not the extensive ordeal it is now, post-9/11. I changed it through common usage, notarizing a document I found in a Nolo Press book, then started with the Social Security Administration and worked my way through all the government systems. A few years later, when I needed a passport, I went through the court system.

At the time, some of my African American friends were losing their "slave names." Mary became Imani, and Sue became Shakira. My mixed friends were changing *haole*-sounding names to something more ethnic. People with names like Cindy Hanson took on names like Luna Gonzales; Jennifer Hamilton became Jennifer Chung. A lot of lesbians were ridding themselves of their father's names by eliminating their last names and just going by their first and middle names, or coming up with something else altogether, like Dykewoman or Blackwoman. I included my Chinese middle name in some of my writing at the time, but after a while my whole name became too tedious and I just went back to being Willy Wilkinson.

Later, I met a lot of trans guys trying to find the right name for themselves, often choosing formal, multisyllabic names like Sebastian or

Hamilton, which reminded me of the Winston Lees and Jackson Chans I went to school with, or my uncles Humphrey Chang and Gordon Chang, who had substantial English names to balance out their mono-syllabic Chinese names.

Over the years, banks and utilities refused to discuss my account information with me, insisting that I wasn't Willy Wilkinson or that he was my husband. Many people on the phone had trouble hearing my name when I said it very clearly. Because I articulated "Willy" but had a female voice, people heard what they wanted to hear, insisting on turning it into a girl name.

But some people, especially black people, saw it as a name that women had. I met a lot of black women named Willy, and that gave me some leeway. And yet the name is distinctly male, with a certain homeboy ring to it in some circles.

A lot of Asian people have had issues with my name, first and last, and assumed that somehow my cultural experience and knowledge were diminished because of my name. Many refused to believe I was Chinese because of my name, except one time, when I called a local auto insurance agent to explore buying a policy; he said he knew I was Chinese because of my name, Wei Lee.

But once the wave of hapa people who were born in the late '60s and early '70s exploded onto the scene, assumptions about me by Asian people, based on my name, started to change.

When I came out as transgender in the mid-'90s and found the FTM community, even though I felt out of sorts culturally, one of the most profound aspects of that experience was that no one had an issue with my name, and that was a huge relief.

*   *   *

In the late '80s, I was the coeditor of *Phoenix Rising*, the newsletter of the Asian lesbian community in the Bay Area. When I took over the role of editor, I was not impressed that the articles focused on softball, recipes, and gossip about who was dating whom. During my time as editor, a small group of dedicated individuals transformed the newsletter from a short, awkwardly typewritten rag into a visually beautiful, computerized, political forum. I wrote about the politics of Asian lesbianism, the necessity for us to articulate our issues and organize ourselves, to self-identify and smash the dragon lady and lotus blossom stereotypes. I wrote about my dreams of visibility, community building, and empowerment. I saw that the newsletter primarily served Chinese American women; I worked with Filipina, Indian, Japanese, Hawaiian, and mixed women to organize a broad base of Asian and Pacific Islander lesbians. In the fall of 1987, a group of twenty-eight Asian lesbians descended on Doreena Wong and Jenny Pizer's house in Washington, DC, for the March on Washington for Lesbian and Gay Rights. I ran all over that march, giving the newsletter to every Asian lesbian I could find, to network and build a nationwide readership.

I got a lot of positive responses to my articles and the work I was doing with the newsletter. One night back in San Francisco, I was at a party. When a tall, inebriated Chinese American woman discovered that I was Willy Wilkinson, the editor of *Phoenix Rising*, she said, "You're Willy Wilkinson? I always thought Willy Wilkinson was a white man!" As if a white man would have written all those Asian lesbian empowerment pieces.

I had long since abandoned my dream of becoming a white man, not just because I came into my identity and pride as a woman of color but because I identified with African American boys and men. Their energy, anger, rhythms, and poetic language spoke to me in ways white men never did.

Over the years, people often thought I was black on the phone, especially black folks, because it was second nature for me to code-switch into a manner of speech that resonated with black people. My word choice, intonation, and/or vibe would change as I spoke, and that felt familiar to a lot of people. When I first started working with an organization that did capacity building in communities of color, the work was all on the phone, because they were in Sacramento and I was eighty-five miles away in Oakland. I was working closely with the youth program coordinator to provide LGBTQ training for youth service providers. When she found out I wasn't black, she couldn't believe it. She kept asking me, "Are you *sure* you're not black? You have a black stepfather or something?"

The training was a huge success, so she and the executive director drove down to Oakland to meet me. When the executive director asked me to be the researcher on a statewide African American HIV–prevention capacity-building contract, a job I never would have applied for, I responded, "You know I'm not black, right?"

She smiled and said, "You don't have to *be* one to *help* one." I took the job and watched the surprised looks on people's faces when Willy Wilkinson showed up to present the findings. For whatever reason, I worked with many black folks who repeatedly renamed me Willie Wilkerson. My 1099 tax statements, bios on their website, and articles I published often saw this amusing, yet uninvited, name change.

At one point, long before I medically transformed my body to male, I booked a massage at a health club. When I met the massage therapist, she breathed a sigh of relief, because in her mind the job wasn't going to be as demanding as she thought it was. "I thought Willy Wilkinson was a big black guy," she explained, looking at my small, female-bodied frame. Then, with the sure confidence of someone who could really see me, she smiled and said, "But Willy Wilkinson is a small Asian guy."

I felt elated to be witnessed, grateful to have named my destiny.

FINDING MY VOICE

*"It's about realizing, painfully, you've kept that voice in-
side yourself, locked away from even yourself. And you step
back and see that your jailer has changed faces. You realize
you've become your own jailer."*

—Tori Amos[19]

When people ask me how I became a public speaker on LGBTQ
issues, I tell them that it was not something that came easily. It
took me years to find my voice, because I was raised to believe that my
voice didn't matter.

When I was growing up—and really, this went on well into my thirties,
when I spoke at the dinner table—it was as if I wasn't there. As the family
gathered around our pockmarked wooden table, I would ask my parents,
"May I please have some more rice?" The silence in the room expanded so
much that you couldn't move or breathe or speak. Everyone averted their
eyes, looking down as they ate. It was as if I were in a room alone, because
not one of my family members—my mom, dad, older brother, or two
older sisters—would acknowledge that I had spoken. After a while, my
mother would address my father, "Does the child want more rice?" At the
dinner table, and often in other situations, she never spoke to me directly
or used my name, just referenced me in third person as "the child."

As a young kid, I learned to say nothing. But as a teenager coming
into my anger, I would shout, "Why don't you ask me yourself?" Still

I got no response, no verbal or physical reaction. From anyone. Every night the game was the same. My mother would speak to my father, who would then ask me, "Do you want more rice?" Diminished, I would hold out my plate so he could serve me.

Since my mother refused to speak to me directly, she used my father as a conduit, and my father was complicit in the ritual by playing his role without any deviation from how it was assigned. My siblings were well trained to condone this behavior with silence; they knew very well that to speak up meant that they themselves would become a target. I had no choice but to be silenced into submission, into nonpersonhood. There was no breaking through. It was clear that I was not worthy of being responded to, that my words fell on deaf ears, and that there was no way I could convince anyone that I was indeed living and breathing right in front of them. That I was fully human.

If I didn't eat my food quickly enough, my mother would reach out and steal it, especially my meat. If I briefly looked the other way, she would likely take a few bites of beef, reminding me again that the "lowly girl child," to use her words, did not need to eat as much as the others. That was the cultural training she had been taught. I was the youngest, and female-born, and clearly gender nonconforming. I was smaller than everyone else, so I probably didn't need to eat as much anyway, and we wouldn't want any of it to go to waste.

*   *   *

My mother was proud that she could feed a family of six on a dollar. She could buy a cheap piece of beef for fifty-nine cents a pound, tenderize it by beating it into submission with a wooden mallet, marinate it in a soy sauce concoction, cook it, and call it steak. I was well into my teenage years before I learned that "steak" did not mean some hard, fatty, grisly slab.

"You don't like steak?" my neighbor queried with surprise. I was a junior in high school when our neighbors invited us over for steak dinner, which was apparently a really big deal. As I chewed tender morsels and discovered that I actually liked steak, these nice white people chatted with my jovial parents and asked me about myself. It was very different from dinner at home, which felt so pinched, so full of ritual and tension.

Back home, my mother would literally count the green beans. This was how we learned math as a tool for managing our limited resources. "There are thirty-six beans and six of us, so how many beans do we each get?" she would ask. It's no wonder I wanted more rice.

As a young adult, I learned to hold my plate away from her, or just to get up from the table with my plate in hand and go to another room, so I could eat in peace without the constant snatching of my food out from under me. But as a young child I didn't feel so empowered. If I needed to go to the bathroom, or if I ran to answer the ringing telephone, I would surely return to an emptier plate.

It's no wonder that I struggled with food addiction as a young adult. Once I left home and headed for college, I felt liberated to eat as much as I wanted without the stress of needing to protect my food. After rugby practice my first year in college, I would load up my tray in the cafeteria with meat loaf and mashed potatoes, all that American food that others found boring but I found enticing. A burden had lifted. But it wasn't long before I was overindulging in food as a way to swallow my feelings. I watched as my dorm's resident bulimic piled up her trays at the cafeteria, snacked in her dorm room at all hours, then quietly stepped out to throw up in an out-of-the-way bathroom. I knew her struggle, but I never threw up, just stuffed and swallowed it all—my anger, isolation, and unworthiness. I read *Fat Is a Feminist Issue*, Susie Orbach's classic 1978 book that proposed that women eat to take up more space in a sexist social system, but felt confused that I never gained weight, which just added to my list of shifting realities as a racially ambiguous, gender-transgressive person.

*   *   *

In high school I had very demanding English classes that required class participation as a percentage of the grade. I was terrified of one hard-nosed teacher in particular, Mr. Drawback, as we called him, because he was harsh with students who didn't speak in class. It was deeply painful to watch him make the quiet Asian girls cry, like Betty Wu, a Chinese girl who was my friend. She broke down as he relentlessly berated her for not speaking up, asking the question again and again with greater volume, leaning over her with nasty breath, and calling her a "ninny" and other names for not answering.

I averted my eyes and looked down. My heart ached as she crumpled into her seat, tears streaming down her face. I knew her pain. I knew exactly why, no matter how smart she was, she couldn't speak up in class.

These were public school honors classes, and we were all driven, college-bound, honors students with teachers who were celebrated for their skills. We worked extremely hard to complete every assignment with flying colors. We read every old-time, crusty piece of English literature. We wrote every five-part essay. But some of us were not comfortable calling attention to ourselves or taking up any space at all in class.

I wanted to hide, especially when Mr. Drawback asked a question I knew the answer to, one to which I could surely provide an in-depth response if it were on a written test. My heart raced in fear that I would get called on, that I would be faced with the unbearable discomfort of demonstrating my knowledge, then sighed with relief when a big white guy with no trauma about speaking up would stretch out at his desk and comfortably shoot off some half-assed answer. It seemed like white people were not worried about speaking up in class. They did not have the cultural conditioning we suffered from—that to speak up was to die a little every time. That to speak up was to be reminded, one more time, that they were not meant to be seen or heard. That their voice didn't matter. That they had no voice at all, because it didn't really exist.

Needless to say, Mr. Drawback laid into me, too. He was supposedly teaching us to speak out, but he seemed to really enjoy making students squirm, especially the Asian girls. As far as I remember, I never cried in class, but I know I disintegrated into intense panic. I knew the smell of danger. I flinched in his presence. I was in a state of fight or flight for the classroom hour, as long as it took to get in and get out, terrified that I would be the one on the receiving end of his harassment this time. But no amount of harassment was going to make it any easier for me to speak up in class. It did not help me rise above my terror. My family training taught me that to speak up was to be punished in front of my family, all well trained to condone the behavior with their silence. And in school I learned that *not* to speak up was to be squashed into a terrified puddle in front of my peers, who were also disciplined into silence.

*   *   *

Now, when people ask me how I got into this line of work, conducting LGBTQ and transgender-specific cultural competency trainings, I have to say that it was not the destiny I ever would have imagined for myself. I always knew deep down that, despite the relentless silencing, despite decades of active dehumanization, I did indeed have a voice, and that my particular path in life carried an important perspective. But my fight-or-flight response was so ingrained, so beyond my control on a physical level, that I was well into my fourth decade in this world before I began to break through. Prior to that time, whenever I was at an event, or in a meeting—even the most homey, comfortable, kicking-back-on-someone's-couch meeting—I was terrified of speaking in a group. One-on-one was easy, but in a group I got profoundly nervous, my stomach flipped, my heart raced, and I worked extremely hard to manage my breathing so I could speak without sounding like a nervous wreck. Often I was too paralyzed, and my body's functions too overcome by my terror, to hide it.

When I began to stand in front of groups of strangers to speak about what some considered a controversial topic, I was terrified. I was uncomfortable with the exposure of me as an out, butch lesbian. I was nervous about the exposure of me as an out trans person, too. I was very aware that people always saw me coming, that they looked me up and down. I was concerned about the consequences of exposing myself to others' ignorance and biases. But most of all, I was freaked out that I had the audacity to take up space by standing proudly in front of a group of people and educate them about how to treat us as equals.

Training after training, as I prepared to begin the session, my heart jumped as I attempted to modulate my breathing. I reminded myself that I was breaking the rules by pushing against inequality. I doubted my knowledge and questioned my ability to speak without looking nervous. But once I began the training, the physical symptoms stopped and I found myself relaxing into the experience.

Ultimately, it wasn't any particular therapy approach, or a witchy ritual to vibe out the silencing and humiliation, that helped me arrive. It was the act of training itself. It was the years that became decades of speaking to groups of people so that they could provide better services for marginalized populations. It was the hundreds of training events, the tens of thousands of participants who listened to me, cared about the topic, asked questions, and engaged in meaningful discussion. That is how I found my voice.

PROFESSIONAL TRAVELER

As a student at UC Santa Cruz in the early '80s, I experienced both an awakening and a boiling-over that filled me with the urge to run. As Ronald Reagan won the presidency in the fall of 1980, I found the academics in my first year both easier and harder than high school—easier because I didn't have to do as much work, or so it seemed, but harder because I was required to stretch in ways I never had before. No longer beholden to a grading system, I was to outdo *myself*, rather than others, to uncover hidden talents, question social hierarchies, and explore complex thoughts—achievements that instructors assessed and documented in written narrative evaluations, instead of grades.

I felt isolated and on unstable footing in my dorm, which seemed to be dominated by rich *rah-rahs* from Southern California with outgrown Farrah Fawcett wings and daddies who bought them shiny new cars. In my first year, I played rugby with strong, vivacious dykes, slept with my first woman, and came down with a severe case of mononucleosis as I struggled to process it all. I had to come to terms with the fact that I was female, even though I had never seen myself that way.

Until the age of eighteen, I was fueled by deep, internalized misogyny, despite my intense, close relationship with my high school girlfriend Kristie, the hippie "best friend" whom I spent long hours with on the phone and frequently slept with in the same bed. She would call me to ask if I could come over so she could play me a love song, which she dedicated with "if only you were a boy, Willy." We loved each other but didn't dare express our love for each other sexually.

But most of my high school friends were guys, because I related to them and because I developed a strong dislike for women, especially Chinese women. In the '70s, women were not often listened to, valued, taken seriously, or considered leaders. Women were often mocked. Asian women were not regarded as having anything important to say. As I observed my mother's Chinese friends sipping tea in our living room, describing the mundane details of cooking and cleaning for the men and boys in their lives, I formed an early resentment toward them. They seemed to accept, without question or struggle, their supposed inherent inferiority. I hated them for listening to men even though men didn't listen to *them*. I hated them for accepting the ways in which men disregarded and derided them. I hated them because I received ample messages from society that women were not to be trusted. I hated Chinese women because they seemed as weak and unimportant as everyone said they were. I rejected them as a reflection of me.

But in Santa Cruz, something shifted. I began to realize and accept that I was a woman, that I was attracted to women, and that I was a woman who loved women. It was no simple process, but the unraveling of years of disdain for women was profoundly liberating.

I felt uneasy on the first day of Introduction to Feminism, the now-legendary course taught by Bettina Aptheker. It was a hot September afternoon in 1981. The room was packed with two hundred women and a couple of men, with one black woman in a sea of white faces. As someone who lacked clarity about both my gender and my race, I wasn't sure where I fit in. But as I listened to Bettina discuss the women's and civil rights movements, I found myself riveted to the topics she addressed and the connections she made. I realized that somehow there was a place for me in this conversation; the social, cultural, and historical perspectives that came with feminist analysis turned me on and refocused my narrow lens.

I began to embrace my experience as a woman. I educated myself about the subjugation of women in the United States and elsewhere, and the ways in which women had fought back. I was struck by the overwhelming male domination in health care systems; books like the seminal *Our Bodies, Ourselves* taught me and a generation of women how to control our own bodies and center our health care experiences. I participated in Take Back the Night marches alongside women who claimed their right to walk safely at night.

I began to come out not just as a woman or as a lesbian, but as an Asian woman, which felt unfamiliar and exciting yet lonely. I wasn't like any other Asian women I had ever known. Though I grew up with a lot of Chinese, Japanese, Korean, and Filipina friends, I had never seen another Asian woman who was even remotely androgynous or gutsy. But there was something very soothing about beginning to view my life within a sociopolitical context. I discovered Ruthanne Lum McCunn's book *Thousand Pieces of Gold*, a fictionalized account of Lalu Nathoy, later known as Polly Bemis, who was traded at age thirteen by her father in China for two bags of seeds, brought to America to be a sex slave, and later won her freedom in a poker game. I began to understand the implications of race, gender, and class that had shaped my own experience, as well as that of women who came before me. Though written documentation about Chinese and Asian American women was limited, and work by Asian American lesbians was virtually nonexistent, I began to piece together a social and historical framework for these collective experiences.

I took a class called Women in American History, which was really just about white women with means. In an effort to counteract the erasure of women who did not fit into this slice of American history, I worked with a group of students who researched the history of women of color and what were known as "passing women"—women who lived as men. Like the others on their respective projects, I provided a thorough bibliography so the instructor could include the history of Chinese women in America the next time she taught the class. Sadly, she shoved that rich information in a drawer, never to see the light of day again, and continued to teach that course about white women for decades.

*   *   *

When I came out as a lesbian, it was messy. I had some parting sexual experiences with men that were less than empowering, and relationships with women that were imbalanced and complicated. The first woman I slept with went home to Southern California over the holidays, at which time her high school girlfriend collapsed while running and died of anorexia. I moved across campus, and my new roommate, who was bipolar, and I had an attraction to each other as we both struggled to come out. Not long afterward, she had a breakdown and was locked up in a mental institution by her psychologist parents.

All the lesbians I knew were white, and I couldn't reconcile my mother's expectation that I be a good Chinese girl with the lesbian I was discovering inside. When I rode the bus or walked through the redwoods on campus, people stared at me. Apparently, people were stumped or fascinated by my race, and sometimes by my gender. A lot of people asked me, "What are you?" People stopped me on the street to *tell* me that, not ask me whether, I dyed my hair, in reference to a shock of auburn up front.

"Did anyone ever tell you that you look like Yoko Ono?" asked my neighbor. As someone who was frequently on the receiving end of unsolicited assessments about my race, which varied widely, I did not have a clear picture of what I looked like. My first response was, "Really? Do you think I look Asian?" Only later did I realize that the comment was offensive because I didn't look anything like Yoko Ono.

When I hung out with dudes from school, they told me that tofu was invented in Santa Cruz. People got up in my face with weird questions about "Eastern philosophy." When I went to a lesbian support group or planning group, women stared at me, then told me, "I'm so glad you're here." I hadn't said a word. I quickly learned that when I single-handedly integrated the lesbian scene, it made them feel better, more important, like they got more cool points and their status improved. My closest friend affectionately called me Willy Tofu Monkey Face, which she frequently yelled from across the room, because, as she explained it, my face "looked like a monkey's face." I felt miserable and restless but couldn't articulate that being enthusiastically and repeatedly told that I looked like a monkey was deeply unsettling. I just knew that I had to get the hell out of there.

I knew I couldn't go home to my parents, whom I couldn't talk to, and the soul-deadening 'burbs I had been so desperate to leave. So the first summer of college I lived in the woods. I hid a flashlight in a hole at the base of a redwood tree at the edge of campus. When night fell, it was completely dark around the grove, but I got to know the terrain well so I could find the tree in the obscure night. Once I found my light, I hiked through brambles and tall redwoods to the underbrush where I had stashed my backpack and sleeping bag. I slept under this low canopy of brush, not a soul in sight. I didn't eat much, mostly nuts, crackers, carrots, and peanut butter, and an occasional hot meal with a five-finger discount at the school cafeteria. I never cooked and didn't want to spend money on prepared food. I got really spaced out from being hungry all the time but found my thrill hiking to a river and skinny-dipping in it. That's how I bathed. The economy in Santa Cruz was very depressed, and jobs were hard to come by. Toward the end of the summer, I finally got a job working graveyard at the local tea factory but still never got enough to eat.

The following summer, I was a camp counselor at a Girl Scout camp up the coast, near Lighthouse Point. It was vibrant with badass, fun-loving dykes. They exhibited the kind of kinship the '80s term "family" referred to. In the '80s, gay people were *family* because it often wasn't safe for us. We had to look out for one another. I loved their "women can do whatever we want" energy, and that they weren't afraid to be themselves. As a counselor, I loved leading the energetic camp songs that all the counselors and campers grew tired of, and taking the kids on backpacking trips through the wooded state parks nearby. I really enjoyed supporting the tortured baby-butch campers, still in high school, who didn't yet realize who they were.

I had affairs with a couple of the camp counselors, who were older than I was, with stable housing and cars, and who made me feel connected to a temporary place of home. These women were white and couldn't begin to understand my kind of crazy, but they were a little damaged themselves, so we found each other. While they didn't know the isolation I felt as a woman of color, they knew what it was like to struggle with demons and feelings of low self-worth because they had been mistreated. I discovered the deeper bonds of lesbian sisterhood.

I went back to school my junior year. As much as I embraced this new, lesbian culture, I felt culturally stranded. I connected with an African American lesbian, and that helped me feel less isolated in this monolithic, Birkenstock-wearing, oddly seasoned, tofu-eating, crunchy-granola scene.

I made plans to get the hell out of dodge. I hadn't finished my degree, but I just couldn't be in Santa Cruz anymore.

In March 1983, as my departure date neared, I attended an event for International Women's Day, where I met Aly Kim, a Chinese/Korean American lesbian who was selling records for a women's recording label. There she was, smiling broadly and sporting an '80s dyke 'do—a business-in-the-front, party-in-the-back mullet of straight black hair. I was so surprised and thrilled to discover that she was a lesbian, I excitedly introduced her to Dafna Wu, a Chinese/Brazilian/Jewish American lesbian whom I had recently met on campus, proclaiming, "Now we are three." Two weeks later, despite having finally found other Asian lesbians, I was on a bus to Mexico.

*   *   *

As a young child, I decided that I should learn Spanish because it was an essential skill to have as a resident of California. In high school I studied with great enthusiasm, honing my accent until my *d*'s softened, my *p*'s mixed with *b*'s, and my *rr*'s curled off my tongue with ease. When I headed for Mexico, the dollar was robust against the peso. I had a couple thousand dollars left from slinging greasy wings at the Kentucky Fried Chicken in San Mateo and from my entrepreneurial endeavors in the suburban street economy.

My mom had taken me to get a bank account at age six, so I could learn about the importance of saving. My tiny hand had reached over the counter to give the startled teller my allowance and the silver dollars that my grandfather had pressed into my palm. Over the years I went hungry at lunchtime so I could save sixty cents, the lunch money I got two or three times a week, and then ran home starving to eat at three o'clock. I had been saving my money my whole life so I could run away.

Though there were many happy moments with my family during my childhood years, I was also deeply pained and exhausted from the relentless ridicule and silencing and the disregard for my name change. I planned to run away from the time I was six, and even made some half-assed attempt then. By the time I was ten, I was studying how to survive in the woods, in case it came to that. I absolutely loved the book and movie *My Side of the Mountain*, about a boy who runs away to the Catskill Mountains, making his home in a big, hollowed tree and persevering through winter storms in his pursuit of independence, adventure, and freedom. In middle school I felt the pang of hunger so deep in my stomach it was concave, but I kept my eyes on my goal as I jingled another sixty cents in my front pocket. During my high school years I had recurring, tortured, Sisyphean nightmares about my parents and eagerly landed a job at the Kentucky Fried Chicken as soon as I turned fifteen and a half. Ultimately, it was my girlfriend and my drive to excel in school that kept me home.

But now, at age twenty, I knew the time had come. I packed my backpack, went to San Mateo, and told my mother I was never coming back. As we embraced in the driveway, she clutched me tightly until her fingernails dug into my side. When I looked up, I saw tears streaming down her cheeks. I was completely dumfounded, thoroughly surprised by her reaction.

I caught a ride to San Bernardino with a fellow student, a sweet straight girl with long springy hair with whom I had had an affair. I stayed overnight with her and her parents, and her father drove me to the bus station late the next night. After being poked awake by a bus station worker, who was checking to be sure I had a ticket, I caught a middle-of-the-night bus to San Ysidro and walked across the border early the next morning. It wasn't the first time I had been to Mexico; I had gone to Puerto Vallarta with two friends in college and had fallen in love with the ocean, people, food, and language. Alone this time, I was excited to be there again and to use my Spanish.

I got on a train for Guadalajara. Standing on the outside back perch of the train's last car as the countryside blew by, I felt my widened eyes tearing from the wind. After chatting it up with Mexican passengers and eating *tortas ricas* and drinking sodas from plastic bags, brought onboard by local women at station stops, I retired to the skinny little bed in my sleeper car. Life was good.

I was sporting an asymmetrical '80s haircut, crafted late one night by a giggling friend. My hair was buzzed on one side and "preppy" on the other, short but styled, with a long, skinny braid in the back. Children tugged at their mamas and said, "*Mira la trencita!*" as they pointed at my braid, which I thought of as my queue, the long braids Chinese men wore in the 1800s. My mother told stories about how Chinese men in America were rounded up easily and entrapped because people could grab and hold on to so many queues in one hand. These queues were part of their masculinity and cultural expression but dangerous to their safety—a fitting expression of who I was.

I went to Mexico ostensibly to study Spanish at a language school, but when I arrived, I found the class boring and below my level, attended by timid Japanese women who apologetically covered their mouths when they spoke. I had already learned all the verb tenses and had an extensive vocabulary. After a few days, I was out of there. It was time for immersion.

I stayed just a few nights in a hostel before I met Laura, an American woman in downtown Mexico City, who invited me to stay with her, rent free. She was a brown Sephardic Jewish woman with flawless Spanish who passed easily as Mexican. She lived with Lois, whom we called Luisa, another Jewish American woman with flawless Spanish; both of them had an upper-class, East Coast, private school background, which felt culturally foreign. But they were so friendly, didn't trip on my queerness or Asian face, and made me feel welcome and accepted for who I was. The other roommates were Nelson, a wealthy, black Nicaraguan guy who had lived in the United States, and Mario, an Italian guy, whose room was mine while he was away. Over the next six months, I enjoyed their many parties with an international group of young people, including many Brazilians, engaged in work, school, and travel in Mexico.

A week after I found this housing arrangement and new group of friends, I met Lola, a short, round Spanish lesbian decked out in Guatemalan garb, who was scoping me out on the subway. I looked over at her short brown hair and outsider energy and thought, *What do you know? A game of "spot the dyke" in Mexico City.* I was thrilled to see her. She and her ex-lover were hitching to Guatemala the next day. Did I want to come?

I was always up for an adventure. I had never been to Guatemala. I said yes without hesitation. At the time, few people—not even my new roommates with means and an American cultural framework— had phones in Mexico, because they were extraordinarily expensive. If

I changed my mind or had a question, I couldn't call Lola. I just had to show up at the subway at ten o'clock the next morning. But I had no questions or concerns. I was open to anything and up for the thrill.

The next day, the three of us headed to Guatemala *de aventón*, riding in the backs of pickup trucks that sped around the curves to Oaxaca, the warm breeze in our faces. There were no more school responsibilities or the English language, just a fast ride into the unknown. I felt alive and happy like never before.

After a couple of weeks, I was dreaming in Spanish.

*   *   *

We traveled to Guatemala City, as well as beautiful Lake Atitlån. The deepest lake in Central America, Lake Atitlån was rich with Mayan culture but also overrun with hippie tourists from Europe. I met many young Germans, Italians, Belgians, and Brits. When one referred to me as "the American," I got really pissed off. Where I came from, if you called someone out by their ethnicity, it was racial. I was tired of being labeled and didn't realize that being an American was just a neutral fact.

One of the other ways I was labeled was as female, with all the sub-jugation and sexual violence that went with it. In Mexico I was harassed every day, all day long, as I walked down the street. "Ehhh, *mamacita*," the guys would catcall in a low, breathy voice. Men rubbed up on me in crowded subways. One time, as I rode late at night in a near-empty sub-way car, a guy stood to my side and pushed himself on my seat menacing-ly. Sylvia, a thirtysomething Mexican friend with two young sons, kept a sharp thorn in her lapel to fight off the assholes on public transportation. In one instance, I was deep in the recesses of a large outdoor market when a vendor grabbed my boob. I kicked him hard in the stomach. When I told Laura, she scolded me for responding the way I did in an isolated setting, exclaiming, "You could have been raped!"

After the parties at the international crash pad, people often stayed the night because public transportation was no longer in service. I awoke one night because the Jamaican guy sleeping next to me was grabbing me and making this creepy hissing sound. I pushed him repeatedly and told him to go back to sleep, but he was insistent. Finally I went to Laura and Luisa's bedroom next door and asked, "Can I sleep with you? That guy keeps trying to get on top of me." The next morning, with the guy already gone, Laura confronted Nelson, the roommate who had brought him to the apartment. "You can't invite men who are going to attack women when they're sleeping!" she yelled.

The threat of sexual violence permeated our collective experience as women in Mexico. A friend of ours had picked psychedelic mushrooms with a ten-year-old boy in Oaxaca who had offered to help her find them. At four o'clock in the morning late one night, this friend recounted how the boy took her farther and farther into the woods, as she ate the mushrooms along the way. He raped her. She was high and tried to resist with all her strength, but he was stronger than she was.

Not only was I classified by gender, I was labeled daily by my race. In addition to calling me *mamacita*, people referred to me as *la japonecita*, "the little Japanese one." It was one thing to get called "Chink" and "Jap" on the playground and quite another to be referred to as Japanese every day, as if it were a simple fact. When I was five or six, I came home and told my mother, "Mom, they call me 'Jap' at school." She responded, "Be proud. Tell them you're Chinese." She had grown up with parents who harbored a long-standing distrust toward Japanese people, from the brutal wars. She would ask her parents, "But what about all your Japanese friends?" Their town was 95 percent Japanese, most of whom worked in the pineapple fields. When Pearl Harbor was bombed, they watched as their Japanese friends were shot down in the streets as they looked up to see the Japanese bombers firing from the aircraft overhead.

When Mexican people told me I was Japanese, I told them that actually I was Chinese, not because I had anything against Japanese people but because I didn't like being misrepresented. They asked when I had left China. I was surprised by the question and told them I had never been to China. That's when I began to understand my experience as an American.

* * *

Lola and Maria had left Spain together but ended their romantic relationship in Mexico and remained travel companions. Their frequent fights, with their southern Spanish accents and escalating annoyance, sounded like a barrage of lisping gunfire. I had never heard language peppered with so much of the *th* sound.

After a couple of weeks on the road, Lola and I became lovers. When we returned to Mexico City, we lived in a $1.50-per-night hotel and got a paid gig as extras in some B movie about the bride of Frankenstein. It actually paid pretty well by Mexican standards, though it was the equivalent of $8 a day, which kept us in housing, food, and supplies.

Poverty was all around us. I often gave money to the young kids who followed me down the street or the women whose heads were completely covered in brightly colored shawls, who held their worn brown hands outstretched while seated motionless. Mexico City had seventeen million inhabitants in 1983, many of whom were homeless panhandlers who had traveled from villages in search of a better life.

Lola and I moved to a little shack on an avocado farm about an hour-and-a-half bus ride outside Mexico City, rent free in exchange for watching over the land. The crisp rural air was a welcome change from the thickly polluted city air, which made my boogers black. We had no electricity, just a bed, a table, and an outside campfire pit, where Lola cooked Spanish tortilla over the fire. I rode a bicycle into town to fetch groceries from the limited supplies available and pushed my legs hard as I rode back up the hill. "*Écha la fuerza, guerrita!*" called a passing guy, encouraging me up the hill and labeling me as a light-skinned person, a *guerrita*, the other term I heard on the daily.

Lola taught me how words for the same common household items differed in Mexican Spanish, Guatemalan Spanish, and *castellano*, Spanish from Spain. When she slept at night, I read books in English by flashlight, my only connection to the English language, since Lola didn't speak a word. After a month in Mexico, my Spanish flowed easily and quickly, with a singsong Mexican flair. I began to pass for Mexican, since there was a small Chinese population in Mexico. Still, I was *japonecita*, *guerrita*, *mamacita*. Guys randomly broke out into kung fu poses and called me Bruce Lee and San Francisco.

I also spent time writing flawed Spanish translations of articles in American gay newspapers, so that Mexican lesbians I had met could read them. It had been one of my goals to connect with the lesbian and gay community in Mexico City. I wanted to see what gay life was like in Mexico, and this urban center in particular, and I wanted to know more about the feminist movement, since lesbians were not represented in magazines or other writing that addressed Mexican women's issues.

I found a vibrant community of friendly people who embraced one another as family. I met lesbians who lived on the fringes, with very low income from service jobs, none of whom had come out to their families. I enjoyed attending their parties, and was impressed that women could cuddle on the subway ride home without so much as a glance, in a culture where people of the same sex expressed affection easily.

I loved that Mexican men regularly walked with their arms around each other. I went to a performance where gay men danced naked onstage and was impressed that they had the audacity and freedom to do so. In 1983 I observed little, if any, discussion about the AIDS epidemic in Mexico.

That June, after three months in Mexico, I was excited to march in the small gay pride parade in Mexico City alongside my new friends, many of whom disguised themselves with masks. Lola wasn't interested in lesbian/gay politics, in Mexico, or in Spain. She had no interest in marching in the pride parade. She stated, "I march every day." At the time I disagreed with her, but over the years I've often thought about her words. She was out to everyone she knew in her small town in southern Spain, where she worked the olive and almond harvests. Even when we're not marching in the streets, we claim our right to live authentic lives by being ourselves with pride and visibility.

*   *   *

Lola suggested that I be her geisha girl. I didn't even know what that meant.

One day, the owner of the farm sat me down to ask me a very serious question. Clearly he had been puzzling over his query and was nervous and intense. He wanted to know if my vagina went sideways, and if so, how Asian women gave birth. I thought to myself, *Is that why men are so into Asian women? It's not just the "wash your back in the bathtub" submissive-doormat fantasy? It's the treasured, freakishly horizontal lotus blossom?*

I was so shocked, I reacted like I did when my mother tried to explain the birds and the bees to me when I was ten. I had played dumb even though I knew the deal, so I could watch her sweat over a conversation that was clearly uncomfortable for her. I acted like I didn't understand what this man was asking me, just to see how far he would take it. He took out his pen and drew a crude picture of an Asian woman, complete with slits for eyes and a horizontal vajayjay, and repeatedly tapped his pen on her genitals. If Asian women's stuff goes sideways, how do they have babies?

I got on a train for Texas, ostensibly for a job that didn't pan out, but I just needed to be in the United States again. I was hitching on a road just over the border, when a woman picked me up because she didn't like the look of me on the street with my thumb out. She took me to the bus station and bought me a ticket to Houston. There I met two guys crouched on the street, one small and wiry and the other big and burly, speaking in a fast Tex-Mex Spanish. They, too, were looking for a place to crash. We went to a homeless shelter, where a staff person ran down the rules for the three of us and a small group of other guys. Afterward, the staff person pulled me aside to tell me that it was a men's shelter and that they couldn't accommodate women. Even though I was reminded every day in Mexico, even though I had developed a prideful female identity during my time in Santa Cruz, it hadn't even occurred to me that I was a woman. In this moment I had completely forgotten.

The wiry dude said he'd look out for me, that he knew where we could all sleep. We set up in a tent in a small field not far from the city center, where we shared a meal. It had been raining, so I hung my forest-green rain poncho on a hook to dry. My last name was written in black permanent pen across the back of the neck. I had had that rain poncho since childhood and had even worn it one drenched Halloween, saying my costume was a string bean. I set my backpack down, listened as they fell asleep, then knocked off in my corner of the tent, the big guy in the middle and the little guy on the side.

When I awoke in the dark of night, the big dude was trying to mount me and the little guy was pulling him off me. Over and over again, the big guy would lie on top of me and the little guy would vigorously pull him off. "I told her I would protect her!" whispered the little guy angrily in Spanish. They argued as the big guy claimed it was his right to have me. Eyes wide open and silently planning my escape, I listened as they argued until they both grew quiet.

After the big guy fell asleep, I waited a while before I got up very carefully, soundlessly grabbing my backpack but forgetting the green-bean rain poncho, that symbol of childhood innocence. I exited the tent, ran forty yards away, squatted to pee, then ran like hell to the bus station, where I wandered around in a middle-of-the-night, nauseated daze. When I'd taken off running, I'd looked back to see the little guy standing at the doorway of the tent, observing me with quiet disappointment that he hadn't been able to give me a safe night's sleep.

I couldn't afford to stay in the United States for long, so I went right back to Mexico to see my friends and continue my adventure. When I got back, I received a letter at the language school from my parents, informing me that they were coming to visit. They hadn't heard from me in four months and were worried. I didn't want to experience the visit alone, so I got a group of ten friends to go with me to meet them at the airport. We took them out to dinner, the English-speaking friends talking to them at length. During their stay, I showed them the sights, interpreted for them so they got what they needed, and sent them home impressed with my Spanish and newfound community.

After that, I went back to Guatemala on my own, to see the lake again and to buy woven crafts for resale. Lola had shown me where to get the best work, which she sold to Mexicans on the streets of Mexico City. One night, while I was staying at a hostel in Guatemala City, I received a visit from a man who was a soldier in the rebel army. He nervously explained their plans in detail, drawing diagrams in my leather journal of the rebel army leadership. He wanted me to go back to the United States and tell President Reagan to stop sending money to the dictatorship of Efraín Ríos Montt, who was responsible for the genocide of thousands of rebel leftists and indigenous people and later imprisoned in 2013. During our conversation, it became apparent that this young man perceived me as male. When I disclosed that I was female, he stopped talking about the rebel army. Surprised, he processed this information, then leaned in and tried to forcefully kiss me. I swiftly kicked him out, struck by the intensity of his attempt to make a connection with me, by the pain of the Guatemalan rebels, and by the uneasy emotion of feeling violated as female once again.

I went back to Mexico but was eager to return to the United States. I was broke. Toting Guatemalan crafts and Mexican jewelry for resale in the privilege of American capitalism, as well as leather crafts and jewelry that I had made myself, I headed to Luisa's private college. We had made a strong connection while walking one night through Mexico City, trading stories, looking in store windows, and goofing around. I discovered that she was *mi hermana de la concepción*,[20] born on the exact day and year as I was: Mexican Independence Day.

In September, after enjoying the grand festivities of Mexican Independence Day with Mexican friends, in which a whole country partied on my birthday, I left for the United States. I wanted to see what it was like to live on the East Coast. I wanted to travel around the world and come back to the West Coast from the opposite direction. I wanted to be a "professional traveler."

*   *   *

Flush with three hundred dollars cash from selling my wares to the private school kids, I caught a ride to Boston. I stayed with a high school friend with a warm smile and fuzzy, corkscrew, dirty-blond hair, the only person at my school privileged and connected enough to attend Harvard. Within a week I found a job, a place to live, and the excitement of the Mel King Rainbow Coalition. Mel King was running for mayor in November 1983 on a platform that celebrated a broad spectrum of people of color, lesbians and gays, low-income people, and people with disabilities. I had never seen anything like it. I was stoked by the idea that everyone was appreciated, especially those of us who were often left out. The Rainbow Coalition concept received a national audience when Jesse Jackson used it in his 1984 presidential run. Sadly, voters were not ready for Mel King or Jesse Jackson, but it was at a Mel King Rainbow Coalition rally that I met the women of Asian Sisters in Action (ASIA).

ASIA was an organization of smart, progressive, mostly straight Chinese and Japanese American women who were articulating the issues of the day: interracial relationships, professional careers, and the cultural clashes of the hyphenated Asian American experience. I was excited to be welcomed into the group. The constant attention to my ethnicity in Mexico, as well as my experiences in Santa Cruz, inspired me to connect with Asian American women and the small, close-knit, forward-thinking Asian American community in Boston. But there was only one other lesbian in ASIA. She asked, "Why did you come this direction? Everyone [Asian] usually goes to the West Coast."

I was excited to explore what it meant to be Asian and female in America, but I needed support as a lesbian as well. Fortunately, there was a new organization called WOZA, a Swahili term meaning "rise up," which stood for Women of Color Organizing for Action. This group was composed mostly of African American lesbians, along with one Puerto Rican lesbian and a straight, gay-friendly Asian sister who was also part of ASIA. They were dynamic, articulate women, most of whom had been educated at expensive private schools. And they knew how to party. We tabled at amazing concerts featuring Sweet Honey in the Rock, Linda Tillery, and Casselberry and Dupree. We danced into the night at house parties with a deep Boston R & B sound.

The group's vibe was down-to-earth, spirited, and soulful but also stiff and upper class. I was pretty goofy. I thought I knew how to dance, but they let me know that though the rhythm was there, the moves weren't cutting it. With my low-rent, thrift-store look, which relied on clothes that I liberated enthusiastically from the local free box, I looked like I'd been hanging out too long in the woods with smelly hippies. When I crashed at someone's apartment after a party, the next morning the woman gifted me one of her many nice cotton sweaters, which looked brand new, to offset my tacky threads.

Boston came with many lessons. When I rode a bicycle on a bitterly cold, windy night, I was surprised and freaked out by the burning pain in my petrified hands. My broke ass couldn't afford to buy oil for my freezing, shared apartment in Dorchester. When the temperature hit fifteen degrees and I curled up in a stiffened cocoon on my mattress on the floor, a coworker invited me to her warm house for the night. As a Bay Area native, I had no concept of cold until I lived in Boston.

At one point I spent my last $3 on a bowl of *jook*, Chinese rice porridge, and went hungry for the next couple of days until the next paycheck. I ran down the wrong street in the wrong neighborhood, and someone threw a snowball at me, yelling, "Go home, Yoko Ono!" I hated that people assumed that because I was young and Asian I must be a student. And I never understood how people could line up down the block in Cambridge, waiting to buy ice cream in thirty-degree weather.

But ASIA and WOZA fed me. I got support for being an Asian woman and a lesbian of color, but not at the same time.

In January 1984, I went to New York City to visit Luisa, now Lois. We attended an event about Nicaragua. During the event, when I went to grab a cookie from the snack table, the woman behind the table asked, "'Scuse me, are you an Asian dyke?" I looked up from that cookie and saw the intense eyes of Katherine Ekau Amoy Hall, a tough New Yorker of Chinese, Hawaiian, and Irish descent. She introduced herself and told me about Asian Lesbians of the East Coast (ALOEC), which she and June Chan had recently founded. She gave me the stapled ALOEC newsletter, a collection of autobiographical stories, articles, poetry, and announcements from networking groups. The cover had a picture of two Japanese women in kimonos standing on a boat, and the words "Watch out, we're coming through," on it. I couldn't believe it.

They were having a Chinese New Year party in a few weeks. Did I want to come? Of course I did. In those days, if you didn't mind being overcrowded and delayed, you could hop a People's Express flight from Boston to New York City for $25.

People at the party welcomed me with open arms. In New York City's Chinatown I found the badass Asian dykes I had been looking for; they were getting down on the dance floor and making out in the bathroom. Around 5:30 a.m., Katherine and I caught a cab back to her Brooklyn apartment, along with Chea Villanueva, a butch of Filipino and Irish heritage. As the dawn light streamed through the window, the three of us stood in a close circle with our bare feet and hands together, witnessing each other and seeing ourselves in each other's reflection. We understood each of our struggles through years of negativity directed at us because we were mixed Asian dykes, rule breakers, different. We held each other close and cried, "Hapa feet, hapa hands, hapa eyes."

*   *   *

In May 1984, I developed a workshop called Asian Lesbianism as a Political Identity, which I conducted at the second annual ASIA conference, held at MIT. I later documented this workshop in an article by the same name, published in August 1984. I asked, "How do we bridge the contradictions of our cultural heritage and our personal and political autonomy? In a culture that defines both Asian women and lesbians solely in sexual terms, Asian lesbians struggle to forge an identity that transcends these stereotypes."

We discussed contemporary Asian lesbianism in Japan, Korea, India, Indonesia, and the Philippines. We talked about the female silk workers in China's rural Guangdong Province who either refused to marry or refused to live with their husbands and were respected as lesbians. In this area, women's feet were not bound, female infanticide was rare, and women earned a substantial living and were the main supporters of their families. We also discussed Qiu Jin (1879–1907), the lesbian revolutionary leader in Sun Yat-sen's army who taught revolutionary politics to women in Shanghai and founded the feminist monthly *China Women's Newspaper* in 1906.

In my article, I also asked, "Why don't we ever hear about these self-sufficient, independent women? After all, this special bonding among women is rooted in our cultural heritage—not the result of 'evil Western influence.'"

When I learned about past efforts to organize Asian lesbians in Boston, I found that Asian women had been experiencing racism in lesbian bars and that every one of them had been asked, "China doll, what are you doing here?" Yet when we saw each other, we often avoided eye contact. I wrote, "For many, seeing an Asian sister in a women's bar creates a mixture of disbelief, contempt, confused identity, and excitement." When ALOEC marched in New York's pride parade, I wrote, "Asian women had different reactions, some joining us, some smiling and waving, most staring right through us as if we weren't there and looking at them." I used this article to organize Asian lesbians in Boston and the surrounding New England area. I met women in their twenties who had never met other Asian lesbians, as well as women in their thirties who had been part of earlier organizing efforts.

I also wanted to address the limited understanding about lesbian experience, and homophobia among some of the women in ASIA. In November 1984, I organized the Dialogue Between Lesbian and Heterosexual Asian Women, which was a powerful, educational, and heartfelt community-building experience.

I had planned to stay in Boston for a few months but stayed for two years. Though I had originally wanted to travel around the world and come back to the West Coast from the opposite direction, I drove across the country in the fall of 1985 with a new lover and landed in San Francisco's Mission district. Fueled by the wisdom of Audre Lorde's *Sister Outsider* and the seminal women of color anthology *This Bridge Called My Back*, I was excited to connect with a vibrant lesbian of color community and a burgeoning API lesbian movement. Audre Lorde's essay "The Master's Tools Will Never Dismantle the Master's House" resonated with me as a pointed critique of racism, classism, and homophobia in the feminist community and a call for an intersectional lens on feminist theory and practice, long before we called it that:

"The failure of academic feminists to recognize difference as a crucial strength is a failure to reach beyond the first patriarchal lesson. In our world, divide and conquer must become define and empower."[21]

I was eager to find community and heal from racism, but in order to experience individual and collective empowerment, I needed to address the exclusion that I and other women had experienced among women of color. I challenged my Asian sisters to expand the narrow rules of community membership to include a broad diversity of API ethnicities, mixed-heritage women, and adoptees. San Francisco was right where I needed to be.

BLURRED
EDGES

FOR ALL THE HAPA GIRLS

Snapshot: 1994

for all the hapa girls who have ever
walked the fine line
done a wild dance
tried on someone
else's shoes

for all the hapa girls who have ever
looked for something
they had lost
in the places
it was not

for all the hapa girls who have ever
painted pictures
in the dark
with many colors
of all kinds
and fuzzy outlines
undefined

for all the hapa girls who have ever
who have ever
who have ever

stayed quiet
when someone
anyone
talked about their nose
their hair color
their skin tone
said nothing
when it was done to their sister
your eyes
your hips
your boobs
stood quietly
your feet
your last name
your size
said nothing
while it was done
by anyone

analyzed
all the hapa girls
picked apart
all the hapa girls
broken down
all the hapa girls
who have ever
who have ever

for all the hapa girls who have ever
struggled through interracial relationships knowing it was
the story of their lives

for all the hapa girls who were ever
told they weren't good enough cuz they weren't the "real thing"
for all the hapa girls who have ever
found a place to hide
behind the full-bloodedness of a lover or friend

for all the hapa girls who have ever
wanted to jump off a bridge
cuz having to be a bridge for everyone else
was too much

for all the hapa girls who have ever
explained
and explained
and explained it again

for all the hapa girls who have ever
walked the fine line
done a wild dance
tried on someone
else's shoes

for all the hapa girls who have ever

MAH-JONGG ACCEPTANCE

I grew up playing mah-jongg with my family as a central expression of cultural and family connection, and we continue to play when we find the time. With much snacking and goofing around, we nickname all the tiles, laugh a lot, and create a cacophony together as the hard tiles collide when we mix them after each hand. We have our own set of rules, which are apparently a combination of Chinese from Hawaii–style and our idiosyncratic family rules morphed over time.

Also known as *mah-jueck*, mah-jongg is a Chinese game that is played around the world. It's similar to the card game rummy, in that players try to get three or four of a kind in a particular suit. In the United States, mah-jongg is played by a spectrum of API folks, and since its introduction to Americans in the 1920s, it has enjoyed popularity among Jewish folks, especially on the East Coast.

Growing up, we played with a plastic set that looked like lime-green and white-almond gelatin. Sometimes we played with a special bamboo-and-ivory set, made before it was illegal to poach elephants for their tusks. My mom illustrated colorful cheat sheets so new players could keep track of the three suits, the three dragons, and, of course, the four winds: *doong, nam, sy, buck*. East, south, west, north.

The game can go on for hours if you have the time. We relax into our silliness as we experience the uniqueness of our cultural fabric, understood without question or explanation. We munch cuttlefish and chocolate-covered macadamia nuts, rub the raised tiles with our fingers, and play it cool during strategically tense moments.

If we haven't played in a while, we rediscover our favorite tiles like long-lost friends, which we announce in Cantonese and English as we set them down for all players to see. There's Stabby, or *Hoong Joong*, the red, swordlike, heavyweight tile that is the character for "central," or "central country" (China). There's Family Camp Stove, *Sei Toong*, four in the circle suit, which looks like multicolored concentric circles on an electric stove. And there's *Baht Mon*, which means eight in the character suit—sung, of course, with a familiar superhero theme song: "*Duh duh duh duh duh duh duh duh*, Baht Mon!"

When we get three of a kind, we yell, "*Poong!*" Sometimes, on closer inspection, we are amused to discover that one of my dad's tiles in his so-called *poong* is similar to, but not exactly like, the others. Once, my dad had a *poong* of the five in the circle suit, known as *oong toong* in Cantonese. The word for "grandfather" in Cantonese is *gung gung* (pronounced *goong goong*). My clever nephew, Weston, a teenager at the time, exclaimed, "Gung Gung *poong*ed on an *oong toong*!" which Georgia and I memorialized on a T-shirt that we gave to him the following Christmas.

And when we win, we yell out, "Mah-jongg!" and do a happy dance and collect our multicolored chips. My sister Sunya famously jumps up and bangs on the walls.

*   *   *

When I was growing up, my mom always said that each one of us kids would get a mah-jongg set when we got married. She looked high and low for four special sets with the numbers only in Chinese. She didn't want any "haole numbers"; she wanted us to know the Chinese numbers. Over some period of years, she found four sets that met her criteria and tucked them away as special gifts for each of us at the time of our matrimony. As a child, I wasn't sure what the future held, but I knew that I had always broken the rules and would likely not live up to this expectation of marriage, which might mean loss of my culture and family togetherness.

In 1984, I was about to publish the article, "Asian Lesbianism as a Political Identity," in *Sojourner*, a women's newspaper out of Boston. I knew it was unlikely that my parents would ever see this newspaper, but I felt that since I was publishing, I should come out to them.

I was living in Boston at the time and came home to visit my family in June 1984 on the occasion of Weston's Red Eggs and Ginger party, the Chinese tradition to celebrate a new baby. "It's just a little piggy!" my people would say for the first few months after a baby was born, keeping the baby's birth a secret so the evil spirits wouldn't steal it away. Since infant mortality was so high in China, it was cause for great celebration when the baby made it a month and was likely to survive, at which time its birth was revealed and the baby was welcomed into the family and community with a Red Eggs and Ginger party.

Soon after my arrival in the Bay Area, I had dinner at my parents' house with my siblings. Not usually one to drink much, I uncharacteristically slugged back a glass of wine as I nervously attempted to eat dinner. When my dad asked me questions, I gave stilted, one-word responses. I was distracted, tense, and not particularly friendly. Awkward.

Finally, my sister Su-Lin pulled me into the bathroom, put her hands on my shoulders, and eyed me close. "You have to tell them. Mom thinks you don't like the food. You have to tell them soon."

I went back out there and began. I was so nervous and freaked out, I couldn't breathe. I was about to burst out in tears or flames. "Mom, Dad, I'm a lesbian." As if they couldn't see by looking, as if they hadn't known me my whole life.

In anticipation of this conversation, my brother had said, "They're not the kind of people who are gonna run you out with a shotgun." But I had been gripped with a terror that knotted my stomach and kept me at a distance from them. I had no idea what to expect. As it turned out, we had a conversation unlike any other conversation I had ever had with my parents.

It was dead quiet as they gathered their thoughts. My dad responded in his measured, soft-spoken way. "I've known that for some time on an intellectual level. Now I have to process it on an emotional level." Surprised to hear his words, I let myself breathe.

My mom asked if I was sure, if I thought this feeling was going to change. I responded that it wasn't a phase. Then she shared with all of us that she had read *The Well of Loneliness* as a teenager and wondered if she was a lesbian because she was different. I couldn't believe my ears.

I showed my dad my article, which he read on the spot and said was good.

That night, as I slept at my brother's flat in San Francisco's Cole Valley, I felt a profound sense of relief. It was Saturday night, and I could hear the loud music playing below at Maude's, the famous and now-defunct dyke bar. As I listened to Anita Ward belt out the lyrics to "Ring My Bell," my body finally let go of the stress I had harbored for years and I drifted off to sleep.

The next day, back at my parents' house, I spoke to my mom in the kitchen. "Mom, I'm never getting married." Never say never, right? It was 1984. I couldn't imagine that people of the same sex got married, or that I would ever want to do that. Marriage equality was not imaginable back then. I followed that statement with something I'd been longing to know. "Can I have my mah-jongg set?"

She shook her head. "No! No! *No!*" was her response, as she shuddered and changed the subject. We both knew that the mah-jongg sets were supposed to be special wedding gifts. I guessed that meant that I was never going to get one.

I returned to Boston and began organizing Asian lesbians in Boston and the greater New England area. In September 1984, three months after my trip to the Bay Area, I came home to discover a hefty, rectangular package on my doorstep. Surprised that my parents would have spent the money to mail something so heavy and costly, I eagerly ripped it open. There, on the steps of my apartment building, I gulped as I took in the gift. It was my mah-jongg set, complete with instructions and colorful, hand-drawn cheat sheets.

Sometimes gestures speak so much louder than words. My parents aren't the kind of people who would tell me they loved me with words, but there it was. It was my twenty-second birthday, and I was holding in my hands the most profound gift a parent can ever give to a child: family acceptance. Two years later, my mother began to call me Willy.

FAMILY PRIVILEGE

"When you heal yourself, you heal seven generations back and seven generations forward."

—Ligaya

In October 2014, I had the opportunity to perform spoken word for a wonderfully savvy, diverse audience at Vassar College. During the Q-and-A period after the show, they engaged me in thought-provoking discussion. A Latin@ transmasculine individual asked me to "speak to the myth that people of color are less supportive of trans family members." His choice of words seemed to imply that he had an agenda, that he wanted me to shatter what he believed was a common misconception. As I responded, I thought about the many layers of complexity I needed to address in my reply. Of course trans people of all colors and backgrounds struggle to be appreciated, recognized, and affirmed by our families of origin. We want to feel loved with our families by our sides. Who can say that folks of color are less supportive of their trans family members than white folks? It's unfortunate that we even have to make the comparison.

But the larger question in my mind was this: What is family acceptance, exactly? And what does that look like for trans people of all colors, cultural experiences, religions, and geographic locations? Some of us are fortunate to receive unconditional love and support. Some of us experience loss of family that is absolutely devastating. Some of us are simply tolerated, rather than truly accepted. Many of us live in the complicated, blended space between acceptance and disrespect.

For many trans and gender-nonconforming people of color, family relationships and community ties hold tremendous importance. In the United States and other nations where we locate our experience outside the mainstream cultural framework, our families reflect our social, cultural, and community experience as people of color within a dominant culture that wields racial, economic, and gender-based power.

To be sure, some cultures affirm transgender experience. In locales such as Thailand, Hawaii, Samoa, India, Pakistan, and the Yucatán region of Mexico, there are indigenous traditions that recognize and appreciate gender diversity, particularly among male-to-female individuals, though the existence of female-to-male individuals is less often acknowledged. Stigmatization and marginalization of trans people still persist in these societies, but people in these regions have a heightened awareness of the existence of transfeminine individuals.

Yet many trans people of color hail from traditional cultures that attach considerable stigma to gender-transgressive behavior. Families and communities exert pressure to adhere to cultural mores. When we don't follow the rules, our families may reject us to varying degrees. For people of color who are living in countries where we are not part of the dominant culture, family rejection can impact us as a devastating loss of cultural context, and of our literal and figurative homes.

While trans folks of color are unique as individuals, many of us view our experience not as individualized, but as rooted within our families and community frameworks, even if we have experienced rejection, harassment, and abuse at the hands of our families of origin and/or communities. In an effort to maintain these ties, many trans people of color, like other queer and trans people, create families of choice. These relationships can be especially important for people whose cultural traditions place great value on family and interdependence. Service providers, community support organizations, and educational institutions can build rapport by acknowledging and honoring these family relationships, and by not making assumptions that these folks view themselves solely as individuals, when they instead might see themselves as part of a larger community structure.

But connections with our original families often give us our most fundamental sense of home. Many trans people of color have maintained relationships with our families of origin, though we may not feel fully respected as trans people. Still, we are at family gatherings enjoying deep cultural connections with multiple generations.

*   *   *

When I was a child, the Chinese side of my family had a harder time supporting me as a trans person than the Caucasian side of my family. I know that my parents were doing what they could with the resources they had. When I came out as a trans kid in the early '70s, there was no public awareness, support organizations, or appreciation for trans people. There was no community, no trans-affirming policies, and certainly no visibility of transmasculine people. There were no visible Chinese trans people, though the goddess Quan Yin, who my mother believes helped her find my dad, was originally depicted as male, a part of Quan Yin's story that's not often acknowledged. There was nothing to help my mother integrate the reality of a gender-expansive child with the teachings of her culture. Even now, while we have come a long way and many support organizations value diversity, very few resources exist to support families of color with trans and gender-expansive kids.

True, my mother had difficulty accepting my gender expression. But, as I explained to the Vassar audience, I got other things from my mother: a rich, multicultural experience; a sense of tradition; cultural and spiritual values; and connection to family and community. My mother educated the world around her about Chinese culture. She taught her first-grade class how to use chopsticks and took them to Chinatown. She educated her friends when she greeted them: "In Chinese culture, you never come empty-handed and you never leave empty-handed," she'd explain as they graciously accepted a small gift. Our legendary Chinese New Year parties were a festive opportunity to share our cultural traditions. I am grateful for the gifts she has given me.

I also feel grateful to have a kind, thoughtful, emotionally accessible father who showed me that masculinity can be capable and caring. Though my dad is of a generation that did not value women as equals, he never embodied his father role in an overbearing way. He was always organizing activities for us, including lots of outdoor exploration. When we went backpacking he would rise before dawn, catch fish in the creek or lake, and fry them on the fire. He'd make oatmeal or bring freeze-dried eggs to life and boil water for hot chocolate or tea. Then he would bang his tinny aluminum Sierra cup to announce that breakfast was ready, as we'd poke our sleepy heads out of our warm sleeping bags, completely unaware that he had been up orchestrating it all for us.

*   *   *

A week before I traveled to Vassar College, I was honored to receive the Vanguard Award from Transgender Law Center. My parents, at ages ninety-two and eighty-eight, attended the event, a demonstration of family acceptance in itself. In my speech I had the opportunity to thank them not only for showing me the beauty of community, but for teaching me the *power* of educating our community about our cultural frameworks. That is a gift that guides me as a writer and public health consultant every day.

Family acceptance is a privilege that many queer and trans folks don't have, and its absence has a significant impact on our health and well-being. Research conducted by the Family Acceptance Project at San Francisco State University found that highly rejected gay and transgender people ages twenty-one to twenty-five had lower self-esteem, were more isolated, felt hopeless, and were at high risk for physical and mental health problems. These young people were eight times more likely to attempt suicide, six times more likely to report high levels of depression, more than three times as likely to use illegal drugs, and more than three times as likely to be at risk for HIV and other sexually transmitted infections.[22]

Family dynamics are entrenched. People of all colors and cultural experiences, including those assigned male at birth, have been adversely impacted by cultural misogyny that polices and denigrates gender expression that steps beyond what is considered the norm. Many queer women and transmasculine people have to undo generations of female subjugation in order to succeed at living our lives authentically and finding our own agency. Even years after medical transition, many transmasculine folks continue to live with the sexism and misogyny that have been directed at us across our life span. Trans guys say that their brothers are accustomed to telling them what to do, and that their fathers ignore them when other male family members are present. They describe a dynamic in which everyone in their family disrespects their name and pronouns.

Certainly, trans people from myriad cultures, whether they are of color or not, feel strongly aligned with their family cultures and larger community structures and navigate families with varied levels of acceptance. In my experience, I've observed that for Asian and Pacific Islander transmasculine people, the concept of family acceptance is layered and not singularly defined. We may be at the table, eating our traditional food with everyone else in the family, but our families' responses to our gender identities and expressions vary. Some families don't talk about it; some recognize it but are unable to update our names and pronouns. When our parents or other older family members misgender us, whether deliberately or absentmindedly, many of us struggle with whether or not to correct them, because we have been trained to respect our elders. We weren't raised to stand up for ourselves and assert our right to be respected for who we are.

*   *   *

In January 2012, when I told my parents that I was medically transitioning, my dad said that he now had to understand that he had two sons. My mom asked, "Are you still gay?" In 2015 my parents often still refer to me with female pronouns, out of habit, not malice, but what's important is that they have taken my medical transition in stride. They accept me as the trans person I am today, and for that, I am extremely grateful. They have helped me financially when times were lean. They have helped me build my dreams, and they believe in me. They have taught me the meaning of family privilege.

LGBTQ people's family experiences vary widely. Many say that the relationships they have with their families of origin can be challenging, layered, and sometimes unhealthy, yet, if given the option, many choose to actively engage with their families even when they question the impact on their psyches. While all LGBTQ people need family support, queer and trans folks of color who reside in countries where we do not represent the dominant culture have a particular need for family connectedness.

The idea that all communities of color do not accept their queer and trans kids is certainly a myth. Many of us experience family acceptance that is from the heart, though sometimes not completely satisfying. Yet many of us appreciate being at the family table, as we challenge ourselves to work to improve our family dynamics so we can experience more respectful interactions. For family relationships are our lifeline to the past, a remembrance of our ancestors, a cultural congruence for our souls—however messy and imperfect they may be.

Providing Support in Communities of Color

I have worked with a number of community-based organizations that effectively give trans folks a place of home and family. An outstanding example is the Asian & Pacific Islander Wellness Center in San Francisco, an organization I'm proud to have worked with over the last few decades as staff member, board member, consultant, and volunteer. Its Trans Thrive program gives trans folks of all colors, many of them homeless or marginally housed, a taste of home where they can meet up for food, peer support groups, caring and responsive wraparound services, referrals, and skills-building opportunities. Like so many other support organizations that care for trans people around the world, Trans Thrive is a healing force for the homelessness of our bodies, minds, and spirits.

Trans Thrive works in partnership with the Transgender Economic Empowerment Initiative (TEEI), a program of the San Francisco LGBT Center. The first program in the nation to address critical trans employment issues, TEEI helps trans and gender-nonconforming people develop life skills, identify career goals, update resumes, navigate the interview process, and connect to trans-friendly employers. I've enjoyed working with TEEI in varying capacities, including launching the pre-employment workshop series, and providing transgender cultural competency training for employers. I am continually impressed by the ways that TEEI helps address the pervasive, systemic inequality that impacts the lives of marginalized trans folks on a daily basis.

Brown Boi Project empowers young masculine of center womyn, two-spirit people, trans men, queer and straight cisgender men of color, and allies by providing opportunities to develop leadership skills, work towards economic self-sufficiency, encourage self-care, and transform the privilege of masculinity into a tool for social change. With a commitment to racial justice and gender justice, Brown Boi has transformed the lives of thousands of queer and trans folks of color through leadership summits, workshops, and conversations that challenge misogyny, examine privilege, and focus on healing. Brown Boi is an Oakland gem that has taken its dynamic and powerful work to a number of cities across the nation, providing opportunities for people of color to embrace their masculinity without shame, build self-confidence, and create family with each other.

I'm privileged to have worked with Asian Women's Shelter in San Francisco, an organization that was one of the first domestic violence organizations to address LGBTQ, and particularly trans, issues. It serves all self-identified women, provides annual staff training on LGBTQ issues, and offers client education on LGBTQ issues quarterly. Its Homophobia Busters program trains allies to address homophobia, heterosexism, and transphobia within API immigrant and refugee communities in order to reduce isolation and create social support for API LGBTQ people. It is the role of the Homophobia Busters, as allies, to stand up for LGBTQ clients, staff, and advocates, rather than place responsibility on the shoulders of LGBTQ people. In addition, Chai Chats is a multiple-session program of training, dialogue, and skills building on healthy relationships in API LGBTQ communities. Since its inception in 1991, Asian Women's Shelter has been rooted in a social justice framework that normalizes and advances LGBTQ issues.

OLD LADY/YOUNG BOY

Snapshot: 2002

The first time I shopped in the boys' department, I was overwhelmed by a complete and utter thrill like nothing I had ever experienced in my young life. I was nine years old. It was a special moment when my exasperated father finally did what my mother and grandmother could not bring themselves to do. My mom's frequent complaint, with all the martyrdom of a hardworking Chinese mother, was that she *thought* she had *three* daughters, as if I had gone missing after spilling out of our Rambler on a sharp turn. She had the most trouble seeing me when she was looking right at me. My grandmother faithfully sent me huge red tents for dresses in the unwavering hope that they would bring me great joy on my birthday, insisting I'd like them as much as the train set I wanted but never got. My *haole* grandmother had a hard time recalling just how small I was and figured if I was eight years old, then I must have been a size 8, not a petite 6X, and that at the sight of the pretty little thing I would snap out of my raging aversion to dresses.

But my dad understood me. It was a simple act, really—giving up on trying to make me like those little flowered prints in the girls' department and crossing over to the land of stripes. I was relieved beyond words. I ran, exhilarated, through dark-colored racks of rough-and-tumble wear, each calling my name in a language I understood. I had found my fashion planet, and what a joyous celebration it was.

That was the year I changed my name from a name I'd always hated to a name that spoke my truth. And whom should I find in the boys' department, ready to party with me? Why, Billy the Kid, of course—the first pair of pants that ever hugged me and told me it was all going to be okay. These rugged, soft cords—the kind of light brown that blended well with dirt—were the coolest. But the best part was that they were emblazoned throughout in dark blue lettering with the words "Billy the Kid" in a Western motif. I wore those pants through patches on the knee and until the words and pictures rubbed bare.

*   *   *

Decades later, having not grown too much bigger than I was in those Billy the Kid pants, I still shop in the boys' department, trying to express my manly, *GQ* fashion sense in a department littered with cartoon-character footie pajamas and too many bright colors in a single article of clothing. It's not an easy task reconciling the holy trinity of mind, body, and fashion.

I drool over the men's ads in the Sunday paper, wondering where I can find a basic button-down shirt with a subtle, classic print that doesn't scream *clubhouse* or *bug collecting*. And yet I jump at the opportunity to express my conflicted inner adolescent. Swaggering in my long, hooded jacket, baggy jeans, and Vans, I'm used to that startled, cutting look from upper-class white ladies who walk quickly away from me. I am so much more than the narrow vibration of an adolescent male, and yet there I am at the intersection of decades of female wisdom and everything that the Target boys' department has to offer.

One night the group that I run for people of color on the FTM spectrum met in a local queer center's youth space. (The youth were kind enough to overlook the fact that some of us were well over the age limit.) The youth program had recently tricked out the place with a large-screen TV and video games. Everybody was all the way into the hands-down, absolute favorite, the Tony Hawk skateboarding video game—not for the skateboarding head rush, but because you get to create your *guy*, your avatar. You get to choose your height; your weight; your skin tone; your goatee, or not; your head wrap, tank top, Jams, tattoos, striped socks, boots—whatever you want. We spent half the night conjuring up our adolescent male alter egos on a video screen. It was *Cosmopolitan*'s virtual makeover for the FTM set.

I wear a boys' large, 14–16. According to the size charts, I'm the size of a twelve- or thirteen-year-old boy. Kids are getter bigger and bigger, and so are the clothes. I find myself getting younger and younger as I reach for a medium. But now that I've hit forty, I've got this old lady/young boy thing going. Mammogram-ready, lurching toward perimenopause, approaching middle age, I'm wondering where this will all take me as the gray hair sets in. Hell, I'm old enough to be my own parent.

And yet I long for ways to express the *man* inside me, cuz that forty-year-old transmasculine individual is certainly no boy. I need to convey the *suave bolo* who brings his lady one long-stemmed rose and sweeps her off to a candlelight dinner of gourmet delectables. How do you construct a man's image when all you have to work with is a simple palette of children's crayons?

Easter is my time of year. There's an influx of boys' dress wear—and it's on sale. I fit a size 16 perfectly. To think I spent so many years buying ragged stuff at the thrift store and hemming and taking it in. But when I put on a nice boys' suit, it's like it was made for me. Maybe I have a career in modeling after all.

Back in the day, I got my suits at the Burlington Coat Factory in downtown San Francisco, before I graduated to Nordstrom. Burlington is a huge, three-floor warehouse full of winter coats and cheap threads. The boys' suits have that slippery polyester feel, but the price was always right for my broke ass. Burlington has always had a special place in my heart. Me and my butch Filipino bud, who was even tinier than I am, loved the place. "Never tell anyone where you get your clothes," my friend would advise, as if our tacky threads bore no resemblance to our top-secret locale. As I shopped or asked that a dressing room be opened, the straitlaced Filipina salesladies would hover, attentively scrutinizing my tie choices. "How old is the boy?" they would inquire with mock innocence. As if it hadn't occurred to them that they were looking right at him. "Thirty-two," I'd respond. "*I'm* the boy."

*   *   *

In my quest for adult male stylings, I walk a tightrope between juvenile rags and this icon of male clothing—the suit. Yet it's really the middle ground I most prefer. Sometimes I find that rare gem—the perfect pair of chinos or a thick, ribbed cotton sweater.

But shopping alongside children has never really bothered me. With most of the stuff under ten bucks, I can get a whole wardrobe for the price of one pair of my wife's jeans. And with tighty-whities at $3.79 for a pack of seven, who needs to do laundry? I'm completely sticker-shocked at the sight of adult prices. But that's cool. So far nobody's pulled the alarm cuz there's an old lady in the boys' dressing room.

One time I was cashing in on a back-to-school sale while my wife browsed. "Get these," she suggested, pulling a nice pair of dress socks from a nearby display. I threw them into the cart, and together we approached the register with my new $30 wardrobe. The cashier never looked up.

"How's school? Do you like your teacher?" she asked, with that saccharine-sweet, talking-to-a-child voice. Georgia and I both looked at each other and burst out laughing at the sudden, twisted revelation that if I were a kid, that would make Georgia my mother. Then I laid down my platinum credit card.

The thing is, I don't really know how I'm perceived. People call me sir, or they call me ma'am. It's a rare occasion when someone addresses me as if I were a kid. Maybe it's the wrinkles, or the spot of gray, or the telltale survivor vibes of someone who has lived through a lot.

I guess I'm the male counterpart to Britney Spears, back in the day. Remember that song "I'm Not a Girl, Not Yet a Woman"? I'm not a boy, not yet a man. Just an old lady/young boy stepping over the puppy-dog tails as I navigate my way through life.

REVELING IN OUR AUTHENTICITY

It was a sunny summer day when I took my wife out to brunch for her birthday at an outdoor café. Our sandy-blond waitress presented our respective plates of food, then freeze-framed with a piercing stare and, in the absence of any finesse one would presumably adopt for tipping customers, demanded, "Are you part Asian? The Asian always takes over!" She then turned to my wife and proceeded to complain about how her half-Filipino kids didn't look anything like her. As my food began to cool, it occurred to me that holding my Asian face responsible for her issues with her family was not a strategic way to get a decent tip.

Our family language was English peppered with Cantonese and Hawaiian, and everything tasted better with soy sauce. As a family we celebrated our multiculturalism. And yet, throughout my life, my features have been picked through, my cultural knowledge evaluated based on my looks or last name. "I didn't think you would know how to use chopsticks, because you have brown hair." My loyalties have been decided and my membership questioned. It hasn't been just "What are you?" but also "What are you doing here?"

Similarly, as a trans person, I embrace and celebrate my unique gender journey. But for most of my life people have been as confused about my gender as they have been about my race, struggling with their need to categorize me. You know the drill. Their eyes bug; their mouth wrangles in an awkward attempt at gendered salutations. Pronouns fail them. They pause in midair without realizing it. "Sir? Ma'am? Uh . . ."

Like many trans folks, many people of mixed heritage are not easily defined or fathomed. People who are mixed are assessed based on their facial features, body type, skin tone, cultural knowledge and mannerisms, values, language, communities, and loyalties. And not just from white folks, but from every direction. There's an authenticity check, just making sure you are who you say you are.

Ah, authenticity—that beautiful thing that we trans people continually strive for. The right not to just live, but to unquestionably revel in our own unique authenticity, even when that expression makes people uncomfortable, curious, and confused. Our masculinity and femininity are measured for realness. Our ability to be perceived as the gender we identify with is evaluated. We are resisted even when we assert our true selves repeatedly.

As trans people, we have experienced the world in different shoes, different realities, different bathrooms. We speak a different language, about T[23] and getting clocked and transfeminism.[24] We use gender-transgressive pronouns and in-house words. We've stepped beyond the expectations of our families, communities, and societies. Many of us know what it's like to live as both female and male at different times in our lives, or at the same time. Some of us are perceived in different ways from moment to moment. Some of us are perceived as clearly one gender or the other yet locate ourselves in the gender galaxy beyond, whether in the present or in the past. And even if our identity or presentation is not ambiguous, our truths, and those of our loved ones, are layered. We may be keenly aware of them every minute of the day, or they may fade from our daily thoughts, but these complexities are there, behind our eyes and under our skin.

That, to me, is where trans experience and mixed-heritage experience intersect: in the ambiguities and complexities, the layers of cultural experience that don't meet the eye, and the difficulties that people have acknowledging and accepting them. The gifts are beyond measure, the opportunity to put a unique lens on the world, to see the views that others don't have eyes for. I view trans experience through a mixed-heritage lens because both are cross-cultural experiences, adventures outside easy categorizations. Living this life means experiencing more than one reality at the same time, code switching into different languages and norms of behavior, cranking up the brightness and color. And in order to thrive unapologetically as mixed people and as trans people, we harness the confidence and courage to defy exclusion and revel in our bold authenticity.

FACIAL INCONTINENCE

Snapshot: 2007

I pulled off my shoes and slammed them into the gray plastic bin, along with my jacket, belt, cell phone, and man bag. Agents in stuffed white shirts and dark blue pants, badges and yellow stripes, sniffed out my belongings under the glare of their monitors. I dutifully held out my boarding pass to the commanding, gesticulating official and slowly walked through the blinking doorway to our collective imagined safety. The place echoed of colliding heavy plastic and smelled of boredom, regulations, and hurry. Like most of the other sleepy weekday travelers, I had the routine down. Getting from one point to another at this moment in time means that you must partially undress in the company of strangers while bossy people charged up by national fear and the power of the uniform tell you exactly how they want you to do it and where they want you to put it.

I sat down on a dull-gray bench to put my shoes back on, then strode up the escalator, got a quick read of the departure monitor, and hustled to my gate. A little out of breath, I came to a stop between the seats in the waiting area and the check-in desk and realized that my flight wasn't even boarding yet. I was cool.

Then I looked down at a woman seated nearby. Her face registered a look of horror, like she was caught in alarm at the sight of the ghost of Saddam Hussein. Her eyes bugged; her mouth dropped. Her face became loose like gravity undone. Though she was upright and clearly awake, she didn't appear to be breathing. She was frozen in time and fright, and staring dead at me—just another random, nicely dressed businessman on a weekday jaunt from the Bay Area to Southern California. Apparently, she had an attack of facial incontinence.

You'd think that I had failed to notice a quarter-size, angry-red zit barreling out of my chin. Or maybe when I'd changed the baby's diaper I'd absentmindedly wiped my exhausted forehead with the back of my poo-poo-soiled hand. What could be so alarming to set off the red lights and sirens at this point in the security check-in process?

Flight or fright, the Homeland Security Advisory System is in effect, the Culture of Fear an indelible part of the fabric of our everyday being. As a nation we are caught in a loop of paranoia, circling from yellow (elevated risk) to orange (high risk) to red (severe risk) and back, with no justification of changes to the threat level. I circle through yellow (*he's a clean-shaven guy with a recent haircut but a very small build*): eyebrows raise; to orange (*wait a minute, what the fuck is it?*): eyes bug, breathing slows, head cocks to the side; to red (*He sounds like a woman. Are those boobs?*): jaws unhinge, pupils dilate, head spins off its axis.

And so it goes, every day, as I mind my own business; everywhere, people in my presence are completely losing control of their facial muscles. Like incontinence of the mind, or of basic social skills, this failure of muscular engagement is uncontrollable, messy, and apparently unprepared for. There are no diapers for this. No training pants with Velcro sides, no extra-absorbent padding.

Even though this has happened thousands of times, I still forget that I freak people's shit. I'm not bad-looking. There's nothing about my presentation that begs for attention, like wildly colored hair or odd tattoos or piercings. In my travels my clothes are about as *GQ* business casual as you can get—dress leather jacket, polished shoes, smart button-down shirt, and Dockers. I iron my clothes. They match. I'm presentable. But the problem here has nothing to do with what I wear or how well groomed I am. It has to do with my incongruity—my mere existence as a transgender person makes people uncomfortable. This day and every day, this experience will happen to me about eight more times. And I'm not just talking about bathroom drama; it also happens during innocuous activities like buying food, getting a seat on the plane, traveling while transgender.

*   *   *

Later that day, on the return flight from SoCal, I handed my ID and boarding pass to the first security pooh-bah and she took a good look at it. "Thank you, sir." Her voice tightened and got higher and faster. "I'm sorry! Ma'am. No, I mean sir. Did I get that right? Yeah, that's right." As she delivered her monologue, presumably glancing at the "F" gender marker, I realized the woman was deep in conversation with herself and not really talking to *me*. As she assured herself that she was okay—she'd gotten it right—it was as if I weren't actually there, or the stage I stood on was too far away to be within earshot.

Navigating between reads on my gender every day is a different kind of traveling, unlike traditional tales of faraway destinations and cultures. Embarking on new soil often means that I *myself* am the culture being visited, an oddity to explore by unsuspecting tourists who arrive unannounced. I am a new food, an exotic cuisine that incites and startles the palate. I am an unusual custom, a hand gesture, a hard-to-pronounce multisyllabic word. I am a natural wonder, shaped into life by the power of the divine, to be gawked at in awe.

Even when I've barely left the house, it's an adventure. There are regulations and unexpected turns, different peoples and cultures, to discover. The rules of engagement dictate that I must be flexible and open to the ways and languages of others. I enter a store, and one salesperson calls me ma'am and the other calls me sir. I respond by lowering my voice and covering my boobs with my jacket. They ask me a question. I abbreviate my answer and don't let my eyes rest on women for too long. They say something that concerns or excites me. I try to modulate my response so I'm not too emotional or effusive. I never know how I will be perceived, so I respond in the moment and try to avoid messy facial incontinence or apologetic freak-outs.

Even though my experience feels extreme at times, I know that everyone experiences some degree of otherness, depending on the situation. And as much as we try to be multicultural, embrace diversity, and be down with folks who are different from us, there's a point where each and every one of us, no matter how hip to the trip we may try to be, has a moment. Deep down we're all wired to be certain that we're the ones who are normal and the other guy is the weird one. And ain't it a good time when someone else is the oddity.

*   *   *

A few years back, I had this odd little experience, another unexpected adventure. My wife said, "Let's go to the mall." I thought, *Oh, man, I don't feel like shopping.* Working me with the urgency of a good deal that comes only a few times a year, she pleaded, "The boys' dress suits are on sale." I reluctantly agreed. We drove out to the 'burbs. Oops, wrong turn off the freeway, and there, like a reverberating glow from Mecca, was a red-and-yellow In-N-Out Burger sign. Giddy and hungry, we pulled open the door and I thought we had walked in on the teenage cast of *Witness*. In the parking lot and throughout the joint were about thirty youth, white with country and innocence like corn-fed folk from the heartland. The boys wore shirts that buttoned up to cut their breathing off at the neck and zipperless, high-waisted blue jeans that were too blue, with two big buttons that held hiked-up suspenders. The girls wore *Little House on the Prairie* bonnets and dresses with some kind of apron deal, all made out of the same pattern, yet with their own, individual drab prints. I kid you not.

It was the day after Halloween so I really didn't know if folks were just trying to eke out as much as they could from their costumes, the school play had just let out, or someone was having a barn raising. I leaned in to my wife and whispered at a safe distance, "What the fuck is this?" As far as I know, I didn't lose control of my face, but when it comes to incontinence of the mind, self-awareness is not primary. For once, it wasn't my turn to be a tourist attraction when I barely left the house for a bite. The woman next to us, who had an Irish accent, which added to the *Twilight Zone* effect, since we were in a 'burb called Dublin, said these folks were Mennonites. So maybe they *had* worked up an urge for a burger at the barn raising.

All I know is, when they called my number and I took my leather jacket, urban ass up there to claim our burgers, and a group of three suspendered boys turned and gawked at me good, doing that bug-eyed, facial-incontinence thing, our eyes locked for a moment and it took everything I had not to bug 'em back, look them up and down and say, "What are *you* looking at?"

Snapshot: 2008

On the strong, small back
Of my mother's mother, my *popo*
Her older sister rode daily
feet broken and bound
and bent underneath
like delicate, crushed lotus buds

Sewing buttonholes on shirts
five down the middle
two on the sleeves
fifteen cents
for a dozen shirts

Turn of the last century
my mother's father, my *gung gung*
arrived by boat
His sisters sold into slavery
To pay his journey to America
My mother chop-chop-chopping the vegetables
in the family restaurant

steering clear of drunk soldiers
sleeping upstairs
above the jukebox

And I
I in my privilege
turn of this century
tried to decide
should I transition
become a full-time guy

Female-born folks in times before us
lived as men
to survive
get an education
or a job denied
who knows how many of the sons
on Gung Gung's boat to America
were born female

Had I been born twenty years later
I would have transitioned
no doubt
But that collective journey
of feminism as survival
stayed with me
I found peace with my
mixed heritage, mixed gender ambiguity
Fought too hard, too long
to change this body now

Young folks
working it out in conversation
not that different from my own
twenty years ago

trans, genderqueer
How can I make things right so I can be me
break the rules forced upon me
transgress
different language, different options
same ideas
Biology is not destiny

I ask them what about feminism
They look at me like I am
truly crazy
Have we come so far that we really can't remember?

ROUGH
AROUND
THE
EDGES

TURN OF THE HEAD

Snapshot: 2008

Turn of the head
I am ma'am
And back of the head
I am sir
And top down I am
What are you?
And face on I am
No where do you *really* come from?

Shape shift eyes
No connection
Shape shift nose
Misconception
Shape shift size
Not deception
Shape shift
Shifting perception

Tone of the voice
I am ma'am
And style of the threads

I am sir
And texture of skin I am
What's your mix?
And flash of the eyes I am
There's something going on there

Shape shift
No attention
Give them
Presentation
Shift
All those opinions
Shape your own
Damn dominion

Stories unseen
No connection
Trans folks
Misconceptions
Mixed folk
No deception
Gender fabulous
No correction
Disabilities
Shifting perception

Turn of the head
I am sir
And back of the head
I am ma'am
And top down I am
Invisible
And face on I am

THE QUEERING OF CFIDS

On March 25, 1992, it hit me over the head when I didn't see it coming. I was young, able-bodied, and strong. I was invincible and too busy for the lessons in store for me. I had no idea I was going to be forced into early retirement at the age of twenty-nine.

I went into the women's room at the end of my workday, washed my lunch dishes, and leaned over the sink to splash water on my face. Down came the thick fluorescent light fixture from above, swiftly whacking my head, neck, and back. My dishes crashed; I was dazed. And everything hurt.

I had a severe concussion. I was in constant pain. For weeks afterward, people would talk to me and their lips would move, but I had no idea what they were saying. My vision blurred. I became extremely fatigued. I would work all day and then come home and fall into bed until the next morning, then drag myself out of bed and do it again. I went on like this for two and a half months after the accident, until my battery flickered out and I had no choice but to stop. And when I finally lay down, when I finally stopped working, I began to realize how sick I really was. Once I lay down, I couldn't get up.

I became a person who could not get out of bed. I studied the cracks in the ceiling, searching for clues, road maps, patterns. I wondered if I was dying. I had compartmentalized my life into race, and gender, and sexuality, and point of view—and yet the real deal was nothing like that. I had been reduced to that basic human place: survival. I wanted nothing more than to get up in the morning, be able to make myself something to eat, and leave the house. But I couldn't. Leaving the house became a privilege that I no longer had on a regular basis. I got really skinny because I was too sick to properly feed myself. My lifestyle had become a long, slow, deadening road, as I desperately tried to stay with the living.

I thought if I had money in the bank—saved up from my scrappy nonprofit job—I'd always be okay. I thought if I grew my hair out, people would treat me better. I thought if I got rid of my glasses, people would stop telling me that I didn't belong. But nothing I could change externally would change the very internal life of not being able to get out of bed. No one would take that exhausting shower—using all the energy I had for one day—for me. No support organization would bring me food. No one could lie in my bed and count the cracks in the ceiling for me, and no one was able to quell my bloodcurdling terror at the uncertainty and unpredictability of not knowing where I was heading.

The people I thought I could count on to support me in what was important in my life had decided that they could no longer be my friends. They turned faster than I could tell them and ran like hell. Most of them never stopped running. I saw only a few of them again, years later, after I was able to get up and go to events or a few of their parties. They rarely asked me how I was doing and interrupted to change the subject if I told them.

My coworkers were done with me—not a single get-well card or phone call. Just an uninspired termination letter, illegal because I went out on a workers' compensation injury. When they ran into my ex, my coworkers leaned in to whisper an inquiry as if I had been convicted or institutionalized and had brought shame upon the family. The thing is, I had believed that my coworkers *were* my family. We worked at the first Asian and Pacific Islander (API) HIV/AIDS organization in San Francisco. I had been recruited to work with the most marginalized people, the drug users and sex workers, because I was the only person on the West Coast who was conducting street-based outreach with high-risk API people. I thought that the camaraderie, cultural affinity, and queer resonance meant that we were one another's family.

In my naiveté, I thought my colleagues in the wider AIDS service community would understand. Not just understand, but be there with support, referrals, resources. Show up at my house with food, or help me with basic chores like I had for so many others. There were many lessons I had yet to learn.

I knew I had to be an actor. It was a familiar role, navigating shifting reads on my race and gender. I thought I could be an actor in my diminished life but have the satisfaction of knowing who I really was. Like straight cisgender people who play trans people, gliding to the stage to pick up their Academy Awards, glittering in gender-normative attire and sitting with opposite-sex partners, I was an actor. I could pretend that I was living this life, that I wasn't really a dirtball collecting disability.

I needed to remember that I was more than a fallen sibling or a dirty piece of toilet paper stuck on the bottom of some power-tripping Medi-Cal worker's shoe. But the gnawing hopelessness of what became years of disabling chronic illness and disability poverty got to me. After a while, I began to believe the version of every government agency or caseworker who policed me: that I was a no-good deadbeat who would never amount to anything. I became that person because I *was* that person—too sick to work, broke-ass, worn down, nothing.

* * *

I was diagnosed with chronic fatigue immune dysfunction syndrome (CFIDS), a condition of epidemic proportions characterized by persistent fatigue and other debilitating symptoms that are not attributed to exertion, ameliorated by rest, or caused by other medical ailments.[27] Though an outbreak was documented as far back as 1934,[28] reports of a 1984 outbreak among two hundred residents of Incline Village, a small Lake Tahoe resort town, launched modern-day concern about CFIDS.[29] It's called chronic fatigue syndrome (CFS) by the Centers for Disease Control and Prevention (CDC), was renamed chronic fatigue immune dysfunction syndrome by activists, and is referred to by fifteen other names, including myalgic encephalomyelitis. The fact that it has many identities is just one of the controversies surrounding the condition.[30] In February 2015, in a 235-page report, the Institute of Medicine proposed that it be renamed systemic exertion intolerance disease (SEID), with new diagnostic criteria, in an effort to acknowledge its authenticity and emphasize the symptom of postexertional malaise, rather than a cause, since no one cause has been identified.[31] Despite this recent development, the condition continues to be commonly known as CFS among the medical and scientific community, or as CFIDS among patients and some doctors in the United States. Shrouded in controversy, dismissed as psychiatric, CFIDS is steeped in social, political, and economic issues, its legitimacy and existence dissed and resisted.

When I got CFIDS, I became a full-fledged pariah and I quickly discovered that CFIDS was as queer and trans and mixed-heritage as I was.

The diagnostic criteria for chronic fatigue syndrome, first published by the CDC in 1988, were deliberately restrictive, in order to facilitate research, and were not intended for the purposes of diagnosis or disability benefits. According to the case definition, basic criteria include prolonged or persistent, severely debilitating fatigue that reduces activity level by at least 50 percent for six months or more; other medical conditions, such as cancer, hypothyroidism, hepatitis B or C virus infection, and clinical depression, are ruled out. CFIDS is characterized by a sudden onset of flu-like symptoms—such as mild fever, sore throat, swollen or tender lymph nodes, general muscle weakness, and muscular aches and pains, as well as headaches, severe joint pain, sleep disturbances, irritability, and impaired vision—that never go away.[32] Some people, like I did, become ill following a physical trauma. Some get a flu, as I had, that doesn't seem to completely leave the body. People with CFIDS also experience disturbing cognitive dysfunction, such as memory loss, disorientation, confusion, difficulty with word finding and recall, and inability to concentrate or comprehend.

As an athletic person who rode my bicycle all over the city, and as a writer who loved words, I was terrified.

As Hillary Johnson's *Osler's Web: Inside the Labyrinth of the Chronic Fatigue Syndrome Epidemic* documents, numerous researchers have drawn connections between CFIDS and AIDS.[33] Longtime researchers Dr. Nancy Klimas and Dr. Jay Levy described CFIDS as an acquired immunodeficiency syndrome that appears as a persistent viral infection, except the natural killer cells are ineffective.[34] Dr. Mark Loveless, another longtime AIDS and CFIDS researcher, stated, "A CFIDS patient feels every day significantly the same as an AIDS patient feels two months before death."[35] This chilling observation was substantiated by specific clinical data from research conducted by Oregon Health Sciences University, as well as by countless other medical experts, and may be true for some portion of the CFIDS population.[36]

But there were two significant factors that separated people with CFIDS and people with AIDS: I wasn't dying and I wasn't contagious.

On the one hand, millions of young people (mostly men) were dying in their prime. Whole communities were crying out for prevention education and care services. On the other hand, millions of young people (mostly women) were so ill they couldn't manage their daily lives but, except for incidents of suicide, were not dying.

Early media portrayals consistently described people with CFIDS as privileged white women who "didn't want to work." It was dubbed the Yuppie Flu. But if you talked to health care providers at San Francisco General Hospital or any other urban health care institution, the word in the field was that CFIDS was an illness that disproportionately impacted poor people of color. Years later, a 2009 meta-analysis of prevalence data concurred.[37] What's more, it is hard to deny the existence of an epidemic that has affected over a million Americans and over a quarter million people in the United Kingdom, affecting more people in the United States than multiple sclerosis, lupus, and many forms of cancer.[38] And yet there are still people who insist that CFIDS is not real, just as there are people who insist that trans people and mixed people are not who they say they are.

When I got sick in 1992, my sisters in the lesbian of color community told me that "women of color are all cockroaches—we can survive anything—and only white girls, or wannabe white girls, get CFIDS." When I got CFIDS I learned about losing community in ways that far surpassed the community I lost later because I was trans. When I got CFIDS I learned about being relegated to the wastebasket in ways that being queer hadn't even begun to touch. When I got CFIDS I learned about disappointment and missing life events in ways in which my later journey to parenthood only brushed against. I got a hard lesson in being broke, not just in my empty bank account, but in the depths of my destitute soul.

*   *   *

THE COLOR OF CFIDS

Snapshot: 1994

Have you ever
wandered barefoot in unknown territory
searching without searching
like a lost, misdirected child?

Have you ever
been enveloped
by thick, insistent quicksand
that took and took and took from you
until your feet could no longer walk
your hands could no longer reach out
your eyes could no longer see
your mouth and nose and chest
could only gasp
with the weight of your grief

Have you ever
woken up in jolts
from shallow nightsnooze
feeling only the fright
or the flight
or the fight
never the restful slumber of everyday people

Have you dreamed of sleep
as if it were a luxury
bequeathed only to the chosen
Instead finding dreams

in broken ceilings
or in the affection of someone not afraid to befriend you

Have you mourned the passing
of life and love and travel and people
as if your bed were
a cold, empty prison cell
its frame
the steel bars
of another nondescript tomorrow

I have banged my empty prison cup
against the bars of my well-worn bed
nearly drowning my lifespirit
in the dense quicksand
of my ailing body

I have fought and cried
and screamed and angered
like a defenseless animal
caught in some evil torture trap
of senseless war

I have lain in bed
weeks that became months
that became years
staring up into an unforgiving ceiling
looking death right in the eyes
until I could smell it
and taste it

And yet
I no longer fear death
As far as I'm concerned
we've already had our affair

and honey,
I'm over it
Death, that is

I am alive
Alive each day living triumphantly
for I am surviving
the daily slow death of CFIDS
transformed from the full life
of an athlete and activist
to bedridden and disabled
as fast as the ceiling could fall
Friends, lovers, and colleagues
clearing the room
quicker than my eyes could open

For two years
I wondered if I was dying
but with no official word
Disappeared friends weren't gonna come around
to say their last goodbyes
Having just enough hello
to tell me what they thought I should be doing
and that I should go away
'til I got better

Two years
I wondered if I was dying
One day to discover
I had three parasites
and that one was actually life-threatening
Wasting no time
I blew them away with Western medicine
like a shotgun to the source
having waited long enough

under needles
and foul-smelling, bitter herbs
that made even my mother cringe

CFIDS
Chronic fatigue immune dysfunction syndrome
It's real
It's debilitating
Not necessarily caused by one entity
Not usually casually transmitted
Not generally life-threatening
CFIDS

Known as the AIDS of the '90s
it has quietly reached epidemic proportions
you know someone
or someone you know
knows someone
Millions affected worldwide
by an insidious, invisible,
some say nonexistent, threat

Because CFIDS
affects far more women than men
so some medical folks say
they don't believe in it
Cuz they'd rather act like they don't see it
Than scratch their heads wondering what it is

C-F-I-D-S CFIDS
a complex illness poorly understood
Devastating
Unpredictable
It'll bring you to your knees
Like so many other illnesses

with no pharmaceutical cure in sight
It is a puzzle of many pieces
where alternative therapies prevail
the whole-bodied connectedness of Chinese medicine
the spirit
of the body's inner healing

They say CFIDS is a white-girl thing
as if women of color
don't have overworked, stressful lives
that bring our bodies
to the depleted ends
of a double-burning candle

It was everything about being
a lesbian of color
that stressed me into a horrendous mono
so many years ago
as I struggled to come out
And it was my overworked, overstressed
lesbian of color lifestyle
that dragged me
and so many other women of color like me
into CFIDS

Be forewarned:
busyness is overrated
Don't lose yourself
in the collective searching
Listen
to the warning signs

Unless you can only learn from something
when it hits you over the head

For illness and disability
are the greatest teachers of them all

Slowly,
for healing is no quick fix
I am pulling myself out of quicksand
igniting my chi with the breath of my focus
coming home
to the teachings of my culture
like a lost American
wandering forgotten soil

*   *   *

When young people with CFIDS graced the cover of *Newsweek* in 1984, long before I got sick, I grabbed the issue and read it with great interest. How could a cluster of previously healthy people in a region radiating natural beauty fall ill to some mysterious, insidious condition that left them unable to function in their daily lives? I was scared about the perceived looming threat and wondered, like so many others, about the possibility of contagion.

Around 1990, as an AIDS service provider, I read what I could find on CFIDS and went to a very well-attended, though largely white, forum at the San Francisco Women's Building that raised questions about an extremely debilitating illness that disproportionately affected women. With no identified cause, CFIDS was understood as a syndrome, or a collection of symptoms of unknown origin, just as acquired immunodeficiency syndrome (AIDS) was considered a syndrome before HIV was identified. Since it was a syndrome, the diagnostic criteria were considered a "wastebasket diagnosis" because diagnosis was done through a process of elimination.

In 1998, the CDC redirected, or could not account for, $13 million in CFIDS research funding, presumably because of bias.[39] Despite having received much less funding than other conditions, vigorous research efforts have attempted to find a causal factor of CFIDS, though none has been identified yet. It is widely speculated that multiple entities cause

CFIDS. In the '90s, some scientists described it as an autoimmune disorder—hence the name change to reflect the immune system's disregulation. Later research explored a possible link to the retrovirus xenotropic murine leukemia virus-related virus (XMRV), though most scientific publications claiming an association have been retracted.[40] Other possible causes include infection; immune dysfunction; toxins (such as mold); abnormally low blood pressure (neurally mediated hypotension); stress that activates the axis where the hypothalamus, pituitary, and adrenal glands interact; and nutritional deficiency.[41] Many in the patient community have been eager to correct the inaccurate assumption that CFIDS is psychologically based or simply depression (those tired, depressed white women) and rather to present it as a disorder with immune abnormalities that are inconsistent with clinical depression. Most of the depression associated with CFIDS is *reactive* to the stress of such debilitating symptoms.

When I became a person with CFIDS, I, too, was eager to deny that depression had anything to do with my illness. Sure, I was deeply depressed about not being able to get out of bed, but I had big ambitions. For years I awoke each morning with a grand dream of what I hoped to accomplish that day. Then I lay in bed for hours, imagining myself doing those very things, a fraction of which I was able to accomplish. Like many queer and trans people denying a mental health link to our identities, I shied away from any admission that I was depressed, because I didn't want it to legitimize the naysayers who repeatedly disrespected and disregarded the severity of the illness.

The '90s saw a rising tide of female-born individuals stricken with CFIDS, many of whom were lesbians and some of whom were transmasculine people. Everyone I ever spoke to who had it had horror stories about being completely disrespected by medical providers and living with the tremendous loss of friends and family members because of the persistent disbelief about the reality of CFIDS, and perhaps fear of contagion, which proved unfounded.[42]

In my own search for appropriate care and treatment, several male doctors disregarded me as "psycho." One looked me up and down, then questioned my work and what business I had doing it: "What is this? Asian people with AIDS? You speak Asian or something?" He then fictionalized my story in a lengthy, decidedly unfavorable report in which he erroneously stated that I had been under psychiatric care for the past five years. This guy was actually hired by *my* lawyer for my workers' compensation case.

Even though I had health insurance, resources, and connections in the San Francisco women's health community, it was years—a decade, actually—before I found a decent doctor. When I first fell ill, the director of a local women's clinic, with whom I had sat on advisory boards, was nice enough to offer a complimentary visit with the clinic's medical director, but I found that she was one more doctor I had to educate about CFIDS. While the women's clinic was respectful, its treatment strategies were inadequate. Some years later, I attempted to get an appointment at the "fatigue clinic" at the University of California, San Francisco, and was told that they hoped to see me in *two and a half years*. The clinic closed before that time, and the appointment never happened. Similarly, the CFIDS Foundation, which ran an information hotline for four hours a week, lost its funding. And no organization would deliver a hot meal to my door.

Fortunately, after strategically jumping through bureaucratic hoops, I was awarded social security disability benefits, a right that not everyone with chronic illness, especially one that is considered questionable, is able to secure. When I got that check, I sought care from an expensive doctor knowledgeable in CFIDS and alternative treatments.

Hence the stereotype of the upper-middle-class person with CFIDS. Only people with economic means could afford the health care necessary to diagnose and treat CFIDS. I found a big, wide world of groovy alternative providers who salivated at the opportunity to take my money. In my desperation, I hustled every under-the-table gig I could come up with to pay for the latest, overpriced stump water from the cemetery touted by the next "noninvasive" witch doctor who claimed they could cure me. To this day, I don't know how those folks can sleep at night in the security and comfort of their million-dollar homes after a day's work of preying on the desperation of extremely ill people. I saw docs who had no qualms about taking my whole disability check in one sitting, then later hiding in their offices while their revolving-door, disgruntled assistants presented me with the bill.

But what especially smarted in the desperation of my everyday struggle with chronic illness was the nagging pain of loss—the friends who never returned, the family who used it against me. One of the things that was difficult about getting sick was that I had to learn how to ask for help, something I have never been good at. When I finally brought myself to ask close friends in my API lesbian community for help with basic needs, they said that they would be there for me. But when I followed up, they never returned my calls.

I know it can be difficult to be there for someone in need; life is busy, and it's hard to fathom how challenging another person's life circumstances are. I myself don't always have the capacity to help others. This illness and the profound grief I felt made me very sensitive, and when my friends left my life, I felt as if they had turned their backs on me. I was heartbroken to lose the community that I had worked so hard to organize and that had been my home for the previous decade. It was a loss I mourned privately for many years. At one point some years later, a community member asked me to help pay for a visitor's medical bills for an acute infection. I was speechless.

Given the many friends I had, and the interdependence of so many of our cultures—a reliance on larger family and community support systems—it was particularly hard to fathom how my Asian sisters backed away from me so quickly and pervasively. In retrospect, I believe that their behavior was indicative of the times and mirrored the dynamic I saw in the larger API community's response to AIDS. As someone who was considered "weird" because I worked with sex workers and drug users in the Tenderloin, I worked hard to provide HIV prevention education for an API community that feared casual transmission and had cultural barriers to discussing death and disease. At the time, lesbians in my community were not prepared to support someone who was young and debilitated by chronic illness.

Honestly, the API lesbian community was the last ethnic group in the lesbian community to get on board with the AIDS epidemic. In my API community and the larger lesbian community, there was some resistance to working in the fight against AIDS because of the perception that AIDS was a men's issue. There was even a misconception in the early days that Asians were "immune" to AIDS. So while there were many lesbians of color working in the AIDS field in the '80s and early '90s, I was one of only two Asian dykes working in the field in San Francisco until the mid-'90s. I had CFIDS, not AIDS, and in my community there was no cultural reference point for how to support a community leader who had fallen gravely ill.

As much as we talk about chosen family in queer communities, how we look out for our own because our original family may not, I learned the hard way that those concepts did not apply when I was dealing with illness and disability. Ultimately my parents came through for me, bringing me food and washing my dirty laundry from time to time. Their caring gestures during this devastating health crisis made me feel supported in a practical family way.

*   *   *

In the early 2000s, the *San Francisco Chronicle Magazine* ran a cover story about the devastating reality of living with CFIDS, the lack of understanding among medical providers and the general community, the widespread disrespect, and the loss of friends and family that can happen in the fallout. In response, I wrote a letter to the editor stating that it was much harder for me to disclose that I was living with CFIDS than it was to disclose that I was queer and trans. They printed it.

I found that CFIDS had its own closet. I learned that no one really wanted to hear that I was living with CFIDS, so I had to come up with a pat response to the question "What do you do?" or "What have you been up to?"

It wasn't just that well-meaning people gave me tons of unsolicited advice: think happy thoughts, drink this, don't eat that, change your life, meditate. It was that people assumed that because I had a disability, I couldn't do things for myself. I wanted people to *ask* if I could benefit from assistance, not assume my limitations, make decisions for me, or do things for me without asking. I didn't want other people to presume that I was incapable, and I didn't want people to think that they couldn't count on me because I was living with a debilitating illness. I was so tired of people treating me like I wasn't a full human being because my life was different. From my own experience and my work with the disability community, I developed an understanding of the profound need for self-determination within the framework of the independent living movement. I knew we needed to centralize and normalize the experience of people with disabilities so that we could be empowered to define and navigate our own lives.

This illness messed with my masculinity on many levels, too, and made me feel as if I couldn't fully express my masculine self. I could no longer be that physically capable person who helped people move, and I also felt that I had to hide my trans status so I would experience one less "ism." I grew out my hair, but still I got run out of the women's room because, even with a ponytail, I read as a guy. Sometimes I got eyeballed and followed around in stores because I looked so sick.

But CFIDS was also a grandiose mindfuck. When I told people about having CFIDS, in the early days, before I learned not to talk about it, people would respond, "Well, you look fine to me," and I'd wonder whether this response was meant to be a compliment or a way of discounting and disbelieving what they could not see. They had no idea that I had spent several days in bed so I could attend this one event. The ambiguity of being sick as a dog while appearing to be healthy was as much of a reality shift as being continually misperceived for my race and gender was.

To be sure, people with visible disabilities have been gravely mistreated. They have been verbally, physically, and sexually abused, locked up, looked down on, and denied access to so many spheres of daily life. They know all too well about being on the receiving end of "facial incontinence." Having an invisible disability allows me to escape this level of harsh treatment and denial of access based on disability status. I also know from experience that when people do not see evidence of a disability, they may have difficulty recognizing its validity and be less willing to make accommodations.

Some positive experiences came of being sick. As much as I felt imprisoned by my body and condition, and as much as I lamented the drama and pain of life with ongoing physical limitations, I had comforts and opportunities. I rested in a soft, warm bed, not a cold, violating prison cell. I learned how to navigate a patchwork of resources for low-income people and people with disabilities, whether it was discounted utilities or an education. I proposed that the Department of Rehabilitation help me live independently by supporting me to obtain a master's degree at UC Berkeley. That's how I became a public health consultant with a master's in public health—because I needed a job where I could control my hours and work environment. Even though my viciously mean caseworker got a charge out of regularly waking me up at the crack of dawn and bossing me around, I was determined to get what I wanted, and I did. They paid for my tuition, books, and supplies, which made it possible for me to further my education and reinvigorate my career.

I learned the fine art of jumping through hoops with the right amount of dumbed-down diligence, the deliberate diminution of my intellect for authorities. When asked to appear, wear clean but worn clothes, be your worst day,[43] and, whatever you do, don't act like you're smarter than the people who police you, because that just pisses them off and won't make them give you what you need.

Even though I would regularly be stuck in the house for three weeks at a time, I learned to accept countless disappointments of not being able to experience the people and events of queer and trans life that would have fed my soul. I made sure I had food in the house, got as comfortable as possible, and enjoyed my downtime. Those lessons in acceptance helped me later navigate the challenges and sacrifices of parenthood.

And disability came with privilege. Despite feeling policed by the Social Security Administration, Medi-Cal, the Department of Rehab, and other entities, I made my own hours, rather than punching a clock. It was an odd luxury that felt simultaneously upper-class and broke-ass, as full of ambiguity as everything else that defined me.

*   *   *

After living with the illness for two decades, I managed to somehow pull myself out of it, one incremental step at a time. Some magical combination of mental, spiritual, and physical transformation transpired. I have much gratitude for a mad-scientist doctor with unruly gray hair and an oversize white lab coat who helped identify and eradicate a hidden chronic infection in my mouth. His approach suggested that for some people, the culprit may be bacterial, rather than viral. I had dental surgery to remove the infection, followed by a long-term course of antibiotics—which may seem counterintuitive for fatigue, but it helped. So did hyperbaric oxygen therapy to reinvigorate the tissues. Like the researchers who go undercover to study CFIDS, some of whom have received death threats,[44] this doc was on the down-low, so to speak, about the treatment strategies he developed for people with CFIDS. Because of his steadfast but unannounced commitment to treating people with CFIDS, I was able to break free from the extreme incapacitation of the illness, though symptoms persist.

After I became a parent in 2006, my health status began to shift slowly. Whether it was from opening my heart to the sheer joy of parenthood, from the outcome of treatment, or from the necessity of caring for my family, I began to be able to work more, until I was busting my ass day and night supporting my family of five. The work poured in, and so did the expenses of mortgage, food, home maintenance, tutoring, speech therapy, a child in preschool for nearly a decade, and so on. I became highly functional and stopped identifying as a person with a disability.

And then I had phalloplasty in 2014, and the disabling chronic pain of an ongoing complication. The thing that had begun in the women's restroom twenty-two years prior and metamorphosed until I could almost believe that it was gone suddenly reemerged when I got a penis. In the aftermath of surgery, my CFIDS symptoms kicked up and I found myself exhausted, in chronic pain, less mentally clear, and needing to nap at least once a day. I began to rediscover my identity as a person with a disability. As I navigated daily life with chronic illness, pain, and a catheter, I found the fierce presence of a whole new community of people with disabilities.

When I got sick in 1992, there was no Internet, just a San Francisco support group you could drag your body to if you had the capacity on that given day and time. There were no specific resources for queer people with disabilities. In fact, the disability community was not particularly culturally competent on LGBTQ issues and was completely out of it on issues of race. This was my experience in Berkeley, the disability hub of the universe.

But in 2015 I found a wide world of people connecting online, and with that, new language and pride. I discovered "sick and disabled queers," a term that didn't exist in my day, and a large community of people of color who subscribe to this framework. People who identify with this moniker embrace the queering of the body, with all its honest truths, disappointments, and rebellious transgression. When I was very ill, I knew only a few queer people of color who were living with disabilities, and we were all struggling to survive physically, mentally, emotionally, financially, and spiritually. But in 2015 I found hundreds, all of whom appeared to be struggling in some way, yet with a certain pride and politicized perspective I'd never known. This community is articulating the intersections between disability justice, queer liberation, and racial justice in ways that I couldn't even begin to dream of when I was first studying the cracks in the ceiling.

At the center of this movement is Sins Invalid, "an unshamed claim to beauty in the face of invisibility," founded in 2006 by Patty Berne and Leroy Franklin Moore, Jr. A longtime social justice activist whom I knew back in the day, Patty describes Sins Invalid as an organization that rejects the historically pervasive notion that people with disabilities are *invalids* and *invalid*, as well as the old association of "sin" with people with non-normative, disabled bodies. Sins Invalid showcases daringly erotic performances that center queer and gender-variant people of color with disabilities, expanding the erotic body well beyond a narrow spectrum of what is considered "hot." As Patty says, "There're as many ways to get down as there are people."[45]

Disability justice recognizes the interplay between the struggles of people who have been historically marginalized. As Sins Invalid states on its website, "We understand the experience of disability to occur within any and all walks of life, with deeply felt connections to all communities impacted by the medicalization of their bodies, including trans, gender variant, and intersex people, and others whose bodies do not conform to our culture(s)' notions of 'normal' or 'functional.'"[46] As a disabled trans person, I feel a profound connection between society's lack of familiarity with and largely unchecked hatred of trans bodies, and the brutal rejection and widespread subjugation of disabled bodies.

God, I wish they'd been around when I was struggling to care for my sick body and decolonize my mind. Back in the '90s, I connected with Patty, who is Japanese and Haitian, around the fact that we were both mixed, another kind of non-normative body experience. Says Patty, "None of us occupies any one, singular experience. As whole beings, we're in multiple relationships with other whole beings."[47] As I began to reconnect with my own identity as a person with a disability, I attended a Sins Invalid workshop, which provided a cultural reference point for queer and trans people of color with disabilities. While it was an appealing relief to attend a workshop that began with each person stating their access needs, it was transformative to push through my internalized ableism and honor my disabled, mixed, trans body in new ways.

The disability justice movement expands the ideology of the independent living movement, which came out of a white-dominated disability rights framework, to embrace intersectional identities and broader cultural values. Patty articulates an aspect of disability justice, a movement led by queer people of color: "Even the idea of independent living is a little difficult. I mean, I support it, obviously. It's incredibly important. But it's a capitalist framework; there's nothing about collective interdependency."[48] I find her perspective refreshing because it suggests complex identities and cultural resonance within the context of self-determination and multiple communities. Moreover, disability justice celebrates the complexities of whole disabled bodies, *powerful because of who we are, not in spite of who we are.* During the first couple years of my illness, I tried to reframe my sense of worth within the idea of "being," rather than "doing." Disability justice embraces our sense of worth as inherent, not predicated on how productive we are, a concept that can run right up against the pace and values of activism in the LGBTQ movement—something I'd always experienced as a cultural disconnect.

* * *

In addition to living with CFIDS, I also have multiple chemical sensitivities (MCS), which flared up during the years I was most debilitated. Highly reactive to perfumes, chemicals, mold, pollen, dust, and other airborne particulate matter, I was often treated like an extreme inconvenience and freakish problem person because I needed people not to wear perfume or use loud detergent.

MCS fueled my shame. In one incident, I was completely mortified when a professor in graduate school announced to the class that I was scent sensitive, ignoring instructions from the university's disability program to request that students be scent-free without disclosing the identity of the student who needed the accommodation.

It was hard to find support for this issue in my lesbian of color community. In the '80s and '90s, there were lesbians of color who rejected the need to create scent-free space as a "white thing" that went against the individual right to use hair products, perfumes, and oils that, understandably, felt powerful and essential for some women of color. In the late '90s I had a Latina lesbian classmate in public health graduate school who told me point blank that while she understood that I was scent-sensitive, she was going to wear perfume as much as she wanted. It was hard to balance my intense physical need for a scent-free space with an awareness of how personally affirming scented products can be for some people.

In 2014, I was thrilled when I began to see a strong show of support for scent-free space from a leader in the queer women of color movement. Founded by Madeline Lim, whom I've known since the '80s, the "Queer Women of Color Media Arts Project (QWOCMAP) promotes the creation, exhibition, and distribution of new films/videos that address the vital social justice issues that concern queer women of color and our communities, authentically reflect our life stories, and build community through art and activism."[49] QWOCMAP demonstrates solidarity with a number of other communities and movements, including trans and disability movements. In 2014, it issued a statement that recognized that many people of color need scent-free space in part because of economic circumstances that can lead to chemical overload.

I was fifty years old before my mother disclosed that I had been locked up without ventilation with a chain smoker from birth to age four, at which time my babysitter died of a heart attack. Yet my family and community seemed to treat me like I was defective because I was scent sensitive. Though my parents briefly considered the impact of that experience on my health, the economic issue overrode any concerns about the delicate sponge of my newborn body. They had found a baby-sitter who charged only thirty cents an hour. As my parents struggled to raise four kids, it's understandable that they went with a low-cost child care option. I'm grateful for a disability justice movement that recognizes the intersections of race, gender, class, sexuality, and other characteristics, and the solidarity of these interconnecting movements.

*   *   *

Since I first became ill, in 1992, some disability issues have greatly improved, while others have not changed significantly. In terms of service provision, I'm happy to say that people with debilitating chronic illnesses can now receive a hot meal delivered to their home in the Bay Area.[50] I'm also pleased that the Affordable Care Act increases access to care for chronically ill people regardless of one's preexisting condition, theoretically without the threat of financial ruin.

Yet two decades since I first got sick, many of the issues that plagued CFIDS in the early days are still present, and some are magnified. In all this time, the condition has won little respect, people with CFIDS are still not treated as full human beings, and honestly, there are times when I am still hesitant to disclose that this illness has ever been a part of my life. CFIDS is as maligned as queer and trans people, assumed frivolous and insubstantial, discarded, mocked, misunderstood. Like mixed people, like trans people, CFIDS is repeatedly instructed that it can't possibly be who it says it is.

This is the queering of CFIDS.

And yet, thanks to Sins Invalid and the burgeoning movement of sick and disabled queers, I now have a transformative disability justice framework from which to own and find pride in my racially nonconforming, gender-transgressive, disabled body.

Ten Principles of Disability Justice

By Sins Invalid, 2015 (www.sinsinvalid.org)

1) Intersectionality: "We do not live single-issue lives."
                                                    –Audre Lorde

Ableism, coupled with white supremacy, supported by capitalism, underscored by heteropatriarchy, has rendered the vast majority of the world "invalid."

2) Leadership of Those Most Impacted: "We are led by those who most know these systems."
                                                    –Aurora Levins Morales

3) Anticapitalist Politic: In an economy that sees land and humans as components of profit, we are anticapitalist by the nature of having nonconforming bodies/minds.

4) Commitment to Cross-Movement Organizing: Shifting how social justice movements understand disability and contextualize ableism, disability justice lends itself to politics of alliance.

5) Recognizing Wholeness: People have inherent worth outside of commodity relations and capitalist notions of productivity. Each person is full of history and life experience.

6) Sustainability: We pace ourselves, individually and collectively, to be sustained long term. Our embodied experiences guide us toward ongoing justice and liberation.

7) Commitment to Cross-Disability Solidarity: We honor the insights and participation of all of our community members, knowing that isolation undermines collective liberation.

8) Interdependence: We meet each other's needs as we build toward liberation, knowing that state solutions inevitably extend into further control over lives.

9) Collective Access: As brown, black, and queer-bodied disabled people, we bring flexibility and creative nuance that go beyond able-bodied/minded normativity, to be in community with each other.

10) Collective Liberation: No body or mind can be left behind—only moving together can we accomplish the revolution we require.

I DREAM OF TESTOSTERONE

Snapshot: 2000

I must have been a dope fiend in another life, boosting to fill the cooker or tricking to hit the pipe. I was taut skin on thin bones, running, quickened breath, heart pounding, piercing eagle eyes intent on finding the next deal, or something to steal, or some human weakness that would get me that next hit. I am keenly focused, darting in withered frame, enslaved to a vision, a fantasy of comfort. My body trembles, adrenals maxed, my mechanical movements the only words I have to describe the want, the want, the want. I close my eyes and imagine the slow drip of nectar, liquid oil of serenity.

I dream of testosterone like the dope on the spoon, the magic elixir that will soothe away my troubles and make everything right. It is the *curandera*'s sweet remedy, the herbalist's concoction, my only drug of choice. It has caught me in a hard stare.

I dream of testosterone coursing through my veins, building me up and thrusting me forward, announcing my maleness with utter certainty. Arms, thighs, back, I am euphoric. I am at peace. I am jumping through fire, the boy coming down from the mountain a man. I am drinking that long, cool drink that quenches the desert-dry thirst of a lifetime. I finally have the chemical my body always knew it was meant to have.

I have dreamed of T like a dripping-wet brush to my tired woes. Let this multicolored palette give way to one solid primary color, a deep dark blue, and after a while I could learn to forget the rich complexity of vivid hues. I dream of a place where the body becomes the soul, where my third-gendered existence finds a home, like the edge of mixed blood becoming a river understood. Wipe away all ambiguity, cleanse this mixture with a simplicity intelligible to all. Burn all the dictionaries—I have found my slot. As with the allure of a monoracial category, I can check one box only, as if to erase the visage of mixed heritage. For so long I wondered if my Chinese features were a scar on my face, or the charred remains of a good Chinese girl who tittered meekly and was designed for winter colors. I dream of T to smother the mix with a brand-new story and take me to another land.

In this new kingdom I find prosperity and walk the streets with ease. I am the picture of vibrant health, my illness fallen away like loosened old clothes. I am transported from everything challenging and difficult. I get a break like the lottery. I feel myself the way I was meant to be—fiercely alive. I swagger, and I am not the lawbreaker, not someone who has defrauded the biological deal. My picture has been taken down from the WANTED posters. No red flags wave; no neon signs flash. The world yawns as I walk by.

I am the straight guy, a new man caught in a seduction. Without a word, men welcome me into their ranks, knowing nothing about me. I am invited to sit at their table and smoke their cigars and drink their liquor. In this new world I am smarter, more responsible, and more financially secure. I am confident. I overindulge. I walk down the street my own way; no rules guide me. I stop hearing the highs and the lows and forget how to cry. I pull up the needle, firmly plant it in the upper-right quadrant of my ass, and fall into a blinded sleep.

I am jarred awake by the shatter of glaciers melting and rivers overflowing. The tonic is a spilled mess on the floor. The image that I have tweaked like a pencil sketch on thin rice paper gets caught in the gush of flood. The world knows not who I am. The ease of my interactions with women has left me. There is no automatic trust. Even though my lawbreaking record has been wiped clean, I am still suspect. People look at me quizzically. My history has been erased, my story written in another language. My past is lost to all except those who know the lost language. My voice announces me in another life. I find myself searching for parts of my soul. My spirit misplaced falls out of body, exhausted from trying to force itself back in. I awake from disorienting dreams not knowing which soil to step on, which food to eat, which language to speak, as if I have erased half of my chromosomes or a familiar scar.

The assumptions are different but still wrong. No longer a manly woman, I have become a womanly man. Yet my masculinity is decidedly female, butch to the core. I am a gentleman of a different stripe. It's the way I take my woman sweet and rough and worship her for the goddess she is. It's the way I know women cuz I am one, the way I will fight for women to the end. It's about being down cuz I'm *there*. I cannot take myself further away from who I am and what I love.

Still, I crave relief from the punishment for gender variance, the shame, the assumptions, the people whose faces register horror as they pull their children away from me. I sink back and imagine what it would be like to go unnoticed, to live a life clearly one thing or the other, pre-defined by someone else. I want to live in a world beyond all the ma'am-ing and sir-ing, all the he-ing and the she-ing. But I cannot obliterate this queerness by injection. No stroke of the brush can mask it or change it or make it go away. Beyond the collage of images of us reflected in the eyes of others, we are never truly seen. I am but a reflection in choppy waters, my dream but smoke and mirrors.

CHRISTOPHER, BADASS DRAGON

The first time I spoke to Christopher on the phone, we were in the middle of a conversation, when he sighed and asked me to hold while he stepped away and threw up. When he came back to the phone, he joked about it. I was surprised that he could feel that unsettled in his stomach and still carry on a conversation, and impressed with the way he laughed it off. As I struggled with my own health challenges, I appreciated his sense of humor about something so ongoing, demanding, and overwhelming.

When I met Christopher in 1993, he was skinny and female-bodied, wearing a wrinkled white T-shirt and jeans with a dark blue bandanna wrapped around his head. He was speaking about living with CFIDS to a small gathering of people at the San Francisco Women's Building. Not long after he began, he said he didn't feel well and proceeded to lie down on the cold, hard floor. We in the small audience craned our necks to view him as he continued to talk.

Christopher and I became close. He was hapa, his father Chinese and his mother Caucasian. We both came from butch identities to embrace ourselves as transgender, as FTM. In the early '90s, we were two of the four transgender-identified people in the API lesbian community in San Francisco, a community in which we were both deeply involved.

But our connection stretched beyond our shared experience as hapa trans people. It wasn't just that we both had a deep reverence for Chinese culture. It wasn't just that we were both gender-transgressive people struggling to navigate acceptance in our families and communities while coming into our true selves. We bonded deeply because we were both living with the same life-shattering, debilitating chronic illnesses: CFIDS and MCS. Though our symptoms and limitations were different, we both knew the gnawing daily struggle of living with a body that worked against our dreams, trying to connect to a world that didn't understand our experience, through years of grinding disability poverty.

My disability undermined my masculinity and confidence, but Christopher wasn't afraid to wear his disability on his sleeve. He pushed people to see him in his wheelchair and surgical mask. When I was extremely debilitated, I was devastated because I had to stay home, but Christopher wasn't going to miss being in the world because he was too sick. And sure enough, there he was, marching down the street in the Lunar New Year parade with a pretty girl pushing him in his wheelchair, expressing himself in all his brave authenticity.

Christopher was family. He was there to mark the occasions—the Lunar New Year and other holidays, birthdays, anniversaries, Oscar nights, Halloweens—with love, respect, laughter, and fabulousness. He was the best man at my wedding. He was a pioneering filmmaker, community organizer, and activist. He was a bold, driven artist. A witty tough guy who once showed up on a dark night to help me fix a flat. A pansexual gentleman who knew his way around the kitchen and had a flair for home decorating. A rebel who deeply honored cultural traditions.

Christopher Lee was another beautiful, talented trans person of color tragically lost to suicide.

*   *   *

Christopher had a tremendous capacity to take risks, whether in the way he loved with so much heart or in the way he celebrated his unique self. He embraced so many different kinds of people without judgment and wasn't afraid to stretch himself in his creative work or the groundbreaking community organizing and community building he did with Tranny Fest.

In 1997 he cofounded Tranny Fest, North America's first transgender film and arts festival, which has since evolved into the thriving San Francisco Transgender Film Festival. In collaboration with cofounders Al

Austin and Elise Hurwitz, he presided over the festival with red-carpet flair and a penchant for community service, providing free Chinese food for a cash-strapped transgender community long before other organizations were doing it. He welcomed everyone, properly painted with black eyeliner and sporting a fly black-velvet suit and his signature flirty, twinkle-eyed smile.

Christopher was an innovative, award-winning filmmaker who produced four films that stretched audiences to imagine a gender galaxy that transgressed race, culture, and sexual prescription. His first, *Christopher's Chronicles* (1996), told his transition story long before the immediacy and prevalence of transition stories on YouTube. *Trappings of Transhood* (1997) was a smart, sexy reflection of early trans pride that documented the lives of a multicultural group of transmasculine individuals at a time when few genuine representations of us existed.

After his first two films, Christopher turned his attention to porn. It was his dream to celebrate trans male bodies and sexuality in all of their beauty and diversity. In 1998, *Alley of the Trannyboys* rectified the absence of trans men in porn, and in 1999, *Sex Flesh in Blood* depicted his special brand of horror porn with a racially, sexually, and gender-diverse cast. Upon the release of each new film and each Tranny Fest, the momentum grew as the Bay Area transgender community built itself from a handful of folks in the early '90s to a vibrant scene by the late '90s, a burgeoning community that was still small enough to know everybody. In 2002, after a successful campaign in partnership with Shawna Virago involving hand-copied flyers distributed at art and political activism events, Christopher was the first FTM grand marshal in the San Francisco LGBTQ Pride Parade.

Nowadays, the word "tranny" is considered pejorative because it is associated with dehumanization and hate violence, especially directed at trans women, but in the '90s in San Francisco, the word was a spirited term of pride. For Christopher, being a tranny was a fierce celebration of individuality, rebelliousness, and beautiful complexity. Whenever I think of the word "tranny," I think of Christopher because he wore it so well.

*   *   *

Between 1995 and 2000, we organized the Dragon Club, a small group of Asian trans guys and butches hanging out and supporting each other. Our big event was the presentation, in June 1996, of the film *Shinjuku Boys*, which documented the personal and professional lives of female-to-male transgender individuals working as nightclub hosts in Tokyo's Shinjuku District. We all dressed to the nines in suits and ties, our ladies in the finest dresses and heels, for a movie in a dank old theater with threadbare seats. When the four of us stood onstage to introduce ourselves as the Dragon Club, it was the first time we'd ever announced our Asian transgender selves to our larger community.

At the time, Christopher was the only one of us who was medically transitioning. As many of us in the API queer and trans community struggled with difficulties embracing our full selves, he was a bold force who celebrated his truth. He educated the API lesbian community about trans issues, and for that I am grateful.

When Georgia and I got married in 1998, I asked Christopher to be my best man. He was so honored and took the job seriously. He was enthusiastic about the ritual of helping me transition into being a married person, organizing my bachelor party and the large, red "double happiness" characters he pasted to my car. He brought our mothers flowers at the rehearsal dinner, and it was hilarious to watch them both swoon. After that, he always gave them little presents at family gatherings for years to come: red roses, a card he got in Chinatown, a lottery ticket, a little trinket. He was all about the charm.

When I think of all the family events we spent together, one Lunar New Year stands out in my memory. Christopher, Georgia, and I drove with good friends Chino and Maya to San Francisco from Oakland to get some delicious Chinese food. We were all *dressed*, but my look was not working. I had this long black coat that Georgia had given me that was too presidential. My shirt was too white and my tie was too wrong. Christopher was known for his well-meaning fashion critiques. He and Chino gave me the hardest time, a memory that still makes me smile.

Christopher was many things: a gender hybrid, a bold trans man who transitioned long before there was much understanding or support, a paradoxical creature, larger than life, intensively creative, and boldly innovative. He had a strong sense of what was right. When he was good, he was so good, so charming, so sweet, so giving. But when he was bad, he was so bad. He was a bad boy who lived at the edges.

Of the twelve animals in the Chinese zodiac, the dragon is the only animal that is a mythical creature, which means it has a connection with the transmuting power of heaven. It's a combo animal, an amalgamation of the tiger, fish, serpent, and eagle. Dragons are free spirits, a symbol of power, getting things done, breathing fire. There's a soft underbelly of compassion yet a sharp tongue. There is no natural predator for the dragon, so they are never cautious and things usually go well for them. They naturally do things—their ideas, gestures, and ambitions—on a grand scale.

Dragons know that rules are for other people. Christopher was a fierce, badass dragon like I have never known.

*   *   *

Christopher and I went our separate ways about seven years before he passed. I felt saddened and confused as to why. Whenever I ran into him at parties, he was warm and joked around with me, though he appeared troubled as he stood at a distance from others. I was always happy to see him; I never stopped thinking of him as family.

As I wrestled with my profound grief after he passed, I wished I had known that Christopher was suicidal and that I had tried to connect with him in his time of need. I felt gut-punched by the loss of him in both life and death, and devastated to learn that he had been in so much pain. With suicide, there are so many questions, and never enough answers.

*   *   *

At Christopher's memorial in February 2013, as I stood onstage before a mourning community, I felt stiff in my body, racked in my soul. I had slept fitfully the night before, replaying so many moments spent with Christopher. My insides ached with sorrow, the whys, the hows, the what-ifs interfering with everything that made sense in life.

I looked out from the El Rio stage at all the people whose lives he had touched: kinky queers, androgynous Asian dykes, leather daddies, experimental filmmakers, presentable lawyers, long-term activists, starving artists, and tattooed rebels. There were many people who, like he and I, had come out as transgender during the '90s. After a month of online grieving, it was moving to see everyone there to mourn in community.

I had wanted to play a music video, but, not being much of an Asian techie, I couldn't make it happen. At the time, Macklemore and Lewis's "Thrift Shop" video was starting to gain popularity. Christopher knew how to work a thrift store; he would be stoked to find slick suits he got for twenty-five bucks, or loud aloha shirts that only he could pull off. The first time I saw this music video, I was convinced the dude had borrowed Christopher's fur coat to shoot it. It seemed like a fitting commemoration of him.

As I reflected on his life, the most difficult part was knowing that the health care system had failed him. I spoke with Chino and Maya Scott-Chung, and Shivaun Nestor, who recounted that at the time of his death, he was in great physical pain in the aftermath of trans surgery, deeply depressed, and was marginally housed. Though he was estranged from his family of origin, he had a dedicated chosen family[51] with expertise in how to navigate the health care system, who worked tirelessly to house him, look after him around the clock, and help him access care. A social worker at San Francisco General Hospital told his friends that he had the strongest support system of anyone she had worked with in her twenty years of service. I was grateful for the way his chosen family had worked so hard to help him, and devastated that even with a well-coordinated support system, he ended his life through suicide.

*   *   *

Though a community-based organization in San Francisco had a dual-diagnosis unit specifically for trans people, the program was designed for trans women and was sadly not accessible to him. Christopher told his friends that when he visited, he found that he couldn't stay because the women's strong perfume set off his MCS and CFIDS symptoms—an important reminder of the need for scent-free access in trans community programs.

After a staff person at an inpatient mental health facility inappropriately disclosed his transgender status to other patients, a psychiatrist told his chosen family that Christopher's problem was that he was not out and proud about being trans—an ironic assessment, given that he had cofounded the first transgender film festival in the United States. The disclosure of a patient's trans status is a clear violation of HIPAA, the federal rule that protects the privacy of patient health information. In a residential treatment setting, disclosure of a trans man's status can gravely impact the individual, inciting his fears of violence and setting him up to be targeted for harassment, ridicule, and physical and sexual assault. This egregious breach of confidentiality made Christopher feel unsafe, threatened, and distrustful of mental health facilities, which made it difficult for him to access the care he needed.

The tragedy of Christopher's story is that a network of Bay Area providers failed to meet the needs of a well-connected and supported, marginally housed, trans man of color with mental health and physical disabilities. Sadly, he was far from the first trans man of color I've known personally who committed suicide. The alarming data speak to this monumental issue in the transgender community, which is unparalleled in any other demographic. As I've stated previously, the National Transgender Discrimination Survey, with 6,456 participants from every US state and territory, found that 41 percent of transgender people have attempted suicide, nine times the 4.6 percent rate for the general population. Trans men have a higher incidence (46 percent) than trans women (42 percent).[52] That means that nearly one in two trans men—or every other one—has made an attempt to end his life. This is not ideation we're talking about, but actual attempts. And the situation is not getting any better. Even though we now have awareness about transgender people, educational opportunities for the general public, and many resources, we are losing more trans people to suicide than ever before. We have so much work to do to stem the tide.

A number of other studies have corroborated this high suicide rate, showing that 25 percent to 43 percent of trans people have attempted suicide at some time in their life.[53] The suicide rate goes up for people who lost a job due to bias (55 percent), were harassed or bullied in school (51 percent), worked in the underground economy (60 percent), or were the victim of physical assault (61 percent) or sexual assault (64 percent).[54]

Rates are high for trans and gender-nonconforming people who experienced homelessness (69 percent), had been turned away from a doctor's office because of antitrans discrimination (60 percent), had a physical disability (56 percent), and had a mental health disability (65 percent). Rates are high even for trans people who are considered "low risk"; people with graduate degrees have a 31 percent rate.[55]

There are so many factors that lead trans people to contemplate or attempt suicide: rejection by our families, schools, and communities; difficulty securing and maintaining employment, health care, and housing; physical and mental health disabilities; and the constant dehumanization aimed at us that still goes largely unchecked throughout society. Structural inequalities and structural violence are clearly a contributing factor, yet one thing is clear: trans people attempt suicide across a demographic spectrum.[56] I don't know a single trans person who doesn't have the scars.

According to the interpersonal theory of suicide, risk factors for suicide include "thwarted belongingness," or a lack of social connectedness, and "perceived burdensomeness," the belief that one is a burden to others.[57] The idea of thwarted belongingness is an important concept given the many ways in which communities can exclude people who do not fit narrow rules of membership. Many trans people and others who challenge social rules experience social isolation, which can put them at risk. This issue of belonging hits home for me as someone who has never fit neatly into community rules of membership. It is a reminder that we need to be gentle with each other and to establish membership and systems that are as expansive and welcoming as possible.

In addition, people who are struggling with economic issues, unstable housing, and health conditions, as Christopher was, become exhausted asking others for help and start to believe that they are a burden to others. His death, and the death of so many others, is fundamentally related to the pervasive structural inequality that plagues transgender communities, especially trans communities of color, which are disproportionately impacted by educational, employment, housing, and health care discrimination.

Data indicate that one of the highest predictors of suicide is difficulty accessing trans-competent care. I find it devastating and deeply unsettling that in his time of great need, and with a strong social support system, Christopher was unable to find a facility that could care for him without judgment or interference. This tragic tale is an important reminder that programs that provide mental health support need to ensure that their staff are well trained on transgender issues.

*   *   *

Christopher's death impacted those around him in myriad ways. Some people whose lives he touched became more resolute about following their dreams, working creatively, and changing the world. But his death left an indelible hole in so many of our hearts. In an article in *Psychiatric Times*, Ronald Pies, MD, described the impact of suicide:

"Any suicide—even in the direst circumstances, and even after much deliberation—leaves a grotesque gash in the emotional life of families and communities. It may take years for such a wound to heal, if it heals at all."[58]

Years later, Christopher's chosen family and community continue to mourn him and the tragedy that led to his death.

Yet, in true badass-dragon style, Christopher created change even after he passed. When the coroner listed him as female on his death certificate, Transgender Law Center worked with Assembly member Toni Atkins and Equality California to pass the Respect After Death Act, which took effect in July 2015. This law helps ensure that transgender people's gender identity is reflected on their death certificates. Thanks to Christopher and the advocacy of his chosen family, Chino and Maya Scott-Chung, no more trans people in California will be misgendered in death.

As I reflect on the beauty and the sorrow, the joy and the tragedy, that are Christopher's story, I am thankful for the gifts of his brotherhood. As I navigate my path as a hapa Chinese trans man with a disability, I carry the gift of his kinship and his ability to juggle all of who he was within all the layers of ambiguity and complexity. As a parent of three small kids, I feel his gift of love and family. And as I work to help people and systems stretch to be more trans-affirming, I feel his presence—not just because he was a well-loved trans person who tragically fell through the cracks of the mental health system, but also because he had the confidence and the fire to take big risks to be his true self. His spirit informs my life and work every day.

The day after the memorial at El Rio, there was another gathering, at a meditation center, a spiritual send-off with loud drumming that vibrated my insides as I wrote words of love and forgiveness to throw into the big outdoor fire. The deep bass tones reverberated to the bone, the heart, and the soul as a grieving community sent our brother off, another trans angel to watch over us.

For more information about Christopher Lee's life and legacy, visit www. dragonsbloodrising.org and www.facebook.com/ChristopherLeeMemorial.

Suicide Prevention Resources

The Trans Lifeline is a free suicide prevention hotline for trans and gender-nonconforming people in crisis. Hotline volunteers are all trans-identified and educated on the range of challenging life experiences that trans people experience: www.translifeline. org; (877) 565-8860 (United States); (877) 330-6366 (Canada)

The Trevor Project provides crisis intervention and suicide prevention services for LGBTQ youth ages thirteen to twenty-four. Its lifesaving programs are available by phone, online, and through text. The Trevor Lifeline is the only national twenty-four-seven lifeline for LGBTQ young people: www.thetrevor project.org; (866) 488-7386

FALLEN ANGELS

Angels are falling in the streets
Our grief more desperate with each drumbeat
Beautiful souls taken in their prime
Being true to themselves their only crime

Chased stabbed shot raped and beat
Every week the horror repeats
Gentle spirits gone but no headlines
Cuz the victims expanded narrow gender lines

Angels are falling in the streets
Not just cuz they startled between the sheets
Fathers lovers thieves laying the blame
Desperately trying to exterminate their shame

A national crisis, state of emergency
Institutional violence, structural inequality
Racism, classism, trans misogyny
When will they see trans humanity

Angels are dying in the streets
Rest in power, loved ones, your spirits ever sweet
Bigotry and hate the vicious shrapnel
Taking beautiful women whose bodies were assigned male

EXPANDING
THE
EDGES

WONDROUSLY LAID

My beautiful femme I dare say
How wondrously did you me lay
The toes they were grippin'
Next day I was crippin'
Yet feeling so happy and gay

IRREVERENT, VOLUPTUOUS GRAD STUDENT

The headline read, simply, "I Like Fun," which sounded reasonable enough and got right to the point. The ad read, "Irreverent, voluptuous grad student seeks brainy, brawny girls to frolic with. If you like wicked laughter, bitchy banter, and opening doors, take the risk and call. I won't bite unless you want me to."

There was no picture, of course, because this was in the days before the Internet. That's right. Gather 'round, children. Grandpa's gonna break it down. Let's talk about life in the last century.

The ad ran in the *San Francisco Bay Times*, the only real option for lesbian personal ads in the Bay Area in the mid-'90s. In a sea of badly written personals, this one jumped out at me. People who placed ads left a voice mail on the phone system, and if you were interested, you left them a voice mail. Though this ad had been published two weeks prior and it was almost time for the next issue of the newspaper to come out, I knew I had to respond.

I listened to her voice message, which struck me as friendly, unpretentious, and, surprisingly, not nervous. I left a voice mail: "I'm sure you have a long line out your door. I know it's late, but I was wondering if that irreverent, voluptuous grad student got laid yet."

She called the very next morning, at ten o'clock, on January 1, 1995. Georgia was the first person I talked to on that New Year's Day. We hit it off right away. We talked about butch-femme relationships and cultural traditions. I talked about *Stone Butch Blues*, Leslie Feinberg's seminal 1993 novel, which sparked a timely conversation about transmasculine experience and butch-femme relationships. We talked for an hour, and by the time we spoke a day and a half later, she had already gone down to Mama Bear's Bookstore, bought the book, and read it. I was impressed.

We talked on the phone for a couple of weeks before we met. I told her I was butch—transgender, actually—and that I had long hair. She said she liked long-haired butches. I told her that her beautiful voice was "mellifluous." She was impressed that I used a word she didn't know. I said that it meant that her voice was flowing like honey. She said she was Greek and confirmed that the word *meli* meant "honey." I told her I was Chinese, and she shared that her two previous significant lovers had been Chinese. I asked, "Is that your flavor?"

That's when the needle scratched the record and the "get into the groove" music came to a sudden stop. I was strongly woman of color–identified and held "white women" in suspicion. What was her thing about Chinese people? Did she think we made ornamental decorations? Were we accommodating? If she had a "rice" infatuation, I was *gone*.

She responded, "I grew up in San Francisco, in the Richmond district," referring to a section of town that was largely Chinese and Japanese in the '70s and '80s. "Most of my friends were Asian. My parents are immigrants from Greece, and I was the kid they sent into the butcher's shop to get the lamb's head, so my parents didn't get ridiculed for their accent. Even though our cultures are really different in some ways, I think there are a lot of cultural similarities." I loved her response but was still wary.

I told her I was in a show at a community performance space and invited her to come by and meet me. Though I normally wouldn't have shared this piece of information, I told her that the show was about disability, that I had a chronic illness. She said she'd check it out.

On the night of the performance, I searched the audience for someone who could be a cute, femme, irreverent, voluptuous Greek American but didn't find her. She didn't show. I later found out she'd decided she was done with me because I had challenged her about race too aggressively. She didn't want to be held under suspicion and have to prove herself like that.

But I didn't know this yet, so I called her again, and we found ourselves in another deep conversation about race, culture, gender, and creativity. We challenged each other to examine our long-held assumptions and pushed through walls of distrust. I was intrigued by a woman who was "white" but whose cultural, linguistic, and immigration framework was so much like that of the women of color in my community, for whom the world was neatly divided into women of color and white women. Georgia's reference points disrupted the ideology of those around me.

I invited Georgia over for lunch at the San Francisco apartment I was subletting while my friend was out of town. She wore a gray, high turtleneck sweater that said "Back off, Big Boy" but cruised me with a twinkle in her eye. I made her some of the few dishes I could put together in the kitchen: chicken adobo, tofu with *dau miu* (pea sprouts), and rice. As I leaned over to lift the lid off the pan to peek at the steaming *dau miu*, I could feel her eyes nibbling on my backside.

Soon afterward, I went to her house on MacArthur Boulevard in Oakland to pick her up for our first dinner out. Crossing the street in the dark, blustery night, holding one long-stemmed rose, I stepped into her warm house and tried to understand the significance of a tall, rusty wire birdcage, which housed sketchy-looking Barbie dolls, at the top of the stairs. I scanned the assortment of flea market finds around the room and told myself that I would never live with her.

We headed out for dinner. After rejecting a brightly lit Japanese restaurant that her coworker had recommended, we found an intimate Italian place that served large quantities of delicious food and left us alone. She told me about the year she lived in Greece. I heard about her rural, agricultural people, their food, and their family life. As I got up to use the restroom, I told her not to touch the bill if it came and leaned in to kiss her. She leaned toward me, and I felt a sense of familiarity, as if we had been kissing each other at the dinner table for years. As we walked to my little green hooptie, she said, "I bet you wish I was a woman of color." I assured her that I appreciated her for who she was. I appreciated her cultural framework, that she had a people, a language, and a home country. She gazed into my eyes, open and sparkling in the moonlight. When I leaned in to kiss her again, it felt magical.

After dinner, we returned to her apartment. As I parked, I craned my neck to read the street-cleaning sign. Just as I registered the words

NO PARKING 2:00–3:00 AM, she quipped, "Don't worry, you'll be gone by then." We talked, made out, and gazed at each other for hours.

Afterward I told her I needed to take a break for five days because I was writing and preparing to audition for a solo performance at what was then Brava! For Women in the Arts, now the Brava Theater. A few days later, I was impressed that she had respected my needs by not calling me, but found myself picking up the phone anyway.

I got the solo show, and we got ready for our first big night out, the annual gala of an organization called ETVC, for Educational TV Channel. It was started by cross-dressers and later became known as Transgender San Francisco. Along with my buddy Chea and his date, we were some of the few people there who were assigned female at birth. In preparation for the big event, Georgia had gone downtown to buy what came to be known as her prom dress, an expensive purple silk dress. That night at the event, we emerged from making out in the bathroom to find a long line of antsy people waiting.

We went back to my Lower Haight apartment and a well-stocked fridge and didn't emerge for a few days. The last Sunday in January 1995, the San Francisco 49ers competed in the Super Bowl, hosted locally. That evening we lay in each other's arms as the sky darkened and listened to the excited revelry of people honking and cheering in the streets. "They won!" we exclaimed to each other, as we began to realize our own sense of winning a seemingly impossible lottery.

Over the next few weeks, she cooked for me and I began to understand just how masterfully she knew her way around the kitchen. We talked all night, shared our past hurts, and snuggled under covers in her heatless apartment, her feet warming my Popsicle toes. She whispered, "I want you to tell me all your secrets." I asked, "Are you ready to heal your life?"

When we met, my chronic illness played a major role in my life; each day I awoke and assessed the state of my energy and abilities against my hopes for the day. Not long after we met, Georgia came to my apartment in the city so we could go out one night, only for me to have to tell her that I was too ill. I was devastated that my body had failed me and that she had to see that so soon. I needed to know right then and there if she was the kind of person who could deal with the unforgiving reality of a lover who lived with the unpredictability of an incessant, debilitating illness. I said, "If you're gonna leave, leave now." She asked questions about what I needed and adapted to an evening in, rather than out. It meant so much to me that she was able to be flexible and that she still wanted to be with me when I couldn't get out of bed or out of the house. I had had a lot of lovers since I'd gotten sick, and they'd tried to get with it, but no one took care of me like Georgia. I knew she was a generous, special person.

Five weeks after we'd first spoken on the phone, three weeks after we met, we were brushing our teeth in the mirror, when I said, "Okay, marry me." It wasn't exactly a proposal. It was an acknowledgment of what was happening. A few weeks before I met Georgia, I had a premonition that someone was coming, that I had better stretch out wide in my lonely bed and enjoy those last moments of being single. After a lifetime of thinking I was not the marrying type, I had come to the realization that I might be. And then I met her. I felt fed in my stomach, heart, mind, and soul.

BECOMING DADA

We had been together nearly a decade when we embarked on a journey to find a roommate. I knew, after spending so many years gabbing until we no longer made any sense, or holding her hot little mitt in a dark movie theater, laughing out loud, that our lives would be enhanced by the addition of someone with whom we could share the joy. And what our new roomie could bring was unquantifiable and entirely unimaginable.

So we looked and we dreamed and we called to the heavens, to Quan Yin, to God, and to everyone who lived before us. Our hearts lifted with the possibilities and sank with every loss, and there were moments of tremendous loss. We wondered if we had found the right "biomagical matter" that would make our dreams come true. But still we persevered, knowing full well that this one who would share our home was just waiting by the curb, waiting for that celestial bus that would bring him or her home. As it turned out, it was no express bus but one that hit every bump, jolted at every stop, broke down in the worst ways. But it came right on time.

We communicated along the journey, in dreams and visions in Morse code, muffled underwater and punctuated by the jab of a singular dance step, leaping through flesh and fluid. He sent us cryptic pictures, flickers of light, a grain of rice, the profile of a round head, a surprise in his lap, a slumbering face. We came to know him as Luvbug, Jr., one who jumped playfully in quiet times but stopped to listen attentively at others.

When the day arrived that we met him, there was still a difficult journey ahead. Mama pushed till the blood vessels in her eyes popped; Luvbug, Jr., was in distress. But in the moment when he could finally lie peacefully and take it all in, the bright lights, doctors, and machines faded as our firstborn son looked me in the eyes as if to say, *I know you.*

We brought him home, enveloped in joy and wonder and amusement. Why was our new roommate so loud? So messy? So small and yet in possession of so much stuff?

He had us from the moment we first saw him: the sparkle in his eyes, his sweet, sensitive spirit, his love of mischief, and his tendency to find so many things freakin' hilarious. Right away he started showing us his hidden talents, like doing sign language with his toes or making a mean pocket of curry stew. He was just two weeks old when he started to put his little lips together to try to pull me in to kiss me, a seemingly impossible gesture for a baby so young. After all the hoping and dreaming we did before his birth, we never could have imagined what it would feel like to experience how precious he would be in person, the innocence and wonder and laughter, the depth of our love-fest. We got hit hard and couldn't even see it coming.

This little guy never wasted any time when it came to flirting with everyone in sight, especially the pretty ladies. At six months, he showed how *dynatos* (strong) he was. As he held his flexed arms up with seriousness and force, he looked like he was going to burst a blood vessel in his forehead, while everyone peed in their pants from laughter. At eleven months he would speed-crawl with total abandon at the sound of the washing machine, just so he could see the *gyro, gyro*[59] spin of the clothes. At two and a half, he jumped up every morning, squealing with delight as he ran into our bedroom to wake us and wish us *kali mera*, good morning. When I arrived home from work, he'd run to me, giggling with abandon. He would steal every last "stawbuddy" off my plate and request "clockit" milk.

One night, at two and a half, my son tried to stall bedtime by announcing, "Let's chat awhile." I held his warm little man hand while he drifted off to sleep. Suddenly he jolted up, threw his arms around me, and exclaimed, "I looove you, Dada!"

I wondered how long his precious spirit would remain unfettered by the trappings of cool, and school, and social rules. Or how our experience as parents of one child would shape us for the next leg of the journey. He was two and a half when, after a grueling attempt at getting Georgia pregnant that ultimately involved in vitro fertilization (IVF), we celebrated the beginning of his sister's second trimester in utero. He nicknamed her after a character in a popular children's story. I tried to imagine the prospect of sibling rivalry, sharing, and double the playful spirit.

*   *   *

Our daughter arrived six months later in warm, low light under the best possible circumstances, with a team of fierce female providers and me coaching Mama on. After all the walking and massaging and bathing and pushing, the baby's head became visible and she finally made it out, tiny and snuggly and sweet. Georgia was incredibly strong; whoever decided that women are weak must not have been around when they were birthing babies. The moment after Georgia gave birth, she rolled over and said, "Let's do it again." Once home, our daughter hung out next to her brother in her bouncy chair while he played in his playhouse. He couldn't wait until she was big enough to play with him.

I would sit on the couch, holding her swaddled in her soft blanket, my head drooping to the side as we both slept. When she awoke, I'd put her in the baby carrier and take both kids for a walk around the neighborhood while Mama got some rest. Though the adjustment was sometimes hard for my son, as it is for any older sibling, he always showed his love for her, at one point telling her, "You're the milk in my cereal."

Like her brother, she giggled and played and luxuriated in the trappings of toddler time—washing her hands in the sink, playing in the kiddie pool, drawing free-form pictures.

When she was two, we decided to try once more. Georgia prepared her body with acupuncture and fertility meds. We had two embryos left from the IVF cycle. It was a one-shot deal, and we were elated to learn that we were pregnant again. My son announced, "We have a boy and girl, so this baby should be transgender, so we have one of each."

At the twenty-week ultrasound, we saw our little baby's fist in a power salute and the clear image of a "frank and beans." We kissed in celebration;

then Georgia quipped, "I see a lot more light sabers in my future, and our bathroom will never smell fresh again!"

After searching for a vehicle that could safely and comfortably accommodate three car seats, we realized that there was no way around getting a minivan. We got a good deal from a neighbor's brother, whose wife and kids had just relocated to the Philippines. The interior of the car looked like a crime scene: seats that had tangled with scissors, black marks of unknown origin, and the putrid funk of spilled milk. We had it repaired so it was running smoothly, then took it to car detailers, who looked us up and down judgmentally and asked, "*How* many kids do you have?"

After they made it pretty, we took it to the upholstery repair guy, a chatty Lebanese man who had spent time in Greece and wanted to try out his Greek with Georgia. As he spoke, I couldn't make much sense of what he was saying but figured that my intermediate Greek just wasn't good enough to catch it, or that he spoke an unfamiliar dialect. But actually it was just bad Greek, ungrammatical and oddly accented.

At one point, Georgia told him that we had two kids and one on the way. He turned to me and said, "He's doing his work." I thought, *Who is this guy talking about, God?* He threw his arms out and looked at me with a knowing grin and a glint in his eye. *Oh yeah, me. I'm so virile.* It was an odd moment, the beginning of life to come, gender-affirming yet crudely sexist. I was only four months into medical transition. Later that day I used the men's locker room for the first time, no sweat.

*   *   *

When I began the journey to parenthood, I wondered what my child would call me as a third-gendered parent who definitely didn't identify as a mom. When my son was born in 2006, I was a transgender butch in a butch-femme relationship and had not yet pursued medical transition. I wanted to ensure that the magical moment when our child emerged into the world was not marred by someone referring to me inappropriately. I told the doctor that I wanted to be referred to by my masculine parent name, and though he was gender-nonconforming himself, he discouraged me from documenting my parent name on the birth plan or patient-room communication board. "There are a lot of lesbian nurses at the hospital who wouldn't support that," he told me. As it turned out, the hospital staff understood who I was as a gender-transgressive parent, and no one called me Mom. In 2006, health care providers had a limited understanding of nonbinary gender identities, and I felt relieved to be seen.

As I cared for my baby, I found that people often said he looked like me, a surprising privilege I never expected as a nonbiological parent. But when I was alone with him, people assumed that I was his mom, which was hard to hear. It felt taxing to have to explain that though I was his parent, I was not his mom.

Yet I also experienced some gender relief as a trans person with a baby. People, especially women, who might have scowled at me or glared with suspicion, now smiled at me warmly. After a lifetime of people giving me dirty looks, it was a welcome change. I found that I could access the women's room much more easily. Prior to having a child, if I wanted to use the women's room, it was best done with Georgia present, while talking, so my voice could be my ticket in. But a baby gave me a solid membership in the women's room, which I often needed, since the sexist, gendered rules of parenthood often meant that there was no changing table in the men's room.

Ultimately, my son named me Dada when he was sixteen months old. It was the perfect parenting title. He always knew who I was.

When he was four years old, he enjoyed playing with a neighbor girl who was the same age. His friendly, progressive mom told us to drop by anytime. So we did. But the girl's unsuspecting grandmother answered the door and was stricken with an attack of facial incontinence. With a look of absolute horror, terror, disgust, and disdain, she made it clear in no uncertain terms that the child, who was standing right there, was not available. I wondered what it was like for my son to experience those moments with me.

Next thing I knew, I was at a kiddie birthday party in Piedmont, a small, wealthy enclave next to Oakland. There was a picture of Laura Bush on the mantel, and I thought to myself, *How the hell did I get here? Who let my queer, trans ass into this house?* Later, we went to another kiddie birthday party, in the backyard of a mansion. When I tried to enter the house to use the bathroom, the maid who had been directing the guests to the bathroom eyed me suspiciously and informed me in a very unfriendly manner that the house was off-limits.

As a gender-transgressive parent, I often felt like I wasn't recognized as a real parent, in the absence of a standard title and gender presentation. Even though people understood us as a queer family, I felt like they saw me as this person who just happened to live with the real family and help out. The world of preschool parents and our Greek community were very straight, and oftentimes it seemed that people just didn't have a cultural reference point for me.

In addition, I quickly discovered that many LGBTQ people lacked a basic understanding of parenthood. No, kids are not furless pets, and no, I could not do whatever I wanted. It was hard for people who had to manage only their own lives, and who had at best a distant awareness of family life, to understand the demands of parenthood or how to be around kids. I still have to explain to people that it's not okay to swear around my kids, or discuss sex, drugs, violence, or scary topics. And people can't go on and on about themselves, as if the kids aren't present, and have ongoing needs for attention and assistance.

Rather than attending a queer community event, I might spend my Friday evening having movie night with the kids, watching the latest, fully merchandised, animated blockbuster or some washed-up, talking-animal movie starring my favorite D-list actors as pigeons or horses. While the kids kick back, I'm busy jumping up to fetch food and drinks, cleaning up spills, and managing some little person's chewed-up food on my plate.

*   *   *

Ultimately, it was my experience as a parent that led me, after decades of contemplation, to decide to pursue medical transition. I needed to be seen as the father I always was.

About a year into my medical transition, Georgia introduced me to a woman who ran a kiddie play center. The woman remarked that she had seen us each there separately but not together. Georgia joked that we never saw each other anymore. The woman responded, "You got together at least three times!" It's an odd thing being perceived as a straight couple, as if we got pregnant easily and are both biologically related to our kids. It felt bizarre to all of a sudden embody other people's idea of a standard, unquestioned way of being, as if millions of depictions of family were made in our image. Yet every time someone referenced an aspect of straight culture, I was slow on the uptake. Despite a lifetime of having been inundated with straight culture in endless ways, I felt as if I lacked the cultural competency to be straight.

Male privilege and straight privilege are astounding, and I'd be lying if I didn't acknowledge that I enjoy being respected as the provider and family man that I always was. Everyone should be respected the way men and straight people are. Suddenly, not only was I seen as a parent, but I became a much better parent, an awesome dad. When I took all three kids to an amusement park or the pool, I was "daring Papi" or "brave Dad." True, it's no easy feat managing three small kids in a public space. But even if I just take them to the park, the general feeling is *Isn't that nice that he's helping out?* Is the bar set that low for fathers? Women are expected to inherently know how to change a diaper or manage a tantrum as if they were born with the knowledge, while men are celebrated for taking any amount of responsibility for caring for their kids. True, I know fathers who are pretty checked out. But I also know many men who are dedicated, hands-on dads.

It's hard for people to fathom that it can be a huge orchestration as a trans father to go to the restroom with my three little kids, bringing them all into the men's room while barking, "Don't touch anything!" With the insight of a three-year-old, my youngest asks, "Why do we always go to the triangle one, not the circle one?" referring to the restroom with the urinal, which points out like a triangle, as opposed to the throne, shaped like a circle. I answer, trying to remember to keep my voice in the male range, and hope that the kids don't see someone's penis. With so many states trying to legislate away our right to urinate, it's hard enough as one person, and a whole other dimension to pee in peace as a trans parent.

I've learned many skills as a parent. I can stumble awake in the dead of night and provide whatever is needed. I can change a nasty poop midair and be fun at the drop of a hat. I can manage a toddler throwdown involving wet sand and hard objects. I can quickly come up with creative solutions to conflicts involving the sharing of toys or the need for attention. I know the racing fear in my heart if I have to give milk to a little person in the wrong-color cup. I can stay extremely focused for hours in order to guard everyone's safety. I can comfort the pain of hurt feelings and boo-boos. I can come up with answers to life's most mystical questions. I can assess mysterious liquids on the bathroom floor and roll with the almost-daily certainty of personal injury and property destruction.

At any given time there are three insanely cute, barely clad little individuals talking to me at the same time and climbing me like a play structure. Barefoot, with deliciously plump, tater-tot toes, they exclaim, "Dada, watch this! Did you see that?" "Play catch with me, Dada! Did you see me do the monkey bars?" "Dad, do you want me to show you my space station?"

From the day they're born, they tell you when, how, and if things are going down. Every night at bedtime for years, I sang a medley of Greek songs, until my youngest gave me the hook. With a serious look, he shook his head and said, "No, Dada." They tell you who is doing what, and often it's Mama they want to feed or comfort or help them. I learned early on not to take it personally if I was considered sloppy seconds. She birthed them, after all. And then, one by one, they charm me with gifts of art or feed me freshly picked tomatoes from the garden.

Three kids means the cuteness quotient has gone through the roof. They brighten my day every day with their beaming smiles and unbridled giggles and "I love yous." And they get me. They have a whole *community* of transgender stuffed animals who all have their individual gender journeys, though most are FTM, thank you. In fact, my daughter has informed me that all but three of the stuffed animals that take up residence on half her bed are trans.

*   *   *

In 1984, I was in Boston when *Choosing Children*, the now-legendary film about lesbians becoming parents, debuted. I eagerly watched it onscreen because I was curious about this new phenomenon and I knew one of the families it depicted. At the time, lesbian families were unknown territory. Over the past few decades, there has been an explosion of LGBTQ-headed families, especially among lesbians.

In 2003, Georgia and I were part of a group of multicultural friends who organized Baby Buds, a group of lesbian and trans prospective parents of color and/or in interracial relationships. We supported each other through conception, birth, and life with baby, meeting monthly for years to build community. We got together less frequently once our kids became school age, while new groups of multicultural queer women started iterations of Baby Buds Next Gen every few years.[60]

In 2015, I am excited to partner with COLAGE to launch the first program in the nation to support the kids of trans parents in a K–12 school setting. I am a member of the early wave of parents who are embarking on parenthood as trans-identified people. Those who went into parenthood straight-identified, and to some extent lesbian-identified, and then came out as trans, have much older kids. But most of us who came to parenthood as trans-identified people have young children because we are part of a new movement that is gaining momentum.

As more and more trans people choose parenthood, providers, educators, parents, and caregivers need to develop cultural competency in the many ways in which trans and gender-nonconforming people identify themselves. At the 2015 Philly Trans Health Conference, I had the privilege of conducting a workshop on trans family issues, where I heard the incredible stories of trans and gender-nonconforming parents from all over the United States and Canada. Over the past few years, I've also had the privilege of organizing and hosting the annual Trans Family Forum through Our Family Coalition in San Francisco. I have come to know many prospective parents or new parents across the trans spectrum, most of whom were assigned female at birth. The number of parents with nonstandard presentations and parent titles is growing. These are parents who locate their gender somewhere in the vast, nonbinary space between male and female. Some masculine female-bodied folks are defying traditional gendered prescriptions by choosing pregnancy while confusing providers and enduring ridicule from trans men who pressure them not to get pregnant.[61] In addition, there are also many trans parents who identify as male or female but have a history that is not visible to the naked eye. This is an opportunity for all of us to question the extremely gendered, pink and blue rules of parenthood. I hope that we as a society can develop greater understanding of gender-expansive parenting.

At the same time, LGBTQ people have an opportunity to develop their cultural competency in the issues of parenthood so that queer and trans parents can find support and family in LGBTQ communities.

As a parent, I feel very protective of my kids. I don't want them to have to experience hatred and bigotry because I am trans. As the transgender movement continues to move forward, I hope to see more images of us in the context of our families, caring lovingly for our kids, to help the world push past the outdated prejudices that paint us as less than fully human, so that our kids can thrive.

TRANSFORMER

I pulled into the driveway in my red-hot, middle-aged hooptie. Small and scuffed rough, with an inconsistent sheen, it had a ragged look that said nothing about its reliability as a mid-'90s Honda Civic. But the jewel was in the cargo. Riding high in the back was my then-four-year-old son—a rugged, sweet beauty of a little brown boy in a navy blue NASA jacket and rain boots. The kind of little guy who could build complex Lego airplanes, work a Transformer in minutes, and use a multisyllabic new word after learning it once. A mischievous charmer who could romance a pretty girl in his Batman gear and get the digits of her captivated mama with his conversational stylings and a flash of his killer smile.

We had just come from one of our adventures at the "waterfall," the landmark Oakland fountain that flows luminescent through redwoods and creek bed. We did our thing, having packed our adventure backpack with rope, binoculars, snacks, juice boxes, and something to scoop up river rocks. It was what my son deemed "boy time" at its finest: he and Dada hanging in the woods, jumping rocks, being dudes together. Never mind the gender requirements. It was our special time.

We established our self-protection as we fought invisible bad guys lurking in the forest. We investigated nature as we gathered flat, smooth rocks and evaluated their colors and textures. And it was a time of immense wonder. "Dada, how old are the redwood trees? How far away is the moon?"

As I turned off the engine, he asked, simply, in his high little voice, "Dada, are you a man?"

I pocketed the keys and thought, *Cool, this is it.* It was time to answer to that parental call of duty, teacher of life's mysteries and miracles, with a continuation of the Pride conversation we'd initiated six months earlier, about men who love men and women who love women, boys who feel like girls, and girls who feel like boys. At the time, he contemplated the options and pronounced, "I'm a boy who feels like a boy, and I'm a man who loves women."

But this was me we were talking about, so I responded, "Sort of. I wasn't born a guy, but I feel like a guy."

"Were you born a girl?"

"Yeah, but I think I'm a guy. I always have. But not everybody sees me that way." I noted my non–medically transitioned female voice and body as I spoke, and considered how it might be confusing to him that people sometimes assumed I was his "mama."

He thought about it.

"People like me are called transgender. Can you say 'transgender'?" I asked.

"Transgender," he said, enunciating very well. I could see the wheels turning. Then his eyes lit up with the fire of a new wonder to behold. "You're a transformer! But not exactly that—you're a person who transforms!"

"That's right!" I said, amazed at his ability to draw connections.

"Dada, there aren't that many people who are transgender."

"Yeah, but I know a lot of people who are."

"Mama's not transgender. You're way more like a man than Mama is. I'm not transgender."

"Yeah, cuz you're a boy who feels like a boy. I super-love you."

"I super-love you, Mister." And he smiled that killer smile.

WINTER OF LOVE

When Mayor Gavin Newsom defied California law and allowed
city officials to begin issuing marriage licenses for same sex-couples in San Francisco on February 12, 2004, it was a pivotal, magical
moment. Queer people, driven by the desire to celebrate our love and be
recognized as fully human, dropped everything to journey from across
the United States and other countries to take part in the emergence of an
exciting new chapter in LGBTQ history.

When I originally published the following article in the *San Francisco Chronicle*, which explored the sociopolitical intersections between
my parents' interracial marriage and my own same-sex marriage, the response was overwhelming. Though the article predated widespread use of
social media, the link was shared throughout the world. People told me
they printed out multiple copies of the article and distributed it among
those they felt needed education, as well as those who were celebrating. I
received hundreds of enthusiastic responses from people I knew throughout my lifetime, as well as those I never met, who wrote to me to express
their gratitude, tears, and congratulations.

"Half a dozen people called me this morning. Have you *seen* this
article?" said Shane Snowdon, who was my editor back in 1984 when I
wrote "Asian Lesbianism as a Political Identity" for *Sojourner*.

"Well, I am undone," wrote a legislative staffer in the California capitol.

"Your article touched my intellect but slammed my soul," wrote an
effusive, conservative family member.

*   *   *

Freedom to Love: Where Same-Sex and Interracial Marriage Convene
First published by the *San Francisco Chronicle* on March 5, 2004:

The morning after my parents went on their first date, my mother's co-workers rushed up to her and fervently admonished, "It's just not done!" "What about the children?" they demanded. My mother simply replied, "We just had one date."

The year was 1949. My father had picked up my mother the night before at the elementary school where she taught first grade, and they had enjoyed a night of dancing. For them, their evening was perfectly innocent and sweet. For others, it was an abomination. My mother is Chinese, and my father is Caucasian.

My mother had just begun her career as an elementary school teacher. [She was the] first Chinese teacher in the Berkeley schools, [and as such], the assistant superintendent told her, "The eyes of Berkeley will be upon you. If you don't do well, you will close the doors to other Orientals coming to Berkeley." For the first two months of the school year, there were two rows of observers in the back of her classroom taking notes on everything she said or did.

When my parents married in 1951, the minister told them that their timing was fortunate, as California's anti-miscegenation law had just been repealed three years prior. Enacted in 1880, the law prohibited the marriage between a white person and "a Negro, mulatto, or Mongolian." It was written to prevent intermarriage between Chinese people and whites, and was supported by San Franciscan and future U.S. Senator John F. Miller, who in 1878 declared, "Were the Chinese to amalgamate at all with our people . . . the result of that amalgamation would be . . . a mongrel of the most detestable that has ever afflicted the earth."

In 1945, Gov. Earl Warren reiterated and expanded the ban on interracial marriage to include "Malays." In 1948, the California Supreme Court ruled against antimiscegenation laws in *Perez vs. Sharp*, calling such laws "by their very nature, odious to a free people."

But social change was less forthcoming. In 1958, the first Gallup poll on the subject found that 94 percent of white people opposed interracial marriage. That year in Virginia, newlyweds Richard and Mildred Loving, a Caucasian man and African American woman, were awakened in the middle of the night by police wielding blinding flashlights and arrested for violating the state's ban on interracial marriage. The judge who convicted them ruled that "Almighty God created the races white, black, yellow, Malay, and red, and he placed them on separate continents because . . . he did not intend the races to mix." It wasn't until 1967 that the federal ban on interracial marriage was lifted in *Loving vs. Virginia*.

Today in 2004, as interracial marriages flourish and mixed-race people abound, these stories seem archaic, mean-spirited, and representative of an era of ignorance left in the past. But are they? Opponents of interracial marriages considered the unions to be "immoral" and "unnatural." Sound familiar?

In 1998, Houston police broke down the doors of John Geddes Lawrence and Tyron Garner, arresting them under a twenty-eight-year-old Texas law making same-sex intercourse a crime. Last June 26, the U.S. Supreme Court struck down Texas's "Homosexual Conduct" law, ruling it unconstitutional and in violation of the defendants' fundamental right to privacy and equal protection rights. Considered a major victory for gay rights, the decision struck down most laws governing private sexual conduct, but it did not affect marriage laws.

On February 24, President Bush endorsed a constitutional amendment banning same-sex marriage. Today we are again at a crossroads between the freedom to love and form families, and the zealous, fearful forces that seek to control these unions.

Call it what you want—codifying and controlling the rights of marriage for heterosexuals only, insisting that heterosexuals are uniquely qualified to love each other and raise families within the institution of marriage, or just plain asserting that heterosexuals know best—it all piles up to unequal treatment under the law, and that spells discrimination.

The U.S. Constitution does not allow marriage discrimination on the basis of race, religion or criminal status. Justices of the Supreme Court have called the freedom to marry a fundamental human right.

Why, then, are same-sex couples legally forbidden from marrying? And why is it necessary to write discrimination into the constitution and declare war on gay America?

Granted, not everyone, straight or queer, is fond of the institution of marriage. Some don't see this as a pressing issue. Fifty percent of heterosexual marriages end in divorce. But regardless of where folks stand on the issue, everyone deserves the basic human right of choice. When in the history of this country has separate been equal?

California has the most comprehensive domestic partner law in the country, yet with just fifteen rights and responsibilities, it provides little more than 1 percent of the more than one thousand state and federal legal protections offered to opposite-sex married couples. Marriage equality is a civil rights issue like any other.

When the smoke clears, it remains to be seen where those of us who married at San Francisco City Hall—arguably the happiest place on Earth—stand legally. Some of us have taken tremendous legal risks, such as bi-national couples whose immigrant partner could be deported, and people with disabilities who could lose meager subsistence benefits. But anyone who has witnessed the marriage rush knows that for many of us, societal validation and affirmation in the eyes of the law outweigh the risks.

When my wife, Georgia, and I tied the knot at City Hall two weeks ago, we were unprepared for the flood of emotion that came with it. Although we had been married six years earlier among family and friends in a ceremony with no legal standing, there was nothing like the feeling of being recognized under the law, whatever that would come to mean.

Despite the many social and legislative victories in the lesbian, gay, bisexual, and transgender arena over the past few decades, same-sex couples have continually been denied a basic human right that so many others take for granted. The deciding moment when we finally obtained this right was immeasurably profound.

When you have been told all your life that your very essence is wrong, when you've tried to play by the rules but got judged anyway, when you've broken all the rules because you had no choice, when you have fought long and hard for the right to be different, your life boils down to choices. We choose whether or not to be the best "me" we can be, to not let the legacy of negativity dictate how we feel about ourselves, and to stand up for ourselves and not be stunned or bullied into silence. Sometimes we go about our business without having to make those choices; sometimes we make them every day. Many times we are required to make those decisions on the fly without any warning.

For Georgia and me, the decision to get married at City Hall was thoughtful yet immediate. Like many others in the community, we followed our hearts and didn't look back.

When I had heard Wednesday evening, February 11, that something exciting might be happening at City Hall at noon the following day, I just knew Mayor Gavin Newsom was going ahead. Yet when we walked into City Hall at 11:15 Thursday morning, it was business as usual. We asked someone at the Assessor Recorder's office in Room 190 where we should go to get a marriage license. Perhaps perceiving us as a straight couple, she matter-of-factly instructed us to go to the County Clerk's office in Room 168.

But when we arrived at the clerk's office, no one was there. We hesitated in the stillness of the air. A city employee who appeared to be a lesbian hurried by. We asked her what we needed to do to get a marriage license, and she told us that they would not be ready for us until noon.

I ducked outside to see what was going on with the Freedom to Marry demonstration. On the steps of City Hall before a small group of reporters was Kate Kendell of the National Center for Lesbian Rights with Del Martin and Phyllis Lyon, who had just wed in a private ceremony. Lightning shot me right back into Room 168. I knew it was for real. By the time noon finally arrived and we got our number to be served, a handful of ebullient couples stood in line, giddy with the buzz of love, excitement, and courage. We were in uncharted territory, with no guarantee that it wouldn't all be shut down before it even began.

After nervously filling out our paperwork, hands trembling and writing our birth dates in the wrong place, Georgia and I stood and waited as people behind the counter ran back and forth, from desk to printer. There was a problem with the software. The licenses only printed out as groom and bride, which would have been fine with us but, since we are both legally female, would have voided our documents.

We had waited our whole lives for this moment, and now we felt impatient. The person who was helping us, a slight, bespectacled man—professional, efficient—whisked by in the midst of all the confusion, turned to us, and confided, "As much as this is momentous for you, you have no idea how momentous this is for me."

After more tension in the back room, he grabbed our form in frustration and exclaimed, "I'm just going to type it in," replacing "groom" and "bride" with "first applicant data" and "second applicant data."

With that, we raised our right hands and swore that we had told the truth. Excitedly taking our license, we wished everyone good luck and walked into Room 190, where Assemblyman Mark Leno was holding a press conference. Leno was introducing the Marriage License Non-Discrimination Act, AB 1967, named after the year that anti-miscegenation laws were repealed on a federal level. In this historic moment at City Hall, I realized I was continuing my family's legacy of fighting for the freedom to love.

Someone called out, "We have our first couple!" and before we knew it, we had been ushered in front of the cameras to become the first couple to have a public same-sex ceremony, officiated by City Assessor Mabel Teng and Leno. I felt awkward and nervous about all the attention. But as I gazed into Georgia's eyes, a wave of calm passed over me, just like at our first wedding. This was about us, pure and simple. We've been loving each other for nine years. We're best friends. She's my family. We'll soon be expanding our family. She cracks me up every day of my life. Her mind is my playground. She's the soft place I land in a world that doesn't always make sense.

Although we had written our own ceremony for our wedding in 1998, there was something surprisingly special about getting married with traditional vows, usually performed for young, bright-eyed couples before they've journeyed together. When they asked if we promised to care for each other in sickness and health, there was nothing cliché about it. We have survived debilitating chronic illness together. For richer or poorer, we felt every word. Then Mark Leno said, "I now pronounce you . . . ," and I turned in anticipation and wonderment about what he was going to say. "Spouses for life," he continued, and I beamed as I registered this perfect choice of words.

Afterward, as we shared our stories with our new wedding pals, we realized that we had been so used to second-class status that we hadn't been able to imagine things being any other way. The caption on an Associated Press photo of us said that these same-sex weddings were an act of civil disobedience. That may be technically true, but all we were feeling was the afterglow and excitement of our ceremony, private and sweet in its meaning yet public in its acknowledgment. A wedding like any other wedding, and that was the best gift of all.

As word spread in the days that followed, ecstatic queers pulled their sweeties out of work or school, jumped on red-eye flights or drove all night. They arrived with flowers, family, friends, champagne, and mariachi bands. They stood in line for hours; they camped overnight in the rain and bitter cold. Straight, transgender, and religious allies brought food, blankets, and good cheer. Through all the sleep deprivation, hunger, and soggy clothes, San Francisco was filled with the spirit of love, dedication, gratitude, and generosity. The community swelled with the sweet triumph of pride like never before.

As the media covered the phenomenon of the busiest wedding chapel in America, we saw real images of our community in all its warmth and complexity. These were depictions of everyday people, living everyday lives, emerging out of the woodwork in droves. Couples who had raised families together, survived cancer and AIDS together, escaped religious and family persecution together. People who knew exactly what it feels like to care for each other, day after day, year after year, in sickness and health, for richer or poorer, through discrimination and equal rights.

In 1959, my mother went to San Mateo to interview for a teaching job. The principal said, "Wilkinson is not a Chinese name. Do you have any difficulties in your marriage?" She replied, "My husband doesn't have a problem being of another race." The principal slapped his knees and laughed so hard he had tears rolling down his cheeks. The next day, she received a telegram offering her the job.

My mother retired after thirty-eight years of teaching first grade. In March, my parents, who live in San Mateo, will celebrate their fifty-third anniversary [sixty-fourth in 2015]. They've raised four children. They've cared for each other through all stages of health, finances, and discrimination. They are our role models for the freedom to love and create family.

Next year, on Valentine's Day, an entire community of folks will celebrate their first wedding anniversaries. Regardless of the machinations of the right, no one will ever take that away from us. And we are fighting, stronger than ever, to end discrimination and file this time where it belongs—in the annals of the historical past.

*   *   *

When I wrote that piece, I knew I was in the midst of an incomparable moment in history, yet I could not imagine the societal changes to come. San Francisco city officials married over four thousand same-sex couples during the Winter of Love before the marriages were voided one month later. For the entire month, the first segment of news broadcasts on every TV channel in the Bay Area was devoted to the city hall marriages. Never before had I seen authentic, unscripted images of my community on TV—Asian sisters carrying each other over the city hall threshold; Chicana couples who arrived with large, supportive families; mixed-race transmasculine folks with their partners; and interracial African American and white butch-femme couples. It was a welcome change from years of sensational Pride coverage and HIV/AIDS reporting. Though visibility of these aspects of LGBTQ life was vitally important, the media until that point had often portrayed us as flamboyant, half-naked, sick, or responding to a public-health emergency. What better way to understand our struggles for acceptance and equality than to hear our stories of love and recognition? It was an image of queer stability that we hadn't yet seen on TV.

Since Georgia and I got married in front of a bank of news cameras, the footage of our wedding graced every news channel daily and accompanied news stories about marriage equality for years to come. Strangers stopped us on the street to congratulate us. People I interacted with in everyday life—a Puerto Rican woman who worked at the post office, our Vietnamese mechanic, an African American guy who was a checker at the grocery store—told me that they were thrilled to see me on the news, happy about this turn of events. I would never have had those conversations about LGBTQ rights with any of these people if the news media hadn't documented what was quickly becoming a profound cultural shift.

Back in 1998, following our wedding, we traveled to Paris for a few days, enjoying sweet and savory crêpes while walking the streets of the City of Light. Then we spent three weeks in Greece with Georgia's extended family. Georgia's mother had sternly instructed us *not* to come out to her relatives. It was the antihoneymoon in living-queer-love color. Though I loved her family and could appreciate that it may not have been safe to come out, this thinly veiled closet wrenched my soul as I tried to shield myself from all the stares and put-downs, as I walked the gossiping dirt roads of the family's village in the Peloponnese.

But in 2004, her relatives saw us getting married on CNN and finally knew the truth. Back in San Francisco, Georgia's father, who chose not to attend our 1998 wedding, exclaimed to his wife, "Georgia and Willy are on TV! Buy a newspaper!" He proudly displayed my newspaper article, with its large, half-page picture of us, until he passed away in 2010.

"I saw you on CNN the night you got married and squealed out loud with delight. What an irony that a transgender person and a female-identified person were the first so-called 'same-sex marriage,'" e-mailed Marcus Arana, a trans man who worked as a discrimination investigator with the San Francisco Human Rights Commission. "Congratulations on making history. And thank you for writing such a thoughtful defense of the right to marry."

Indeed, the Winter of Love provided a platform for education by displaying LGBTQ people engaging in a familiar, joyful, archetypal rite of passage, as well as experiencing the overwhelming emotion that came with disrupting the status quo. For people like Georgia and me, who came out in the '80s, a very difficult time to be out in our daily lives, we had no basis for reexamining the unwritten assumption, wired into our DNA, that we weren't full citizens like non-LGBTQ people.

In order to show our stories and facilitate this collective learning process, messages about marriage equality were often simplified. When my article was published, the *Chronicle* scrapped my title for a headline that did not reflect my gender identity: "Family Values: Lesbian Newlywed

Breaks Barriers Just as Her Parents Did More Than 50 Years Ago." At that point, I no longer identified as a lesbian or used female pronouns.

In 2004, few people in the general public and even the larger LGBTQ community had a basic grasp of trans issues. As I trained substance use disorder and mental health providers throughout California, I watched them puzzle over the spectrum of gender identity, straining their brains as they quizzically searched for a way to understand. The concept of non-binary gender identity had not yet come into use. In my article, when I said that the terms "bride" and "groom" would have been fine with us, and that we were both "legally female," few acknowledged or understood this nuance. Because I was a trans person who had not medically transitioned, my gender identity was inconvenient and complicated the larger message of equality for same-sex couples.

Following the publication of my article, I was pleased when a friend, transgender author and activist Jamison Green, contacted me to ask if he could submit my article to the National Lesbian and Gay Journalists Association (NLGJA) to be considered for an award. In his cover letter, he described me as a trans person whose identity was erased by the article's title. When I heard that I was to be honored with a NLGJA Excellence in Writing award, Georgia and I traveled down to LA for the event. During the ceremony, the white gay man who presented the award to me referred to me as a "giddy lesbian." Aside from invisibilizing my trans identity, the comment felt like a sexist dismissal of a writer's authentic rendering of a profoundly emotional, historically momentous experience and overrode James's attempt to right a wrong. This comment was another example of the oversimplification that occurred.

Over the years, the movement's messaging often used sanitized images of nice, middle-class, mostly white people. Largely absent were images and stories of trans and gender-nonconforming people who also benefited from marriage. Moreover, the marriage equality movement didn't help the general public understand the profound ways in which LGBTQ people experienced discrimination in all aspects of society, or the pervasive physical, emotional, and structural violence perpetuated against us.

But despite the limitations of the marriage equality movement and its messaging, it was successful beyond measure. Who knew that a little over a decade later we would secure comprehensive, federal marriage recognition?[62] Indeed, these victories have been won by the hard work of so many dedicated activists and the power of storytelling.

* * *

On August 12, 2004, the Supreme Court of California ruled that the City and County of San Francisco exceeded its authority and violated state law by issuing marriage licenses, and voided all same-sex marriages performed during the Winter of Love. Though considered a hero by many in the LGBTQ community, Gavin Newsom was blamed for causing the Republican backlash in the November 2004 elections, in which eleven states passed ballot initiatives banning same-sex marriage and high voter turnout among conservatives helped secure Bush's reelection. LGBTQ people were heartbroken and devastated.

But several years later we experienced the elation of the May 15, 2008, California Supreme Court decision, which made California the second state, after Massachusetts, to legalize same-sex marriage. Thanks to the brilliant efforts of lead attorney Shannon Price Minter, highly accomplished trans man, longstanding legal director of the National Center for Lesbian Rights (NCLR), and a dear friend, this landmark marriage equality case argued that same-sex couples have the fundamental right to marry, and that laws that prohibit rights based on sexual orientation are inherently discriminatory and unconstitutional.

Alas, the excitement was short-lived. Two weeks later, Proposition 8, an initiative to overturn the court's decision and enact a state constitutional amendment eliminating the right of same-sex couples to marry in California, qualified for the November ballot.

One morning during the summer of 2008, I opened my front-window drapes and saw several yellow YES ON 8. RESTORE MARRIAGE signs in the front yard of the house across the street. My heart sank. As I stood on the street to put my son in his car seat, I saw more YES ON 8 signs two doors down, on our side of the street. The people in these two houses were part of the same family, and they each had five YES ON 8 signs in their front yards pointing in our direction.

As the weeks went on, Oakland became a nightmare for LGBTQ

people as mobs of forty people at a time stood on street corners throughout the city, every day, rain or shine, frantically waving these menacing yellow signs, sometimes screaming, "Repent!" People with opposing VOTE NO ON PROP 8. UNFAIR AND WRONG blue signs got screamed at and sometimes physically attacked. Police presence at these corner rallies was frequently necessary.

The energy that people had to campaign for Proposition 8 (commonly referred to as Prop. 8) felt overwhelming. I wondered why they weren't talking about the war, injustice, the Oakland murder rate, or our country's financial crisis. But the idea that two people of the same sex could get legally married presented a crisis of grand proportions. As eighteen thousand same-sex couples rushed to marry before the November elections, we felt the sting of the increasingly inflammatory Prop. 8 campaign. It falsely claimed that without Prop. 8, churches would be taxed for refusing to marry same-sex couples and kindergartners would be taught in school that same-sex marriage was okay. The implication was that children would receive sex education that was not age appropriate.

During the campaign, LGBTQ people and our allies discovered who our friends and enemies were. The ugly came out. Though the Mormon Church repeatedly lied about its involvement in the Prop. 8 campaign, it raised $25 million for Prop. 8, over half of all campaign contributions in support of the measure.[63] The First Presidency of the Mormon Church sent a letter that was read in every congregation on June 29, 2008, urging church members to "do all you can to support the proposed constitutional amendment by donating of your means and time."[64] At the center of these "Yes on 8" demonstrations in Oakland was our neighbor Joe, two doors down, a bishop in the Mormon church, who organized his congregation to campaign for Prop. 8.

Back in the year 2000, Joe and his family members had pointed multiple signs that supported the Knight Initiative in the direction of our house. Also known as Proposition 22, the Knight Initiative explicitly defined marriage as the union of a man and a woman, and the only valid form of marriage recognized in the state of California. Ultimately, it passed by a wide margin.

Despite our neighbors' politics, we always said hello to members of

these two families, who threw large, multigenerational parties and practiced their intricate Polynesian dances in the street. But they were very
unfriendly, scoffing at us and even mocking me. Except Joe. He was the
kind of neighbor who would offer to jump our car, or knock on the door
to remind us to move our car for street cleaning so we didn't get a ticket.

Our relationship improved with these families when we had our first
child in 2006. As we strolled by, Joe's wife, Anita, would stop us to coo
over our baby and offer us leftover baby formula, which we politely refused. Suddenly she became very friendly with us, and some of her family
members followed suit.

And then came Prop. 8. Mobs of "Yes on 8" people, organized by
Joe, stood on nearby corners, screaming us down as we drove by. We
felt betrayed by our neighbors. It seemed as if our progressive Bay Area
enclave had imploded into a close-minded, ignorant, and mean-spirited
nuthouse. In an effort to take back the neighborhood, I organized many
progressive neighbors to counteract the hate with blue NO ON 8 signs,
which they gladly displayed in their front yards and windows.

One evening, as the election approached, the demonstrations had
escalated, and the campaign ads had become especially inflamed, Anita
knocked on our door. We were surprised to see her. Though she often
stopped us to talk on the street, she had never come to our door.

She entered quickly, crouched furtively, and asked that we close the
front drapes. She was concerned about being seen. Offering us gifts of
soap that had been freebies to her, she recounted how her African American coworker had explained that there was a time when interracial couples
had not been able to marry, and that not allowing same-sex couples to
marry was similar. Like her husband, Joe, she had been worried about the
impact of Prop. 8 on children. But a light had turned on for her that day.
She was beginning to see the issue differently, and she wanted us to know
that she supported us even though she couldn't do anything to change the
minds of her husband, family members, or church community.

As I listened intently to what she had to say, I felt a sense of relief and
vindication. In my mind she was family, always had been from the moment we'd moved in and I'd seen her auntie sporting a brightly colored
muumuu that looked like something my mother would wear. I told her

my parents' story. I knew the street demonstrations were only getting more upsetting, but I felt happy to know that in her heart, she stood with us.

On November 4, 2008, Prop. 8 narrowly passed, which immediately ceased same-sex marriage in California. But Barack Obama won the presidency. At 9:00 p.m. on election night, folks were dancing in the streets of Oakland. Queer people battled mixed emotions, and some wrongly blamed black people for the passage of Prop. 8.

Ultimately, federal judge Vaughn R. Walker ruled Prop. 8 unconstitutional in August 2010. On June 26, 2013, the US Supreme Court denied the appeal to the 2010 ruling of unconstitutionality, legalizing same-sex marriage in California. That sunny June morning right after the victory was announced, standing on the steps of San Francisco City Hall before a bank of news cameras on live TV, Kate Kendell, oblivious to the live coverage, famously uttered the words on the lips of so many: "Fuck you, Prop. 8."

At the time, some speculated that dropping the *f*-bomb would hurt the movement, but after a video clip of Kate putting a dollar in the "bad-word jar" was released, all was forgiven. The same day that Prop. 8 was finally dust, the US Supreme Court ruled that Section 3 of the Defense of Marriage Act was unconstitutional. Nine states won marriage equality in 2013, and an astounding eighteen more in 2014. By the spring of 2015, thirty-six states and the District of Columbia had won the right to marry. Same-sex marriage became legal nationwide on June 26, 2015, when the United States Supreme Court ruled in the landmark *Obergefell v. Hodges* case that state-level bans on same-sex marriage were unconstitutional. Denial of marriage licenses and refusal to recognize marriages performed in other jurisdictions violated the fourteenth amendment.[65]

The insults of Prop. 8 and so many other anti-LGBTQ assaults around the country galvanized the unwavering strength of the movement to change the course of history.

* * *

In February 2014, Kate Kendell contacted me to invite Georgia and me to attend the ten-year celebration of the Winter of Love. On February 12, 2014, along with our three little kids, we walked down the steps of San Francisco City Hall in a small procession as cameras flashed and the media documented this milestone. There was much to celebrate as we remembered that day when it all began and reflected on how far we'd come.

As Kate spoke eloquently about the many states that had won the freedom to marry over the past decade, the crowd clapped and cheered. As she described the many injustices same-sex couples had experienced and the ways in which marriage equality helped correct years of indignities, the crowd went wild. But when she said that in California we had won rights for trans kids to be treated fairly in school, the crowd fell silent. It wasn't until I made some noise that they halfheartedly clapped for *the rights of trans children to have equal access to education like everyone else.* I was appalled. I was reminded of how far we still needed to come so that everyone in the LGBTQ community cared about the struggles of trans people.

The next day, Facebook announced that it would include over fifty options for users to describe their gender. Publicity about this move provided opportunities for education about trans issues and the complexities of gender identity. I saw many of my non-LGBTQ training participants question their assumptions about gender and seek learning opportunities that explored the spectrum of gender identity.

By the end of 2014, thirty-five states had won marriage equality, a tremendous victory that no one could have imagined ten years prior. But in fourteen of those states, you could get married on Sunday and be legally fired on Monday. Only seventeen states and the District of Columbia had legal protections in employment, housing, and public accommodations based on sexual orientation and gender identity.[66]

In late 2014, a reporter asked me where I saw the LGBTQ movement going as we moved toward comprehensive marriage equality, and whether I thought the marriage equality movement influenced public discussion of trans issues. I said that, as someone who conducted a high volume of LGBTQ and trans-specific training, I thought that the marriage equality movement had *humanized* lesbian and gay people and, to some extent, larger LGBTQ issues. I would often hear people say, "Gay people—I get that. They're just like us!" In my trainings, I witnessed many participants who were touched by these powerful stories of love and discrimination.

And yet because trans people were largely invisible in the marriage equality movement, I said that I didn't think the movement had helped people understand trans issues. That the general public had a very low level of cultural competency in trans issues, and that there were many ways in which LGBTQ people, especially trans people, continued to be impacted by discrimination, violence, and dehumanization.

Many people in the larger LGBTQ and trans movements haven't loved the marriage equality movement. People have been concerned for years that limited financial resources have been distributed disproportionately to marriage equality while our community has struggled with underemployment and unemployment, poverty, homelessness, criminalization, incarceration, injustice, violence, and difficulty accessing culturally competent, affordable health care. Marriage equality has seemed a privileged cause in light of the state of emergency among trans women of color, who were murdered weekly in the United States during the summer of 2014 and the winter of 2015.

At the same time, donations to LGBTQ rights organizations that have poured in from community members who might not otherwise have contributed to trans issues have helped fund trans justice projects and other LGBTQ causes. What's more, the frequent images of queer people in love, however simplified or washed out they may have been, have put LGBTQ issues on the radar and made the larger society question the legacy of LGBTQ inequality.

Though marriage and trans issues have been distinct and separate, I do believe that the marriage equality movement has helped, rather than hindered, the trans movement. For years, trans rights and LGBTQ rights organizations have partnered to pass trans rights legislation and ensure gender identity protections alongside sexual orientation when possible. The cultural shift that has been an outcome of the marriage equality movement has, to some extent, helped the general public confront their homophobia, which is often tangled with transphobia when trans people are feared. Marriage equality has provided a platform to highlight the injustice that LGBTQ people face. If marriage had not been such a high-profile subject for years, would trans issues be discussed in the mainstream media with the frequency and depth we are beginning to see? Would Laverne Cox have graced the cover of *Time* magazine in 2014 with the headline "The Transgender Tipping Point"? No one can say for sure, but I believe we owe more to the marriage equality movement than many of us are willing to concede.

As we move past the marriage equality movement and the long, unsuccessful struggle to pass the Employment Non-Discrimination Act (ENDA), it is time we have broader goals. I am excited about the 2015 push for comprehensive federal nondiscrimination protections in employment, housing, public accommodations, education, and lending. It may not be as sexy to talk about the multiple ways in which LGBTQ people are still treated like dirt, but it is the reality. The marriage equality movement displayed our humanity in all our beauty and love; the time has come for full civil rights protections akin to the 1964 Civil Rights Act. In order to remove the myriad structural inequalities we continue to experience, we need a cultural shift, and we need legislation.

Comprehensive Nondiscrimination Protections

The United States has taken action to ensure federal civil rights protections for various marginalized populations since the end of the Civil War.[67] Most notably, the Civil Rights Act of 1964 barred discrimination on the basis of race, color, sex, religion, and national origin in voting, public accommodations, education, and federally funded programs. The Voting Rights Act of 1965, the 1968 Fair Housing Act, Title IX in 1972, and the 1990 Americans with Disabilities Act (ADA) are other notable pieces of legislation that have addressed fundamental civil rights. These key legislative victories weren't always fully inclusive, however; LGBTQ Americans were explicitly excluded from the ADA.[68] In fact, while other segments of society garnered protections, a number of laws that *denied* the civil rights of LGBTQ people were adopted—most famously, the 1996 Defense of Marriage Act.

Over the last few decades, LGBTQ rights have been won in a patchwork manner, on specific issues and in specific jurisdictions. In December 2014, the Center for American Progress (CAP) and the Human Rights Campaign (HRC) each released reports detailing the widespread discrimination that LGBTQ people face and the need for comprehensive nondiscrimination protections in employment, housing, education, public accommodations, credit, and federal funding.

Though a Human Rights Campaign poll found that 87 percent of Americans believe that it is illegal to fire an LGBTQ person,[69] there are still no comprehensive employment protections based on sexual orientation on a federal level, despite two decades of efforts to get ENDA passed in one form or another. However, the landmark 2012 Equal Employment Opportunity Commission decision in the *Macy v. Holder* case, brought by Transgender Law Center, affirmed that trans and gender-nonconforming people are federally protected from employment discrimination at companies with fifteen or more employees under Title VII of the 1964 Civil Rights Act.[70] Despite this victory, the ruling leaves out some transgender employees, and though there are protections for federal workers and contractors, LGBTQ workers are not protected in a majority of states.

LGBTQ people are routinely passed over in hiring and promotions and fired at much higher rates than non-LGBTQ people. One study, conducted in the Midwest and the South, found that if applicants changed their résumé to state "progressive organization" rather than "gay organization," they were 40 percent more likely to get an interview.[71] Ten percent of LGB people report being fired for their sexual orientation, while 47 percent of trans workers report being fired, not hired, or passed over for a promotion because of their gender identity.[72] Trans people are four times more likely to live in poverty than the general population. Discrimination based on LGBTQ status is compounded by discrimination based on race; the median African American same-sex couple earns $20,000 less than the median white same-sex couple.[73] Clearly, we need comprehensive employment protections.

As the CAP and HRC reports describe, rates of discrimination are alarming in every other aspect of society, such as, for instance, the area of public accommodations. The term "public accommodations" refers to any establishment, public or private, that provides goods or services, or makes its premises available, to the public. This includes restaurants and movie theaters, as well as health care institutions and restrooms. A 2010 study conducted by Lambda Legal found that 70 percent of trans people and 56 percent of LGB people reported having experienced discrimination in health care settings.[74] Restroom access is a critical issue; one study found that an astounding 70 percent of trans people report having been verbally harassed, physically assaulted, or denied access in public restrooms.[75] Yet opponents of LGBTQ rights often focus on restroom access as a viable reason to deny civil rights, claiming that such laws will allow "men dressed as women" to harass or harm women in the women's room, despite no cases of physical or sexual assault as a result of these protections over the last two decades.[76]

The Center for American Progress and the Human Rights Campaign recommend that Congress pass a comprehensive LGBTQ nondiscrimination act to ensure consistent and uniform federal protections, based on sexual orientation and gender identity, in all aspects of society. Since laws are only as strong as their enforcement mechanisms, fully financed equal opportunity and civil rights offices that can review and respond to complaints in a timely, fair, and comprehensive manner should be established. CAP recommends that these agencies issue regulations that include the removal of transgender exclusions in health insurance, as well as mandate respectful treatment of trans people, including appropriate name and pronoun use, access to all gender-specific facilities, and confidential documentation of trans status.

In addition, CAP recommends that states and local jurisdictions pass nondiscrimination protections in employment, housing, public accommodations, and educational institutions, both public and private. Government and private institutions should collect data on LGBTQ status, and LGBTQ cultural competency training should be mandated across all sectors so that staff members are better prepared to provide equal treatment for LGBTQ employees and patrons. Finally, CAP recommends that the Religious Freedom Restoration Act be amended to explicitly state that the law cannot be used to discriminate.

As we move past the struggle for marriage equality, now is the time to push for comprehensive legislation banning discrimination based on sexual orientation and gender identity. No one can say how long and how hard we will have to fight for these basic protections, but one thing is clear: our humanity can no longer be denied.

SCULPTING THE EDGES

OLD-ASS MOFO IN PUBERTY

I got a zit constellation for my gender galaxy
I'm an old-ass mofo in puberty
AARP is coming after me
I'm an old-ass mofo in puberty

The leaves have turned but the sprouts are sprung
I'm an old-ass mofo in puberty
Like all trans guys, my junk is well hung
I'm an old-ass mofo in puberty

My growth spurt is coming any day now
Got as much mustache as Chinese genes will allow
I'm a teenage old fart who's not understood
Waking up every day with stiff morning wood

Convertible top on my head is soon due
I'm an old-ass mofo in puberty
I remember the old and learn from the new
I'm an old-ass mofo in puberty

Clinging desperately to youth, sticking at 35
I'm an old-ass mofo in puberty
True to myself and fiercely alive
I'm an old-ass mofo in puberty

My growth spurt is coming any day now
Got as much mustache as Chinese genes will allow
I'm a teenage old fart who's not understood
Waking up every day with stiff morning wood
I'm an old-ass mofo in puberty

MY AGE IN TRANS YEARS

A trans guy whom I'd just met asked me what my gold necklace represented. I responded that it was my year, the Year of the Tiger. He enthusiastically exclaimed, "Nineteen eighty-six? Me too!"

I responded, "Are you fucking with me? Cuz I just got asked if I needed a senior discount the other day." He shrugged and said that we all look young. Seems like five minutes ago I was a thirteen-year-old boy. Such is the life of a trans guy.

TRANSITION IN THE FIERCE

YEAR OF THE DRAGON

The blast caught me by surprise, slicing the still nighttime air with rapid-fire explosions. Faster than my heart, louder than my excitement, the deafening release announced Lunar New Year's Eve at midnight in a cloud of smoke wafting to the sky. It continued for about ten minutes, a long time for firecrackers, a little extra firepower chasing away the evil spirits and welcoming the auspicious Year of the Dragon in 2012.

Minutes before, I had launched my own firecracker on Facebook. "*Gung Hay Fat Choy! Chuc Mung Nam Moi!* Did you clean your house? Don't sweep or wash your hair tomorrow. I want to announce my fierce dragon year news. I'm finally transitioning to male, a process I started when I changed my name to Willy at age nine."

Responses blew up my e-mail with the same rapid-fire succession as my next-door neighbor's explosive fireworks. As the firecrackers went *bang bang bang*, my iPhone went *ping ping ping*.

"Thanks for the reminder, and congratulations on transitioning! What an awesome way to start the new year!"

"I'm so proud and happy for you. I did clean my house, and again, you rock, brother!"

"Hoping this Year of the Dragon brings you happiness through your transition, Willy."

When I was growing up, we celebrated Chinese New Year, as we called it, with the following edict: Clean the house ahead of time but never on New Year's Day, because you wouldn't want to sweep away your good luck. Wash your hair ahead of time so you start fresh, but never on New Year's Day, so as not to wash away any good fortune. I once went to the club on the Lunar New Year, and a hapa Chinese dyke told me she had gotten into a car accident that day. Her mother told her, "That's because you washed your hair!"

You're also supposed to pay all your debts. Well, I always say two out of three's not bad.

No matter how American I might be, I consistently adhere to these Chinese traditions. I clean my house before but not on the Lunar New Year. I display a pomelo, a tangerine, and *li-see* for the sweet life. Even if I go to the pool on Lunar New Year's Day, there's no way I'm going to wash my hair, drenched as it is in chlorine. These traditions and superstitions are ingrained in my core.

In my family, we prepared for Chinese New Year by getting new clothes that we were to save until New Year's Day. As a small child, I felt excitement about the buildup toward that day, tampered by my loathing of the frilly red dress I was expected to wear. Despite my intense discomfort with the female clothing assigned me, I enjoyed the heightened anticipation of stepping into those untouched garments and performing an annual ritual that centered us within our family structure while valuing our legacy and our hopes for the future.

I remember that special year when my mother finally grudgingly realized that I needed Chinese New Year clothing from the boys' department. I was fourteen. She took me to a sleepy downtown store, which seemed really fancy, and let me pick out a fly polyester jersey button-down shirt with a fat collar and a black-and-brown artistic print, which reminded me of my year, the tiger. Combined with my slick polyester white pants with stylish pockets, it made me feel like I had arrived. Though the opportunity to wear the right clothes came with an extra dose of ridicule and shaming, some of my family members did respect my name change and started to call me Willy a little more consistently. The anticipation of getting into those clothes on

New Year's Day had such meaning for me that afterward I wore those superfly threads into the ground.

Every year on New Year's morning, my three siblings and I got up early, donned the new garb, and waited to be called to the living room for the traditional tea ceremony, oldest to youngest. First, my brother, Steve, would pour tea for my parents, then pass them the tray with ginger and other goodies for strength and the sweet life. My sister Sunya would get called next, while my other sister, Su-Lin, and I waited and watched in the hall, whispering the play-by-play. Then, after what seemed like a long time, Su-Lin would be called, and as the youngest I remained, waiting alone. Finally, I would get called in to pour tea, first for my parents, then for my siblings, in birth order from oldest to youngest.

I felt conflicted about the hierarchy of birth order, compounded by being the youngest girl and a gender lawbreaker. And yet there was also allure in the precision and order of things and I couldn't have imagined it being any different. A little nervous, I would serve the tray with ginger, coconut, and other treats, to be placed in the tea. I would then say the blessing: "Remember your ancestors, because they paved the way for you. Honor your parents. And always respect your teachers, because they prepare you for the better life." Then we would receive *li-see*, red envelopes with a piece of silver, or a few dollars, for something sweet and auspicious in the new year.

*   *   *

Chinese New Year was the most important holiday in my family and has always felt very special to me, so it was fitting that I would announce my transition on the eve of the new year. I loved the rituals and the festivities, the loud clash of energy that welcomed the new and disposed of the old.

My family celebrated with a flair and flamboyance unparalleled in our San Francisco 'burb. Every year starting on January 1, my mother would make three dozen almond cookies per night until the Lunar New Year, the date of which changed year to year but which generally arrived in late January or sometime in February. She used her father's special recipe, which used almond extract, rather than almonds, to cut down on the expense. The goal was to bake delectable cookies that mirrored my grandfather's, which famously melted in your mouth but could be dropped from three feet high without crumbling. Maybe that said more about the Crisco trans fats, but people walked miles for the chance to savor my grandfather's cookies in Hawaii, and in the Bay Area, they received ours with eager anticipation.

My mom froze all those cookies she baked, saving them for the Lunar New Year. Then I would ride around with her in our banana slug-colored Dodge Dart and distribute handmade Lunar New Year greeting cards with *Gung Hay Fat Choy* written in Chinese, party invitations featuring a picture of the animal of that particular year, and cookies by the dozen. Each year we threw four Chinese New Year parties over two weekends, filled with a multicultural array of hors d'oeuvres and the continual sounds of the gong. Though the inebriated guests usually addressed me by my birth name, which irked me, and I wasn't thrilled about having to be the dutiful daughter who was expected to serve treats with an accommodating smile, I appreciated the enthusiasm with which we honored our traditions as a welcoming way of educating people about Chinese culture.

During the celebrations, as each person or group passed through the front door, we rang the gong to chase away the evil spirits. Grabbing these two bronze cymbals connected by a red rope, we sliced the gong up and down, rather than banging them head-on, to get just the right reverberating sound. The flustered guests would inquire, "Why, do *I* have evil spirits?" The answer was always the same: "We have to chase away the evil spirits to be sure they don't come in."

As the legend goes, Buddha, the emperor of the heavens, called upon the animals to share in the New Year's celebrations, rewarding their loyalty by naming a year after each one in the order in which they arrived. The twelve animals that answered the call raced to see what order they would be designated. The ox was in first place. But the clever mouse, riding on the ox's back, jumped forward at the finish line to take first place. The names of the animals are not consistently described; some say rat rather than mouse, snake rather than serpent, rabbit rather than hare. The sequence that was etched in my brain as a child goes as follows: mouse, ox, tiger, hare, dragon, serpent, horse, ram, monkey, rooster, dog, boar.

Every year we would make a papier-mâché mask of that year's

animal so we could dress up and chase out the old year. At a certain point during the parties, one of my sisters and I would each don a mask and costume, one of us representing the animal of the old year and the other the animal of the new year. The Year of the Tiger was special, not just because it was my year, but because I got to wear animal-print boys' pajamas, with fly, along with a tiger mask, as I pursued the Year of the Ox, the old year. My dad and brother would light a string of firecrackers out front, and my mom would stand at the front door, clanging the gong. All the drunk people would jump back, clutching their dim sum and gin and tonics, while we jostled through the crowd, broom in hand, sweeping out the old year. We chased away the evil spirits as we welcomed the new year in style.

Evil spirits are the demons, the negative elements, that can bring on bad luck, whether it's poor health, economic challenges, or disharmony in the family. People who promote hatred and bias are not evil spirits, per se, but rather have opened themselves up to be influenced by evil spirits. Though evil spirits are external, they can be self-generated, like when we internalize negative messages about ourselves. So while my family fended them off at the front door, it didn't occur to us to consider how they impacted us in our daily lives, such as in the form of gender-based shame and ridicule.

*   *   *

It was Lunar New Year's Day 2012, the first day of the Year of the Dragon, the day after my next-door neighbor's fiery festivities and my own Facebook blast, that I announced my medical transition to my colleagues via e-mail.

"*Gung Hay Fat Choy! Chuc Mung Nam Moi!* Happy Lunar New Year! By all accounts, the Year of the Dragon is going to be bold, innovative, and full of good luck. Ideas will flow, creativity will abound, and love and life will blossom in the Year of the Black Water Dragon. I look forward to our continued collegial brilliance and collective successes.

"I'm writing to share my fierce dragon year news with you"—and I announced my transition. "Oh, and my lovely wife, Georgia, is gestating our third child, due in July."

Responses exploded with the same rapid-fire succession as the others. "I knew you were a fierce dragon when I met you."

"CONGRATS & HAPPY LUNAR NEW YEAR, WILLY!!! How exciting for you and the family. . . . Wishing you good health and peace in your transition and a BIG WOO-HOO on baby #3!!!"

"We also rejoice with you as you make continuing changes in your life that are consistent with fully expressing who you are and thus modeling dignity, self-respect, and love of self, enabling and strengthening love of others. In so doing, you clear a path for many others, and that truly makes a world of difference. Congratulations, and thank you for making the world a better place."

I never expected that congratulations would come with my decision to medically transition. I'm just one person trying to find my way, just doing my best to live as my authentic self. As the messages poured in that day, I felt overwhelmed by the exposure and elevated by all the good energy. The positive responses were so loving and oddly devoid of challenge and difficulty. My house was clean; there were no evil spirits on my street.

As it is understood in Chinese and Vietnamese culture, the dragon is a profound symbol of power. It is the only animal in the Chinese zodiac that is a mythical creature. A dragon year is a blessing, a time to improve oneself and to make a major transition in one's life. It's a good year to take calculated risks, accomplish a mission, encourage change, and embrace innovation. This is the year when we may be able to achieve what seemed impossible before.

Before I knew it, the fierce Year of the Dragon was already instigating change. Three days into it, I awoke in the deep night and showered long and scalding hot in a cloud of lingering steam. It was late January 2012, the morning of my long-awaited surgery with Dr. Brownstein, the legendary surgeon who'd performed chest reconstruction for thirty-five years. The house was dark and cold and quiet. I dressed in the kind of comfortable clothing I would never normally wear in San Francisco, ate and drank nothing, and caught a ride into the buzz and hustle of workday predawn headlights. Once at my destination in the Castro, I adjusted my eyes to bright fluorescent lights and handled the paperwork. I was instructed to don a homely gown, recline, and go to my happy place.

I drifted out to the delicious warm water of the Hawaiian islands, my home country of sorts, where deep blues were sprinkled with brightly colored fish and my movements carried my soul through a gentle ocean. I pushed my arms in a breaststroke, kicked my legs into the depths.

As I swam farther out into the ocean, my surroundings changed into a white room with searing bright light shining through a lone window. I knew the place well but had never been able to get the window open. The room had held an energy for so long that it had settled in with a lingering odor. From time to time this energy would get restless, gnaw at me, make me feel uncomfortable and anxious. Then it would calm down. But lately it had become more resolute. At first it started knocking, then it began banging, on the window. Then it started to run laps around the room, circling, panting frantically. It couldn't sit still, and I couldn't breathe.

I had always wondered if I would ever be able to open the window, or if I really needed to. The doctor knew without my having to tell him that it had been painted shut, so he brought a knife.

Every time I wore a seat belt I felt this anxiety, this reminder that this energy was caged in my chest. Every time I got dressed I had to manage them, cover them, keep them at bay. I was never one to bind or wear a jog bra. I couldn't stand feeling constricted. Every day I wore a white tank top and a button-down shirt. But the anxiety I was feeling at their presence on my chest was escalating. They wanted to be gone, and I was losing my mind.

It had been only two months since I had decided to medically transition, and it was just three days after my announcement. Sure, I had circled around it for decades, but every time I came to the realization that I wanted to medically transition, that I *needed* to transition, I talked myself out of it. But I had reached a point now where I was uncomfortable and pissed off every time someone called me "ma'am" or "she." But was it the right thing for me? Couldn't I just continue being a trans guy in a butch's exterior? Did I really have to radically alter my body to live authentically in my gender? Couldn't I just be the complex gender creature I was without going under the knife?

Over the years, my body had been referred to as "the petite ideal"—the kind of female look that the magazines idealize, an impossible standard.

People were always checking me out in my swimsuit, a sports bikini or board shorts with a bikini top. When I looked in the mirror, I was satisfied. I didn't have a problem with my body.

My wife had a deep appreciation for what she called my "A-plus chestesses." I never let her come near them, though; my instinctive reflex to her proximity was to elbow my arms into an automatic "defensive block," as she called it. They were there on my chest, but unavailable and trying miserably to hide.

As much as others liked my look, I came to the realization that the body I had was not letting me be me. In some sense, yes, it was finally cooperating after my years of struggling with a disabling chronic illness. I was swimming several times a week and living my dream as I used my body to work hard to support my family. But I was getting "ma'am-ed" and "she'd" and relegated to the women's locker room.

I finally realized that the notion that my body should stay female was not my own. I was dining with a colleague at a restaurant overlooking a swimming pool, and she asked me, simply, why I didn't live as my true self. I turned from her and stared into the depths of that expansive pool, caught in that underwater breath, struggling to emerge at the surface. I did *not* want to hear it. Afterward, I conducted a transgender cultural competency training for an organization that provides substance use disorder treatment for troubled youth, a large percentage of whom are transgender. When I saw how they supported these young people, I felt pained in my grief. I thought about how I tried to socially transition at age nine, but without family or school support, there was nothing I could do but insist that people call me by the appropriate name. My emotions spun through the roof on the drive back from rural Northern California, but by the time I got home, I had talked myself out of it. Again.

Still, this nagging feeling was not going away. Over the next couple of months, the realization rose again and again, until one day, as I facilitated a preemployment workshop series for homeless and marginally housed transgender people, it came to stay. I was surrounded by these wonderfully smart, insightful trans folks, whose emotional presence taught me so much about staying strong. When I, as facilitator, asked them to brainstorm about what they do to boost their self-esteem, they were quick to respond: "Talk to supportive people." "Don't listen to negative messages." "Nurture your gift." One day we invited transgender entrepreneurs to speak about their careers, including a buff personal trainer. I liked his physique and how he carried himself. I decided I wanted that for my-self—to be a guy, a physically fit guy.

My long-awaited moment had arrived; it was finally time to medi-cally transition. It was a long time coming, or perhaps it was the next step in a very long transition. I was ready to take steps to change my body to fit my mind. It was time.

As I tell training groups, transition refers to the process by which people change their gender expression to something other than the sex they were assigned at birth. It can mean different things to different peo-ple and can involve many different pieces. Social transition can include changes in clothing, personal styling, name, and pronoun—things I did, or tried to do, at a very young age. Medical transition can involve hor-mones, surgeries, and other transition-related procedures. The myth in the general public is that all transgender people get "the surgery": they check themselves into the hospital one day as one gender and emerge the next day, magically transformed. The reality is that the vast majority of trans folks never access any surgery at all. Moreover, transition can take years and varies depending on the individual's preferences, finances, health status, and health care access.

In some ways, I had been living as male, or transmasculine, for many years, but only people who understood my trans identity saw me that way. I identified as third gender and had tried the gender-neutral pronoun "ze" for a while, but it was too hard to work with. Very few people were used to gender-neutral pronouns in the '90s and early 2000s, whereas nowadays there is an evolving understanding of individuals with complex gender identities who might locate themselves between or beyond male or female. People had not yet started using the pronoun "they," and no one was announcing their gender pronoun in introductions, on name tags, or on their e-mail signature. Over the years, more and more people, mostly trans guys and colleagues, called me "he," but many, especially lesbians and the straight parents of my kids' friends, assumed I was "she," based on my biological status and my wife's insistence on referring to me with female pronouns. I didn't feel empowered, energetic, or entitled enough to continually assert and explain who I was.

When I navigated a third-gender identity in the '90s, I was one of only three people in the San Francisco-based FTM community who identified as trans but weren't changing their bodies. As the years went on, it became less of an anomaly to claim a complex gender identity. After Annalise Ophelian's film *Diagnosing Difference* debuted in 2009, I became the poster child for a nonbinary gender identity, as we were beginning to call it. I am featured in the film saying, "As a third-gendered person, either way, transitioning or not transitioning, there'd always be something that wasn't totally congruent for me." Since I've medically transitioned, I've found that that hasn't been the case.

I never identified as genderqueer, though people often labeled me that way and still do. It wasn't a term that resonated for me, though I suppose that technically I was genderqueer, since I inhabited a gender identity that was not uniformly male or female. I saw myself as a trans man who had not pursued medical transition. I always knew that I was male, but in my generation it hadn't been an option to express myself as such, so I had to be some kind of female. In the process of discovering what that was, I fell in love with women and the world of badass female empowerment. I loved being butch in a butch-femme relationship. I loved the connection I had with women. Yet, at the same time, I felt myself pulling away from women because I knew that I was a different gender. I was nearing the exit for nearly two decades before I was truly ready to leave the world of women.

When I was on the verge of transitioning in the '90s, I was a grad student in public health, where I was struggling to get support as the only out trans person I knew of on campus, and extremely debilitated by chronic illness. I was too sick to attend class on a regular basis, getting notes from classmates who were paid by the disability program to take them for me. I was always "those people" that my classmates talked about—*those people* on Medi-Cal, *those people* with Medicare, *those broke people* who had health issues and needed services. As much as I felt deeply pained about not being perceived as male, I didn't pursue medical transition at that time because I felt I lacked the confidence to stand tall as a man.

I also needed to find some peace with my family. My family of origin had been a painful mess since 1997, the year my sister got together with a man who changed all our lives. After he picked a fight with me, two of my siblings vilified me, and interactions over the next decade were painfully unproductive. But once she left the man in 2011, we all began to heal. Georgia and I hosted a family reunion in October 2011, the first time my parents and siblings had all been together in one room since 1995. Two weeks later, I was ready to medically transition.

I had reached my tipping point. I had recently turned forty-nine and knew that I was not going to arrive at fifty in a female body. I came home from the trans preemployment workshop and informed Georgia, between responding to the needs of our interrupting little kids, that I wanted to medically transition. This wasn't the first time in the seventeen years we'd been together that we'd had this conversation. She had always been against it; I had always known I wanted it, but I wasn't sure if it was the right thing for me.

When twenty-four hours passed and I hadn't talked myself out of it, I knew. This time I was sure. We were waiting to hear whether Georgia was pregnant with our third child. Her recent focus on trying to get pregnant again, plus the fact that we had two kids already, ages two and five, meant my announcement was more than she could handle in the moment. "I can't deal with this!" she told me.

But I could no longer prioritize anyone else's needs over my own. After circling around it for decades, I became filled with a sense of urgency. I immediately made an appointment with a doctor who could prescribe testosterone, and Dr. Brownstein, the surgeon known for excellent results with "top surgery," or chest reconstruction: removal of the breasts and creation of a male chest.

A few days later, we learned that Georgia was in fact pregnant. She was conflicted about my decision, which was one of five or six other family priorities, including addressing our kids' emotional and developmental needs. At the time, I felt upset that she didn't support me. She knew from our first date at a trans event that medical transition was something I contemplated. What I didn't fully understand was how difficult it felt for her to envision an end to the unspoken visual display of our queerness. She needed me, in my butch expression, to convey the queerness of our relationship and family, since her femme expression led people to assume that she was straight. She had fought hard to come out as a lesbian at age sixteen within the traditional Greek cultural framework of her family. Understandably, she did not want to have her experience erased. But eventually she adjusted to the idea that I was transitioning and assured me that she wasn't leaving me, and not just because she needed my help with the kids. She loved me no matter what, and as time went on, she saw how happy I became.

*   *   *

It was a couple of weeks before my initial intake appointment in November 2011 at a trans-friendly clinic, the first time I sought care for medical transition. Since Georgia was busy with the kids, I went alone in midafternoon and filled out pages of paperwork about my gender identity. How long had I known? Since before I could talk. Did I understand the risks of testosterone? Yes, I was well aware.

I was escorted to the treatment room, where they took my vitals. And then I waited, alone, in the empty room. The next person to come in was an intern who began to go over my paperwork. As she reviewed my responses, I felt a sudden typhoon of emotion. It ripped the house down to the studs and everything in it—the meanness, shame, pain, grief, dismissal, lack of access, ignorance, years of contemplation, exhaustion, prohibition. I was finally, finally there in that room, at age forty-nine, asking without reservation for the tools to become my authentic self.

The storm rushed from deep inside, pushing itself into the room, as I struggled for air. Her eyes widened in alarm. My breath stilted; I managed to sob, "I've been wanting this my whole life!"

Two weeks later, in early December, my lab results in, I emerged from a follow-up appointment, script in hand. Within one month of having made this enduring decision, I received the package with the juice I had been longing for for decades. I ripped open the box, quickly loaded the syringe, and shot it into my ass, shaking and hurried like a down-and-dirty dope fiend. Relief couldn't come fast enough.

Six weeks after I started testosterone, the surgeon took out his knife and pried open the painted window in that stuffy white room, and when I woke up, I knew immediately that this imprisoned energy had left the building. I saw the evil spirits leave through that open window like the haze of the dragon, the smoke of the firecrackers welcoming the dragon, the dragon breath itself. As I came into consciousness, I smiled into Georgia's eyes. The anxiety had lifted. They were gone, and it couldn't have felt better. That's when I began to feel free.

CELEBRATING A PARENT'S TRANSITION

IN AN ELEMENTARY SCHOOL SETTING

Georgia and I moved in together in September 1995, after dating for nine months. Times were lean, and we laugh now about the time she found her boss's discarded clothes in the trunk of her car and how excited she was that she could try to sell them at a consignment shop. We relied on $14 "share packages" that consisted of a big block of bright orange government cheese and odd groceries that didn't go well together, like celery and piecrusts. Every week we would go down to a church on Grand Avenue to pick up our share package, along with big hugs and airy smiles from old ladies in dusty sweaters. But no matter how broke we were, we always maintained our credit. It was a tremendous accomplishment a few years later when we managed to buy our first home with no down payment, back when you could get a loan with no money down.

It was a tiny two-bedroom bungalow in a mixed Oakland neighborhood: sweet and homey, with a small backyard where we spent many afternoons relaxing with family and friends over Georgia's scrumptious home cooking. Shortly before our son was born in 2006, we tore down the rat-infested, wood-rotted garage and built a beautiful, detached home office from the foundation up. The house itself was only about eight hundred square feet, so small that a visitor could take a few steps into the front door, do a 360, and have seen it all.

We enjoyed neighborhood walks and felt very connected to our home and community. After 9/11, the neighbors started organizing an e-mail list to notify one another of sketchy activity, developed a bunker of emergency supplies, and held a few neighborhood potlucks each year so we could get to know each other and build relationships. But the neighborhood was oddly divided between progressive people who had no problem with our being queer, who were primarily white, and not-so-progressive people who were not so friendly to us, who were primarily people of color.

Once we had a second child, our tiny house felt too small and we began to wonder if there was any way we could get into a bigger house. Our son was approaching school age, and our concern was not just how cramped our living space was. The school was just around the corner, and most of our lovely, straight, white neighbors seemed happy enough with it—at least those who hadn't fled to the 'burbs. But we knew all too well that the school community included loyal Mormon supporters of Proposition 8, which outlawed same-sex marriage in California in 2008. There was no LGBTQ affinity group at the school, nor was there a history of LGBTQ support from any of its revolving principals, and we didn't feel like creating a whole support program.

One of our greatest accomplishments, besides buying our first home and bringing our vibrant, fun-loving children into the world, was buying a big house so we could all live comfortably without feeling like we were on top of each other. It was no easy feat running all over town for six months, touring homes for sale and attending school information nights, securing a home loan when our money was tight, in an era of immense banking scrutiny, and bidding on and losing several houses. Nor was it cheap dressing up our starter home to sparkle like the belle of the ball.

With intense research, perseverance, and good fortune, we managed to leverage the equity from the small house we had bought years earlier, with no money down, into a much larger house, a Craftsman with original architectural details, space for my office, and a large backyard with room for our kids to run freely. Thanks to a shrewd Chinese American realtor with good game and a poker face, we were able to sell our old home well over the asking price to rich cash buyers and buy our new home from rich people who were in a hurry to sell and who amiably dropped the price to meet our loan limit. Miraculously, it was in the neighborhood with our top-choice public elementary school. Our new school demonstrated strong educational outcomes and a long-standing commitment to diversity issues, and housed a relatively large, active LGBTQ affinity group. We knew it would be a good fit both for our kids and for us as parents. We closed on our dream home three days before our son's kindergarten application was due.

We had made the unusual request to have the utilities turned on before the house was even officially ours, so we could have the appropriate documentation that we lived in the neighborhood. Georgia trembled and got teary as she handed the district staff person our son's paperwork, along with a letter stating our case for his acceptance into our neighborhood school. Her nervousness demonstrated just how badly we both wanted this school to be our kids' educational home, and the opportunity to engage in an active community of parents and caregivers with similar values. In Oakland, even if you live in the neighborhood, it's not a given that your child will attend your neighborhood school. We were thrilled when we learned that he was accepted.

After fixing up our new house, we moved in with great excitement. Every day we were filled with gratitude as we wandered from room to room in disbelief that this home was actually ours. One evening, a few months after we settled in, I was stunned to see the principal of our new school on every news channel, fielding questions about the school's move to provide Gender Spectrum training for the students. I later learned the training was provided in support of J, a female-to-male third grader who was questioning his gender. Gender Spectrum provides education, support, and advocacy for families of transgender and gender-expansive children and conducts workshops for elementary school–age children. The curriculum used age-appropriate exercises that called into question the hypergendered world of young kids. "Is this a girl toy? A boy toy? Both? Is this a girl color or a boy color? Neither?"

When Fox News got wind of the workshops, the principal had a media circus breathing down her neck. She was asked whether the curriculum, which didn't address sexuality at all, was appropriate for the children. "We're working to create a caring school community where all kids feel welcomed," she responded. "What's wrong with teaching kids to accept and appreciate everyone?" I felt a profound sense of relief knowing that we had somehow managed to arrive at a school that just might be able to contain everything we were as a family: queer, trans, interracial, mixed heritage.

It was an exciting day when we walked our son to his first day of kindergarten, with our two-year-old daughter riding in the stroller. Though we had gotten to know some of the families in the community, we were pleasantly surprised to see our new school community in all its color and vibrancy. As we lined up with our son's class, we saw people of every hue, religion, language, and immigration story, students with disabilities, and people of varying socioeconomic status. We turned around, and right behind us was a lesbian family, to whom we introduced ourselves with the warmth of family recognition. We looked up the line and saw another lesbian family, and beyond that, a two-dad family. We were astounded to discover that we were one of four queer families in our son's kindergarten class. One of the lesbian moms commented, "They really stacked us up." There were no queer families in the other kindergarten class; we were purposely grouped together, a practice that is used to create support for marginalized populations.

Over time we came to experience how this dynamic, multicultural group of faculty and staff create a positive educational environment by fostering kids' academic, social, and emotional development. Utilizing the Caring School Community model, this school engages students, families, and staff in community building, cross-cultural exchange, discussion of issues, problem solving, and collaborative activities. I appreciate the school's emphasis on the restorative justice model, which utilizes nonpunishing approaches to conflict resolution by offering a role for all parties involved to engage in dialogue, determine just outcomes, and work against society's assumptions of guilt based on color, class, or other characteristics. One staff member described her work this way: "The best part of my day is when both of the students involved in a dispute feel empathy for each other, say they're sorry, and give each other hugs."

Underfunded, like other public schools in California, our school finds many ways to raise needed funds, about $160,000 a year, for mental health and academic support, library, music, gardening, the arts, and other pro-grams. There are several key fund-raisers, spearheaded by the Parent-Teach-er Association (PTA), which bring the community together. There are ample opportunities to join a committee, whether it is the PTA, the Dads' Club, or a group that strategizes on how to close the academic achievement gap. Families and kids build community in many ways; for instance, the school engages kids in mentorship programs where kids in the older grades help younger kids with their reading and other academic skills.

As a new kindergarten parent, I was impressed that the principal communicated frequently with the school community and always invited people to share their concerns, suggestions, and celebrations. When she welcomed us all to the new school year, she announced that she hoped to learn the name of every student, as well as their family members. I couldn't imagine how she could endeavor to do this, but I felt confident and pleased that we were in good hands.

Yet, despite this open and accessible leadership, an active, welcom-ing, and fairly progressive parent community, and a school that truly em-braced diversity, I was miserable. Every time I was at the school, I felt like I was jumping out of my skin with discomfort. Parents responded to me the way a lot of Bay Area parents did—with an inaccurate assumption: "Oh, two moms. I get that." Some even called us "ladies," which made me upset and frustrated. As if you could look at me with my butch pre-sentation and think I was a "lady." I would explain, "No, I'm Dada. I'm transgender." Some people got it, but most had a hard time understand-ing that even though I was female-bodied, I was not a mom. I struggled to be perceived as the transmasculine parent I was.

While most of the kids at the school seemed to take my parenting status in stride, ironically, the hardest part was dealing with the kids with lesbian and gay parents who would insist, despite my son's objections and my efforts at clarification, that he had two moms. While I appreci-ated the strong queer presence, this continual misgendering was upset-ting. They thought they knew who I was, and what my son's experience was, through their own lens of reality, which was understandable but problematic. I was misconstrued and rendered invisible with respect to something fundamental to my being—my relationship to my son.

Oddly enough, my son's preschool had had no problem understanding and accepting me as his dada. There we were, the only queer parents, mixed heritage and interracial, with a deep discount, at the blondest preschool in Oakland. Despite their lack of commitment to racial and ethnic diversity, they were exceptional at working on the kids' social and emotional development. When a little girl loudly whispered and laughed that I was my son's second mom, the teacher used the opportunity to invite questions and settle the matter well without making either my son or me feel like a spectacle. "I can see how you might think that his dada is his mom," she said to the little girl. "But I don't think that's how his dada feels."

But kindergarten felt different. This was elementary school, not preschool, and we were beginning to develop relationships with families in the neighborhood, with whom we would be in community for many years. A couple of months into the school year, I was at a birthday party with all of my son's classmates and their families. Held in a kiddie sports facility, it was loud chaos as the kids ran wild and the parents connected in gender-specific groups. I was hanging out with my family, making sure our youngest was safe. A mom spoke animatedly with the women about shoes. I looked around. Did she think *I* was part of that discussion? I didn't know what to say to the dads, either. I noted that I was the smallest adult there. I contemplated transition and wondered whether I would be perceived as male, given my size. I also noted that I was the only one who didn't fit into a gender-specific group. I was Dada, a female-bodied, transmasculine parent, something few could understand. And I was *so* tired of having to explain it. As the sounds and motions of delight and abandon swirled around me, my soul ached. I occupied this unseen, misunderstood parenting space. I felt stricken with the deepest sorrow and discordance. I understood in that moment the profound pain that many trans people feel when the complexities and incongruencies of life become too hard to bear.

Trans people who are considering medical transition have asked me what my tipping point was, what made me decide to transition and how I knew it was right. Perhaps there was no one moment but rather thousands of moments over five decades. Something was shifting inside me, from a female-bodied, third-gendered identity to something else, a male identity. I was in uncharted waters, a wide-eyed kindergartner myself, embarking into new territory. I knew I could not go on not being seen as the father I always was.

*   *   *

A couple of months later, I met with the principal to discuss the professional development diversity workshop she had asked me to provide for faculty and staff. "Oh, by the way, I'm transitioning," I mentioned. She responded, "This is so exciting! Thank you for sharing this with me! This is a celebration!" Her enthusiasm was unexpected. At that point, my medical transition was still this challenge that had to be dealt with at home, not something people were celebrating.

Not only was I surprised by her elated response, I was impressed that she had the foresight and leadership to suggest that Georgia and I meet with my son's kindergarten teacher and her to discuss how they could support my son through my transition. It was an act of brilliance, really, that I never saw coming. Faculty and administrators at my son's school cared enough to explore how to create a nondiscriminatory learning environment for my child and wanted to develop support systems for our family? This compassionate response was so supportive and unexpected, I was stunned.

As much as I immersed myself in the depths of my self-actualization and longed for a more affirming experience as a parent at the school, it wasn't about me. I pop in and out. My son goes to school there all day, every day. This principal was just doing what she would do to support any student whose family is experiencing a major shift, such as a divorce or a change in a parent's medical condition.

We sat down with the principal and teacher and talked about how best to prepare our kids for my impending chest reconstruction surgery, how the teacher could anticipate and respond to any potential negativity in the classroom, and how we could all work to protect our son from bias. We wanted to ensure that we were all prepared for any pejorative comments and hoped that our son's experience at school would continue to be positive. "I'll do the Gender Spectrum curriculum next Tuesday," added the teacher.

As Georgia and I left the meeting, my legs moved along but my eyes focused ahead on some distant point as I tried to process it all. I was stunned. *Did that really just happen?* When I came out in the early 1980s, my queerness was something I had to exercise great caution about, even in San Francisco. There certainly were no support systems in place in any sphere in my life. As a transgender person, I had been coming into myself and shedding my shame for decades. I never imagined that I could tell the principal of my son's school that I was medically changing my body and that she would immediately suggest creating systemic support for him as a student in her school.

I flashed on her heartwarming comments and beaming smile during the meeting: "This is a celebration! I feel honored to be a part of it." I felt deeply moved that the leader of my son's school had framed this profound moment in my life in a way that I hadn't even allowed myself to anticipate or imagine.

*   *   *

As I transitioned, I was afraid that the people who had started the Internet firestorm and intense media attention surrounding the Gender Spectrum workshops would create some very unpleasant moments for my son and me. But those fears were unfounded. By the time my son started first grade, things were going well for me as I began to be consistently perceived as male by people who hadn't known me previously. Guys in the Dads' Club would say, "Hey, bro," from across the street, and faculty and staff just knew me as my son's father. Some of the kids would greet me excitedly from across the playground, calling out to me, identifying me as my son's dad. Most important, my son didn't experience any negativity.

Sure, I experienced a full-throttle, freaked-out look of horror—another incident of facial incontinence—from a woman who had previously referred to my wife and me as "ladies." Like other parents, I was just grabbing a front-row seat at my son's play, camera-ready, to watch the cat-herding of first graders in drama class. I sat down next to her, and her breathing stopped, her eyes bugging out of their sockets. I guess my studly manliness just caught her off-guard.

But the parents in my son's class—those I disclosed to—embraced me and rolled with it. Before the school year began, we announced the birth of our third child. When school started, I sent out an e-mail to a select group of parents, saying that I wanted to share a family update because we valued their families as part of our community. I officially announced that I was transitioning to male, that the principal and teacher were very supportive, and that our priority was ensuring that our son's school experience continued to be positive. I told them they could support me by hitting me back on e-mail or saying something to me in person to acknowledge that they had received this information, and by referring to me with male pronouns ("he," "him," "his") and terms ("dad," "father," "husband"). I indicated that as someone who trains community health providers and educators on transgender issues, I would be happy to answer any questions they had.

Their immediate responses blew me away.

"Thank you for providing us with this update, and I appreciate and admire your openness. We wish you and your beautiful family the best during your transition. We feel lucky to be part of this school/community that supports all families!!"

"Thanks for sharing this important news with us. We've always perceived you as a wonderful father, and our son has as well."

"Congratulations and thanks for helping me to grow in my understanding around your journey. I got your back, man!"

"Way to go, dude. You have our family's support 100 percent."

*　　*　　*

In the spring of my son's first-grade year, I was hanging out with a multicultural group of moms during the annual walkathon fund-raiser. It was a blazing-hot May afternoon, and, after hoofing it for a few miles with my son and his friend, I realized that he was old enough to walk on his own among his friends and that I could just chase my nine-month-old baby and drink smoothies in the shade of a pine tree. I held my grinning baby firmly under his arms as his chubby little legs took upright steps, something he could not yet do on his own. The discussion among the parents ranged from getting our kids to bed on time to connecting with people from our past on Facebook to goings-on at the school. It was a fun group of folks, including Alex, one of the school's enthusiastic community builders, who often chatted and joked with parents. She began to tell us about the fifth-grade sex education classes.

Alex said that they were going to get sex-segregated presentations that coming week by guest speakers. She had her doubts about the guy slated to speak to the male students, as he was encouraging the boys to be "players." She turned to me and said, "I wish it were you, Willy. You want to speak to the boys? I'd trust you a lot more than him."

I smiled and laughed, "You want *me* to do it?" I was asking for clarification, not because I was making a commitment. I felt uncomfortable as I grooved to the old-school tunes blasting on the speakers, wondering whether she would feel the same way if she knew I was trans.

Then Alex said that the kids were asking where J, the transmasculine kid, would go during the presentation. I felt caught off-guard by the conversation and distracted by the loud music. I couldn't hear her clearly. "To Be Real" burned up the speakers, and, seizing the irony, I imagined myself getting up to bust a move.

"Say what?" I asked, wondering if she had just said what I thought she'd said. I felt nervous that the conversation was heading into trans territory. I didn't want to disclose my trans status in that moment and potentially become the focal point for invasive questions about my genitals or my family's reaction, or get misgendered from that day on.

"The kids were asking where J should go. You know, there are girls who don't really feel like they're girls, and boys who don't really feel like they're boys. We have to be aware of kids like that and support them."

"Oh," I said, not ready to disclose. I turned and looked at one of the moms seated under the tree. She looked at Alex, never at me, and said, "That's one of the things I love about this school, how great they've been with J." The other mom nodded but never looked at me either.

I couldn't believe it. Neither of these two moms, whose kids had been in the same classes as my son in both kindergarten and first grade, who had witnessed my transition, ever gave me a wink, a nod, or a smile. They never made a move to bust me out in any way. They knew my business was my business to disclose or not, on my own terms. I was stunned that people were treating me like any other parent at the school—not like a freak show or a curiosity object. It was yet another occasion when I was shocked that I was not being disrespected, but that instead things were as they should be, that I was being treated the way everyone should be treated.

Not long afterward, Alex enthusiastically approached me to tell me that she worked closely with a colleague who was a lesbian. I didn't understand why she was telling me about her lesbian colleague, until I realized that she had found out that I was trans and was expressing her enthusiasm. An African American woman in graduate school to become a mental health clinician, Alex was supportive and eager to learn more about trans issues and my work. I felt relieved during moments like this, when it was clear that disclosure did not invite invasive questions or inappropriate pronouns. I could be myself and be respected for it.

The handbook on how to transition in your kid's school setting has not been written, as far as I know, but it has made a world of difference to have the school system and community on my side.

Recommendations

There are many components to creating an LGBTQ-affirming environment in K–12 schools, whether by addressing larger issues of family diversity or by supporting the needs of students who may be different from the norm with regard to their gender identity and expression and/or sexual orientation. This work can take many forms and involves making an institutional commitment to training, policy development and implementation, advocacy, and curriculum integration of LGBTQ issues.

The following are my recommendations for how K–12 schools can institutionalize LGBTQ-affirming support systems. I've highlighted trans-specific issues, since that is an area that is sometimes overlooked.

- Engage key stakeholders to assess school readiness, and develop and implement plans for creating a school climate that welcomes diversity in all forms, including LGBTQ-headed families and young people. The more educators, families, and administrators can collaborate, the more likely the work is to be successful.

- Utilize professional development tools, resources, and lessons developed by Welcoming Schools, a project of the Human Rights Campaign Foundation. Work to adopt the Welcoming Schools curriculum in your school.[77]

- Adopt the Caring School Community model, which engages students, families, and staff in community building, cross-cultural exchange, discussion of issues, problem solving, and collaborative activities. This model is a nationally recognized, research-based program developed for grades K–6, which builds classroom and school-wide community while developing students' social and emotional skills and competencies.[78]

- Create a K–12 school environment that celebrates gender diversity and is prepared to support transgender and gender-expansive students. "Schools in Transition: A Guide for Supporting Transgender Students in K-12 Schools" is an excellent resource that was developed by Gender Spectrum, the National Center for Lesbian Rights, the American Civil Liberties Union (ACLU), the Human Rights Campaign, and the National Education Association.[79] It provides comprehensive best practices for working as a team to support students at various ages and stages of development. The guide addresses gender-specific settings, transition plans, privacy, community resistance, dealing with the media, and student records in K-12 schools. In addition, the National Center for Transgender Equality, in partnership with the Gay, Lesbian, and Straight Education Network (GLSEN), developed a model district policy.[80] The Toronto District School Board has also developed helpful guidelines.[81]

- Develop a written district policy that explicitly states that it is the responsibility and goal of the school district to ensure every child a safe and welcoming environment that is conducive to learning, and to protect students from harassment and discrimination based on the actual or perceived sexual orientation and/or gender identity of them, their family members, and/or their caregivers.

- Principals and teachers can create a welcoming community by inviting questions, concerns, and celebrations from everyone.

- Transitioning parents can involve the administration, faculty, and staff in the process so everyone can be prepared to anticipate and respond to bias from staff, students, parents, and caregivers.

- Integrate academic, age-appropriate issues of gender and family diversity, LGBTQ studies, and transgender studies in various subjects in the curriculum, including social studies, language, science, art, etc.

- Provide regular professional development training opportunities for faculty, staff, and administrators on the limitations of society's gender expectations and the concepts of gender identity and expression and sexual orientation.

- Provide opportunities for advocacy, program development, and social support for parents and caregivers through a school LGBTQ affinity group.

- Create a school community where all families are welcome by providing opportunities for community engagement and artistic expression of issues of diversity. Examples include community forums, digital storytelling, photo exhibits, and multicultural fairs.

- Provide opportunities for learning, program development, and mentorship by partnering high schools with lower-grade schools. For instance, high school students can design a program and present on LGBTQ issues at the elementary school.

- Learn more about the work of Our Family Coalition, an organization that supports LGBTQ families through support, education, and advocacy. (See Sidebar.)

- Connect with COLAGE, an organization that supports kids of LGBTQ-headed families nationwide. (See Sidebar.)

Systemic Support for LGBTQ Young People and Families

I've had the privilege of working with these amazing, long-standing Bay Area organizations that are enhancing the lives of families with LGBTQ members.

Our Family Coalition (OFC) works to remove barriers and create positive conditions that allow lesbian, gay, bisexual, transgender, and queer families to thrive and prosper in schools, institutions, and communities. It cultivates leadership among LGBTQ-headed families and partners with allies to advance social justice and equity. OFC has a number of programs that foster peer support and build community. Among other programs, it runs a monthly transgender-parent support group, which has been the only support group of its kind in the nation. It educates community members about how to navigate the legal landscape of second-parent adoption, wills, and other legal issues. It holds workshops for prospective parents, models how to talk to kids about their biological origins or adoption, and explores white privilege while raising kids of color.

For several years, I have organized, moderated, and presented at OFC's annual Trans Family Forum, which gives visibility to diverse trans parents, our partners, and our allies. It's been an incredible opportunity to witness powerful storytelling about gender identity, with an intersectional lens, and how it influences our roles as parents.

OFC's Welcoming and Inclusive School Program (in partnership with Welcoming Schools) collaborates with families, teachers, administrators, and other professionals who work with children to ensure that curricula, policies, and services are respectful and inclusive of LGBTQ experiences. It provides professional development trainings nationwide for schools, offers educational workshops on embracing family diversity, and hosts events about LGBTQ-inclusive schools.[82]

COLAGE is the only national youth-driven network of people with lesbian, gay, bisexual, transgender, or queer parents. Programs include local chapters, thriving online communities, visibility and support resources, youth activism development, local and regional events, and national education and advocacy. The organization runs community groups nationwide that support young people with LGBTQ parents and holds biannual national retreats at various locations around the country. The Kids of Trans program offers resources and programs specifically for people with one or more transgender parent. COLAGE has a Kids of Trans online community for youth ages thirteen and up to ask questions and post resources, articles, and events. The organization also distributes the Kids of Trans Resource Guide, which offers stories, advice, resources, and validation for young people with trans parents.[83]

COLAGE facilitates peer support among young people to become skilled, confident leaders. I am thrilled to partner with COLAGE to pilot the first school program in the nation for kids with trans parents, which launched in fall 2015. Kids work with peers, mentors, and school staff to reduce isolation and feel more connected to their school community, learning tools for how to talk about their family stories and respond to intrusive questions. These youth-led activities build community and leadership skills. In addition, professional development training builds schools' capacity to support the program and the kids they serve by developing the cultural competency of school staff and by identifying best practices for working with kids with trans parents.

Gender Spectrum provides training, consultation, and events for families, educators, professionals, and organizations to develop understanding of gender identity and support gender-expansive youth. I've had the privilege of working with this organization to develop its capacity to respond to the needs of families and communities of color, and I've been impressed with the diversity work it has done. Gender Spectrum is best known for its annual conference, which brings together families of trans and gender-expansive youth, as well as professionals who are eager to develop their skills for how to best serve these families. There are workshop tracks for high school, middle school, and elementary school youth; parents and caregivers; and professionals.[84] One of the highlights for me has been conducting writing workshops with trans and gender-expansive teens, whose creativity, honesty, and bravery are an inspiration.

SCULPTOR

Snapshot: 2013

When I was in middle school, my father endeavored to whittle away the stressful demands of the workplace, so he enrolled in a night class on woodcarving. It began with a challenging task: to take a small, rectangular piece of soft plywood and carve a ball, as round as possible, within a frame. A ball in a cage, if you will. The ball had to be able to roll within the four corners of the frame, yet it could not get too small or it would fall out. The trick was in taking away just enough to create the round shape yet leave the material necessary for its containment. Over several nights, I watched his quiet demeanor and focus slowly reveal the spherical form, and the thrill and pride as his thumb pushed the ball in motion without escape. I was impressed by the transformation of this nondescript piece of wood into a dynamic and seemingly impossible creation.

His next task was to whittle a wooden chain from a cylindrical stick of plywood, again shedding what was unnecessary but leaving enough to keep the chain intact. Crudely executed yet smooth to the touch, the oval links inextricably interconnected themselves, like a strand of DNA or the linkages of life, solidifying my father's destiny as a fine wood sculptor.

Around this time, I often tossed a football with my dad, refining my spiral and even winning a physical education award in seventh grade for my football skills. My best buddy was a female-bodied person who, in retrospect, seemed transmasculine, though she may not identify that way even today. Susan embodied a strong male energy and was confident and smart, and sometimes overbearing. Caucasian and stocky, with short brown hair, she stretched a boys' white T-shirt and blue plaid button-down shirt over her large, early-developing breasts. She was my pal who understood my gender without explanation, like the girls we chased and goofed around with. We did well in school, wore our boys' button-down shirts, and watched football on her big color TV in her mansion of a house. Her mom, raised rich from Texas oil money, transported me daily from school, along with her two kids, in a large, wood-paneled station wagon, the '70s minivan of choice.

But Wednesdays were different. That was the day our seventh-grade social studies teacher had a standing substitute, Mrs. Winkelberg, who dodged many a spitball in the chaos of our honors class. On Mrs. Winkelberg's first day, Susan became Steve and I, already Willy, enjoyed trying to fool her into thinking that we were guys as we put our arms around our stand-in girlfriends, who seemed to enjoy the fun.

Wednesday was also the day my mom picked me up in our tried-and-true Dodge Dart and bribed me to go to Chinese school with the rare treat of McDonald's cheeseburgers and chocolate milk shakes. Though I have always loved learning languages and have a knack for it, I continually struggled with being in the milieu of Chinese people honoring our linguistic and cultural traditions. I thought Chinese people were nerdy and uncool, and as much as I was curious about learning Cantonese, I didn't want to associate with people who made me seem uncool.

"Eyes on the board and repeat after me," the teacher ordered sternly. Along with the hands-folded obedience she demanded and a disciplinary approach that was heavy with shame and scorn, there were clear gender expectations, which meant that I was supposed to be a good Chinese girl—quiet, respectful, and eager to obey.

I imagined the arcs of spitballs headed in the direction of the teacher's head but instead did what I and all the other students were raised to do: follow directions, do the homework, and have the right answers. Though I felt a certain kinship with the few kids in my age range, I also felt ruffled by them. They were the people I was trying so hard not to be—awkward nerds ridiculed for their fashion expressions, lunch food, intelligence, and introversion. Their proximity pushed my internalized racism buttons and made Chinese school emotionally wrenching for me. Though I actually enjoyed mastering such written and spoken gems as "The cow went up the mountain. The sheep went down the mountain," I felt caught between my mom's insistence that I attend and my own inner conflict and difficulty owning my heritage.

"It's Winky-Dink and Chinky-Dink Day, Wilkinson," Susan informed me every Wednesday in her caustic, amused tone. That meant that I wouldn't be carpooling with her that day, of course. It was also a reminder of who I was: a Chink headed to Chinky-Dink school.

I wanted to whittle away the part of me that got called Chink but sculpt myself into the boy I always knew I was meant to be.

*   *   *

My father knows wood like an extension of his hands, rough logs transformed into the gentle graces of a woman's curves or the fearless leap of a dancer. He begins by turning the wood in his hands, examining its every twist and blemish, then shaves away and refines its natural beauty into a new form that was already there, intrinsic. While some work originates from fallen tree branches, other pieces are carefully selected for the wood's properties. But no matter the source, they all get sculpted into fine art, diligently sanded to a smooth caress and stained to deep, rich tones.

As a young adult I began to sculpt, first focusing my efforts on the internal framework, before venturing to carve and sand the rough exterior terrain. My psyche grew like a gnarled tree on the Pacific coast, the stiff ocean winds pushing, pulling, wrenching, twisting it into its unique form, outstretched arms, jagged and vibrant.

Decades later, in puberty for the second time and still sculpting, I jump into the massive outdoor pool and slice the water until I push back the shame, the violent gaze, the racism, and all the insidious barriers to my being. I build my pecs, and I am stronger in my ability to stand tall, with my chest out. The girth of my neck expands to hold the weight of all the noise in my head. My legs thicken so I can walk the extra mile. I shed the subjugation of being an Asian female in this society, so I can present myself as the proud Asian man that I am: a husband, brother, father.

But somehow I am not the only one at the chisel. I feel the expert hands of others sculpting me into being, the wooden chain of interconnectedness. I sense the rough, crooked hands of my *haole* father in his shop and the brown, smooth hands of my uncles mixing mah-jongg tiles. I sense my father's father in dark blue overalls, tinkering in his wood shed, and my mother's father, sitting on the ground, weaving baskets from coconut palm fronds. And I feel how my three young children shape me into the dad that I am, as I divide my time between working long hours as a public health consultant and caring for them in a daily way.

At a party with my family, my four-year-old daughter runs to me, smiling broadly, giggling, arms outstretched, and jumps into midair as I bend to catch her, lifting her high into the sky, spinning her around and around, legs horizontal, like a helicopter in flight. We are one, twirling in joy, smiling to our ears, and laughing as we dance to the music. I am there to catch them, comfort and teach them, walk hand in hand with them, protect them. They sculpt me with their certainty that I will catch them and hold them.

*   *   *

Engrossed in my work on my computer, I drop from time to time to do fifty push-ups, to sculpt the arms that carry my sleeping children into our home and the shoulders that bear the financial burden of supporting a family of five. I tone and hone my torso into the male physique I was meant to have, releasing the past and reveling in the present.

My father's rugged hands caress the finely sanded, beautifully stained figure of a person in flight, arms outstretched, jumping into the unknown, the ball in a cage and the wooden chain long lost in time but not forgotten.

MONORACIAL BONDING

"Are you gonna go all monoracial on me?" Georgia joked as I reclined in the bathtub, my naked body illustrating a new and different, multilayered image. "Now that you're all male, are you going to be all Chinese, too?" We laughed ironically. For years I had identified as third gendered, my liminal gender expression inextricably linked to my mixed heritage. After decades of a flirtatious "Come here! No, go away" courtship with medical transition, I had finally taken the leap over the edge.

But why would I go all monoracial? How would it even be possible to do that? I had never been understandable. I was coming and going at the same time. I was sir, ma'am, he, they, her. I was him until I opened my mouth. I was "*not* Chinese" and couldn't possibly know anything about it. I failed the qualification tests for membership in all the groups I laid claim to. I was the epicenter of the confusion. I stepped over the line of exclusion. I was the exclamation point *and* the question mark.

But then, as I medically transitioned, things began to shift. Five months into the process of changing my body, I began to be read as male most of the time, especially when I was outside the gender-aware Bay Area. At eight months I began to be consistently perceived as male. On the streets and running errands, people stopped buggin', freaking out, doing a double take. I was he, him, sir.

What's more, Chinese people began greeting me on the street with *joe sun*, "good morning" in Cantonese, my shrimpy ass clearly of Guandong heritage now. I was Chinese, close to the ground, and male.

And then it happened, long after Georgia first jokingly posed the question. Three years into medical transition, I got treated as if I were monoracial.

I got into a crowded express line at the supermarket with my five-year-old daughter. We had run in for a few essential items—milk, juice, and ice cream. I looked over at the rag stand, and there was Ms. Jenner on the cover of a popular celebrity magazine. I grabbed it, eager to read the story, though Jenner herself hadn't come out yet and the media was making a buck off a purported scoop from a "close associate" of the family. I had been waiting for her to come out and was hoping her announcement was imminent.

"Someone doesn't know how to count," said the woman behind me in a loud volume.

Absorbed in my excitement about seeing Jenner on the cover, I looked up to see that an elderly Chinese man ahead of me had at least ninety items in the fifteen-items-or-fewer express line. The woman behind me was a fortysomething Chinese woman with straight black hair down her back. I nodded at her as I continued to flip through the magazine to find the story I was looking for.

"Someone doesn't know how to count!" she said again. Her volume had ratcheted up a couple of notches, in hopes, apparently, that the checker would kick the guy out of line. I winced as I reflected on how tired and ineffective this Chinese passive-aggressive style of communicating felt. How powerless and publicly shaming, I thought, then remembered it had taken more than a few friends and lovers, and my evolving sense of self over several decades, to teach me to communicate directly.

"Someone doesn't know how to count!" The third time was a charm. The checker finally told the man that he was in the wrong line, and the old guy nonchalantly stated that he thought the sign was for the other line.

I turned to look at the woman, who was studying my visibly mixed daughter squirming around, contemplating the candy rack. She surveyed her from head to toe, squinting at her facial features, her mouth hanging slightly agape. It was all too familiar, the look of someone who had engaged her internal racial processor with hard-nosed scrutiny and calculations of racial sufficiency. As she scanned my daughter, she assessed the golden highlights and soft curls of her hair and made her evaluation. The woman smiled knowingly and shook her head with disappointment. "My daughter has green eyes and curly hair! Can you believe that?"

I thought, *Really? Are you monoracial bonding with me?* What did she think—that I was full-blooded Chinese and that I would somehow share her disappointment in the look of our daughters? I had never had that experience before. Once, in Boston, a white woman had tried to white-bond with me. This also took place in a supermarket—coincidentally, with a checker. Her eyes landed on my freckled arm, never my face, as she made a disparaging comment about Puerto Ricans, which made me feel uncomfortable and complicit in her racism.

But this time, this mouthy, passive-aggressive Chinese woman was monoracial bonding with me, and in the worst possible way. Emboldened by her sense of racial superiority, she treated my beautiful, visibly mixed daughter as if she were defective, the way I had been treated my whole life, with continual assessments of my face, skin, and hair, and the disappointing outcome of my statistical breakdown. I was aghast. *How dare you speak about my child like that*, I thought, relieved that the tone of her comments didn't appear to register with my daughter. I felt dirty inside and out.

Could it be that the more I was consistently perceived as male, the more I was also perceived as Chinese, even monoracial? Had testosterone changed my face to look more Chinese, or was it that my short, slight, male stature screamed famine-stricken, Cantonese-speaking ancestors? Had I really reached a place of monopresentation, no longer ambiguous and confusing? Were people so relaxed around me now that they thought they could bond with me in their entitlement? I was used to people cocking their heads to the side, looking me up and down, backing away, or following me around. Now they wanted to connect in our right to oppress others?

Truth be told, simplicity is alluring. I don't mind getting a break from the contortions and assessments of freaked-out people. But this newfound privilege is nothing but a short-lived joy ride in a stolen car before the gas runs out, and my true self reawakens uneasy. I will not monoracial-bond with people so they can evaluate, judge, and dismiss my mixed people. I will not male-bond with men so they can denigrate women. My complexities will not be erased. My privileges will not be pirated. My loyalties are not with those who exclude.

I took my daughter, with her beautiful Chinese eyes, chestnut-brown hair, and radiant smile, and basked in the affirmation of our racial nonconformity—far, far away from the passive-aggressive insults of monoracialism.

A few months later, I attended the National Queer Asian Pacific Islander Alliance (NQAPIA) conference in Chicago, where I met fierce activists from all over the country who were standing up for immigrant rights, the #blacklivesmatter movement, and trans justice. On the first night, I asked a group of young, queer Asian men a logistical question about the conference when I saw them in the drugstore. They hesitated for a moment before responding. A couple days later, after I spoke on the trans plenary, one came up and explained why he had hesitated that night. At the last conference there had been a "creepy old white guy" hanging around whom they'd had to ask to leave, and he wondered if I might be this year's creepy old white guy. "But now I know who you are."

I learned a long time ago not to base my self-image, validity, or membership on the insensitive microaggressions and entitled assessments of monoracial people. Still, sometimes it's too much work managing the calculations of people who don't respect the layered complexities and racially transgressive beauty of mixed bodies.

THE POETRY OF SCARS

It runs along the inside elbow of my left arm, the scar that drew a line through my gymnastics career. I was ten years old, perched on a chin-up bar across the middle of my bedroom doorway, which had been secured in position for months. My dad hurt himself too many times running into that bar, treacherous for anyone who stood above three feet tall and wasn't paying attention. I spent hours twirling on it, one leg over the other, round and round, or two legs behind it, spinning backward until I was hanging vertical, head down and legs pointed to the ceiling.

That particular day I was taking a rest between moves, crouching with my feet balanced on top of the bar, steadied by my hands. Suddenly my rubber sneakers slipped and I dropped forward headfirst, down down down. I didn't panic. I was used to being upside down in flight. I would just curl and land softly on the thick, bright green carpet.

I turned so my left side would bear the impact, bending my arm to break my fall. I hit the ground with a crunch that initiated my nerve cells into a searing rite of passage.

I jumped up and ran to the mirror, my eyes widening to see if my arm was still there. I held my left arm with my right and saw that it was thicker now above the elbow, then ran out to the kitchen to tell my sister Su-Lin. It was five thirty on a weeknight. My parents were out, and Su-Lin was watching me for the evening. She sat me down and said I'd feel better if I ate something. I tried to eat rice and meat and warmed-up frozen peas. The pain only worsened.

A couple of hours later, my parents returned. My dad took me to the emergency room, where I lay on a table to be x-rayed. The technician held my arm up to show me where she wanted it, then let go. My arm crashed into the table painfully. Later, when she saw the image, she was very apologetic. I had broken the humerus, the bone above the elbow, so severely that the two pieces crossed each other. Someone asked me how much I weighed. "Fifty-six pounds," I responded, which they couldn't believe. Since I had eaten, they called in a special anesthesiologist so I could be put under for surgery. When I woke up at one o'clock in the morning, my arm was suspended high above me in traction and my dad was sitting next to me, waiting for me in the dark.

For the next ten days I lay in a hospital bed, watching the black-and-white TV that hung on the wall. The last two fingers on my hand felt itchy inside, so I scratched them until they bled because I couldn't feel the surface of the skin. Most of the time I was miserable with bladder discomfort because the nurses wouldn't respond for hours to my calls for a bedpan. When they finally came, they'd leave me on the bedpan for a couple more hours. My parents came by when they could, to bring me cards my friends sent me and get me the bedpan.

After the bones in my arm were pulled to the right position, I had surgery again and emerged with a body cast that held my arm upright with a supportive pole, which Su-Lin painted with green ivy. The cast covered my whole torso, so I moved by pushing off with my right arm. I wiggled a metal coat hanger down my back to scratch the increasingly itchy skin trapped under the cast. Three weeks later, they removed the body cast and placed my arm in a new cast and sling for another three weeks.

I tried to feel the pinky and ring finger on my left hand, but I felt them either partway or not at all. The ulnar nerve was severed. My mother had me squeezing oranges and pushing hard on my extended arm in the hope that my arm would eventually stretch out all the way. Her mother had instructed her to do the same exercises when she injured her arm as a teenager. I did eventually get my arm to straighten all the way, but I couldn't move my fingers from side to side. Mr. Spock's Vulcan hand salute was impossible.

* * *

My mother took me to Hawaii to stay with relatives and to see an acupuncturist her brothers trusted, because "the acupuncturists on the mainland [were] all quacks." My nerve still wouldn't awaken. Back home, my mom took me to an herbalist down the street, who placed my small hand on a little red-velvet pillow, his smooth brown fingers pressing into my wrist as he listened intently to my pulses. He sent us home with packets of carefully measured herbs that looked like river bracken and damaged hair, which my mom boiled until my dad paced out of the house, away from the overwhelming stench, and the curtains crawled with a pungent story of their own. My mother strained each dose of the thick black liquid into a white Chinese bowl with small, colorful designs. Twice a day I held my breath to choke them down—my first foray into the bitter, foul, funk of Chinese herbal medicine. Five sweet golden raisins were my reward.

I still couldn't feel part of my hand, so I went to a Western doctor, who zapped me with an electrical current that made my arm jump on its own and the rest of me light on fire from the painful surge through my core, but the ulnar nerve was still unresponsive. Five months after the accident, I went back into the hospital for surgery to sew the nerve back together, and when I woke up in a nauseated blur, I felt pain so sharp, so gnawing, that it sliced through me and taught me the power of endurance. That line of scar tissue that runs along my inner elbow narrates the story of the most pain I had ever experienced in my life, until phalloplasty.

Before the injury, I had been having a blast in gymnastics after school. At home I tumbled a string of back handsprings across the front lawn while speeding passersby honked their appreciation. After I broke my arm, I continued with one-handed cartwheels and walkovers but eventually moved on to other sports, which was fine because my gymnastics buddies were starting to get pressured to take ballet and go on a diet, both of which were way too "girlie" for me.

When I broke my arm, I had to miss the weeklong, highly anticipated science camp that everyone in my class went to. But I received more stuffed animals than I knew what to do with, immersed myself in

The Secret Garden, and ate lasagna and tuna casserole when my mom's friends arrived with dinner for our family. People I didn't even know showered me with get-well presents. My favorite gift was a blue circular AM radio that I kept tuned to KDIA, Lucky 13, the soul and funk of the Bay.

One night after my nerve surgery healed, I was cleaning the table with the moldy pink sponge we used for the dishes, table, and floor. It was stinky and sticky with everything it had wiped in the last couple of months. As I swept the crumbs into my left hand, I had trouble holding my fingers together to form a cup that could contain the crumbs without letting them slip through. My mother turned to my sister. "Look at that. She can't even wipe the table. It's a deformity." My sister laughed and responded, "Yeah, she can't even wipe the table right. She only has eight fingers that work now."

I was shocked and silenced. I had thought my sister was on my side. A light went on, and I realized how it worked now. If you agreed with Mom when she was talking about somebody else, she didn't say stuff about *you*. I was the youngest, so if they all repeated the mean things Mom said about me, Mom wouldn't go after them.

I decided that I was going to get ahead of this, that no one was going to use it against me. I went to school and announced to everyone, "I'm an eight-fingered geek!" I held out my left hand, with the last two fingers perpetually curled up, and paraded it for all to see. It was my badge of weirdness. When people asked to see my hand, I showed them gladly, announcing that I was an eight-fingered geek. Then I'd strike a martial arts pose, one leg up, with hands out in defense. "Watch out—I practice kung fu!"

* * *

Scars have written volumes that traverse my body. They speak in poetic whispers, creative tales, and journalistic essays. They have written their own memoir.

Scars hold the glare of violent gaze, the harsh sting of words that can't be undone, the crisscross of fences closed tight and gates opened wide. They have raged against a detached cleaver, bubbled into a boil, and healed into smooth dispassion.

They are the crudely drawn lines of continual assessment, the snap and clench of disregard, the demarcation of access denied. Scars are the forced indentations of a legacy of punishment for the natural incongruence of our beauty.

Scars contain the voluminous bloodshed of too many wars perpetuated against us—under muted street lamps, in shadowy bedrooms, and in the blind of studio lights. They are the jagged, imperfect weave of this eternal loom of threat, the archetypal artifacts of our determination to survive.

They are our collective, tragic tapestries that recall the beloved and the lonely, reluctant soldiers who resisted and succumbed all too early.

They arrive uninvited and unannounced, like houseguests staking claim to a bare cupboard, creeping up on us insidiously, before we can see their incessant stalking.

Scars are the measured stretch marks of forgiveness and rebirth in motion, documenting the loosening and tightening of skin and the expansion of change.

Sometimes our scars come with grandiose invitations and fund-raising campaigns, complete with excited itineraries to a profound, uncertain destination, fearless and exhausted.

They are the eventgoers, the fabulous ones, dressed to the nines in medical glue and silicone gel. They wear their pride in handsome body parts that have shifted in and out of existence, bearing the seam of two lives stitched as one.

Scars are the starting lines and the finish lines of marathons, the path to happy and the road we thought would remain untraveled.

Scars are the ink of our stories, the poetic tattoos of valiant warriors.

*   *   *

It runs around my left forearm, the scar that denotes my membership in the club of men on a journey to body congruence. My five-year-old daughter explained it to me the day I returned from the hospital.

"They used skin from your arm to make your penis, Dada, and then they took skin from your leg to cover up your arm."

"That's right!" I said, amazed at the education process my wife had done in my absence and my little girl's ability to understand, without judgment or question, the masterfully stitched quilt of my trans body.

I thought I would need a tattoo to cover up this scar, this blemish that marks me as one of those people, with deficiency and difference. But at seven months I found myself sporting it around town, this armband, this fashion statement, this salute to the changing landscape of access to care. I wear this scar with pride, and it carries with it legends.

THE
EDGE
OF
LIBERATION

SWIM JUNKIE

Snapshot: June 2014, on the eve of my July 2014 phalloplasty surgery

My wayward schlong dislodged from my dripping swim trunks and landed on the funky, wet locker room floor like a freshly caught fish flopping and struggling for its last, desperate breath on the bottom of a well-worn rowboat. It was 2012, early in my medical transition, and I was still getting the hang of being a gender-gifted swimmer with a new body and gender presentation. I glanced at the black Durafast trunks in my hand, then bugged at the sight of my silicone packy, which was strewn, balls out, on the floor. Furtively scanning the area and relieved that no one was near, I quickly grabbed and concealed my errant junk and made a mental note: *That can* never *happen again.*

When I'm in the men's locker room, I get dressed the same way every time, like a trans person. I don't engage with anyone until I've changed from my junk-packed trunks to my underwear, prepacked with its own set of genitals, and jeans. Then I put on my socks and sneakers before I even entertain a thought about deodorant or a shirt. If there's going to be an ass kicking in my future, I need traction on this slippery floor so I can run. I am there at the pool three or four times a week, basking in the sweet serenity of that inviting, delicious weightlessness, against the backdrop of the ever-present, insidious threat to my destruction as a human being.

I am a locker room magician. Sleight of hand is my trade; swimming is my addiction.

On any given day, there may be several muscular men twice my size who stand but two feet away from me in this tiny postage stamp of a locker room. Like the Terminator's visual statistical feed, I am constantly assessing the capacity and activities of every one of them: their strength, their state of mind, and their readiness to leave. I know exactly where they are in their process of getting ready, how likely they are to turn their backs and for how long, and when they are likely to be in my personal space or facing me. I am an undercover agent, skilled at getting a read without ever looking like I'm checking them out. And, like a stealth trans Houdini positioned an arm's length from danger, I get my junk-packed underwear and swim trunks on and off in a blink, carefully covering myself with a casually placed towel and pretending I'm not stressed every time.

After all, I've got other things to worry about, like getting home quickly so I can send my kids off to school in the morning, or watching my sleeping baby in the afternoon while my wife picks up our older kids. I'm a busy dad just trying to get my swim on.

Like a cat lollygagging without a care, I prefer the warm kiss of a sunny afternoon, but my addiction has progressed to the point where I will swim in all kinds of weather, at any time of day, in order to ensure that I get my time in the water. In the wintertime I creep out in the cold, dark edge of dawn, bundled in a puffy down jacket, waiting until I pull out of my driveway to turn on my headlights, filled with a compelling need to strip down in thirty-degree weather and get into the numbing expanse of an outdoor pool.

Sometimes I'm the first person to get into the hot tub in the dark morning drizzle. I turn on the jets and slide into that exquisite liquid heat, my muscles breathing a sigh of relaxation. I lean back, and the cold rain peppers my head like chocolate sprinkles on a perfect cup of coffee.

And then I emerge, contemplate the edge of the pool for a moment, and glide into the meditative bliss of immersion.

I am that way. Cool, warm, or hot, I want in.

*   *   *

I arrived early one morning and warmed up in the hot tub before staking out a spot in the pool. It was wintertime at the crack of dawn, so there was plenty of room in the pool for me to have my own lane. I wanted to stretch my body as wide as my wingspan could get.

I hesitated for a moment at the edge of the water, my body flushed with steam. Then, when I was ready for that counterintuitive leap, I plunged into the deep end. As the cold water hit my warm skin, there was a split second when I felt as if I had left the house naked, like a recurring stress dream of outrageous social transgressions that I become aware of after it's too late. I am privileged by my hipless Chinese body and barely detectable chest reconstruction, performed by a highly skilled surgeon. And yet in that moment, an ancient taboo surfaced to remind me that I had forgotten to cover up my torso.

And then I remembered that I had earned this most prized expression of male privilege: shirtlessness. It is an archetypal symbol of freedom that cisgender men often throw around with zero consciousness of their privilege, a reminder to every female-bodied adult of an aspect of male privilege that is decidedly off-limits. The idea that we could claim that privilege, that our breasts were allowed the freedom of naked expression, was one of the most profound aspects of attending women's music festivals back in the '80s, long before trans-exclusive policies. It was the unbridled freedom of shirtlessness in a world that imposes bosom management and lockdown.

Each time I plunge into the water, it is my chest that goes first, my heart, my core. I feel the singular impact of a warm, flat surface submerging itself in liquid blue, the vast body of water enveloping me in a cool embrace. I am outstretched, pecs out, my wingspan as wide as can be.

Like a sharp kitchen knife extracting the pit of a sweet, ripe peach or an archeologist exploring the past, I employ my arms to slice open the water to see what's inside. Perpetually curious, forever compelled, I am caught in the seduction. I immerse myself in muffled sounds and blurry visions of reverie and possibility. I stretch out the kinks and heal old injuries, my naked male chest claiming the water.

*   *   *

I wasn't always a swim junkie. I rarely swam as a kid. For years I harbored a tremendous fear of water, after I almost drowned at the age of four. We were in Hawaii, visiting family, one of the few times we went to the "islands." Playing in the warm ocean water, I got caught in the insistent undertow, pushed facedown into the sand, and paralyzed with panic as I struggled to breathe. Though the water was only two feet deep, it tossed me and I could not find stable footing or a way out for air.

Fortunately, my brother was nearby, saw me struggling, and pulled me up. "Steve saved her life!" my mother loved to joke, as everyone laughed raucously. It was so hilarious to everyone in my family, the idea that I believed that I was drowning and my brother saved me. As a parent, I know now that kids can drown in two inches of water. All I know is it was real to *me*, and I was afraid of water for years.

My family members eventually taught me the breaststroke, and as a young adult I began to discover the alluring sensation of buoyancy that being in the pool gave me. As a student at UC Santa Cruz, I discovered the university's tiny pool and the severe but invigorating cold of the Pacific Ocean.

One Thanksgiving break, I caught a ride home up the coast with several rambunctious women. It was so windy and bitter cold, our little Volkswagen bug was getting blown around the coastal highway. We stopped at Bean Hollow, and I dared everyone to go skinny-dipping. One woman was game. In a flash of spontaneous spirit, we stripped and jumped into that icy winter ocean, splashing and floating and swimming until we struggled for air and our parts went numb, laughing breathlessly with the pure joy of butt-naked fearlessness.

In the summertime I spent hours in the freezing Pacific, way past the crash of waves, my friends watching anxiously from the shore. After an hour my nipples had frostbite, but I loved the bounce of salt water, the resilient expanse of the dark ocean.

Later, when I lived in Boston, I would ride my bike at night, in the bite of wind, to the local university and swim. I relied on a breaststroke with lopsided frog legs, pushing, kicking, pushing, kicking for an hour in meditation.

When I returned to the West Coast and settled in San Francisco, I swam in the crowded public pools in the heart of urban frenzy, before discovering a quiet pool on the outskirts of the city. One day I was the only one in the pool during lap swim. The lifeguard, a Chinese American man in his fifties, watched my cockeyed crawl and taught me how to cup my hand and pull the water toward me from below. Cup, pull, curve, cup, pull, curve.

After that, there was no stopping me. I was even more in love with the sensuous rhythm of the water. Swimming became my thing—that and biking all over the city. My work with homeless and drug-addicted people on the streets of the Tenderloin was stressful. My clients were good people with extremely challenging life circumstances, at the intersections of so many barriers. There was only so much I could do for them, and understanding the possibilities and the limitations was an essential part of staying sane on the job. My colleagues cautioned, "Don't expect to be the drop of water that spills the bucket over." But when I was swimming, I opened up my stomach and stretched through my emotion. With each stroke I pulled the grief and desperation of the HIV/AIDS epidemic from my head through my core. The expansive, clear blue pool could hold my compassion, emotional support, and resources and remind me that I was making an impact every day.

Everything stopped in 1992, when I fell ill with CFIDS. I could no longer ride my bike all over the city or make it to the pool. I lay in bed for two years, staring at the ceiling and wondering whether I was dying.

After a couple of years, I began to venture out to the pool. It was hard to imagine engaging in any exercise when it was a monumental struggle just getting out of the house and into my car. But somehow I made myself go. I would arrive and park, rest in my car, then slowly force myself out of the vehicle and into the gym, where a beautiful, sparkling pool was beckoning. I'd say my hellos at the entrance as if I hadn't just spent the last three days in bed, head to the locker room, and emerge into a slow, labored rhythm at the far end of the pool. It was infrequent and in slow motion, but I did it. I felt privileged to have the opportunity.

*　*　*

Over time, my illness continued and I fell out of swimming altogether. I had been sick for well over a decade when I made my tentative return to the water. It was 2005. I was skinny, female-bodied, trans-identified, and struggling to regain some hold over the fatigue in my body.

I stood at the edge of the pool, my bare feet gripping the curved, concrete bevel on the border between solid and liquid. Clothed only in two thin blue strips of faded, man-made fabric, tattered from the bite of chlorine, I felt the crisp air whir around me in a stage whisper and I tried not to listen. *I can do this*, I thought. *I can slip into this cool water on this cold winter night, pierce and pull back on its body with the wave of my cupped palm, or just glide as my arms and legs push circles and circles of liquid snow angels.*

I was standing practically naked in forty-five degrees, trying to convince myself that I should get wet. There was a retractable roof on this particular pool, with air holes that invited crisscrossing side breezes and thick vertical lines of water that poured into the pool on rain-soaked nights. I knew I was some kind of fool.

I shivered as I lost myself in reverie. I wanted to reconnect with this quiet pleasure with the intimacy of a lover. I wanted to feel the consistency of the water on every pore of my skin. I wanted to travel to that visceral plane where meditation meets sport. I wanted to enter my dream.

I thought back to the many times I had backpacked in the rain, hail, and snow, crouching under a tree during a storm, or sleeping with soggy toes in the bottom of my sleeping bag. I started backpacking with my family in the Sierra when I was eight, marching up and over mountains, then jumping into freshly melted lakes at the end of each hot, dusty day. On one trip with my brother and father when I was nineteen, my dad opened up his plastic container of matches just as a stream of rain landed in it. We did eventually manage to get that tricky stove going, as we shivered under a thin tarp, each cherishing a Sierra cup of hot chocolate and a belly full of laughter.

During one college backpacking trip, my group created a sauna with a tent, a long strip of metal, and red-hot rocks from the fire, gingerly placed inside the tent without scorching the delicate fabric. Eight of us crouched naked in the tent, and once we were good and steamy, a few of us dared to jump into the stone-cold stream, our hearts pounding and our breathing strained from the shocking intensity of hot flesh dipped in ice and our own squeals of delight.

I'm that kind of fool. The one who frostbit my tits in the Pacific Ocean, the one who bicycled across the United States, sleeping in fields and abandoned barns. I thumbed my way through Mexico. I went on solo bike trips and backpacking trips. I am a sucker for adventure.

But something had happened between the daring adventure of youth and this fortysomething foray into a new gym membership. I was the same size, the same essential spirit, but my carefree self had been hibernating.

I looked into the still blue water of the pool. I was the only swimmer braving the cold on this brisk winter night. I imagined that I was twenty-nine, that mythical number that marks the end of an era and the beginning of the unknown. Maybe it's the point at which we leave childhood behind and make greater strides toward adulthood. In some cultures, it's middle age. In the privileged party of queer America, most of us are still clubbing into the irresponsible night.

When I was twenty-nine, I was riding my bike up and over the saddle of San Francisco, conducting street-based outreach with the hardest-hit folks in the Tenderloin, Chinatown, and South of Market, and venturing from meeting to training to speaking gig to interview. I was active in the Asian lesbian community, lived with my lover of several years, and had a regular group of friends. I was fit, strong in body, with the legs and butt to get me there. From the outside, I was an athletic public health professional with a strong presence in the community. But on the inside, I was a child just trying to make my way to adulthood.

When I was twenty-nine, I was miserable in my relationship and had initiated a breakup with my lover. I was out of sync as a mixed-heritage person in what was then a full-blooded world. I was freaked out about my gender issues but couldn't even begin to access my trauma and identify my feelings. I was burning out from the post-traumatic stress of working in an HIV/AIDS war zone. I was angry but didn't have a clue why, and I didn't know how to ask for what I wanted. That was the year I became very, very ill.

There I was, fortysomething, dreaming of my youth. Shivering at the edge of the pool, I stared past my bare feet and reminisced about how strong and able I was in my body when I was twenty-nine, before I got sick. Back then I was overtraining as a means of coping, buff on the outside but shattered on the inside. I was a strong athlete who could swim for a half hour, or an hour if I really needed it, the jock who worked the weights and bicycled all over the city.

The dream of my past self put me into the water without a whimper. I slowly submerged into the incongruity of winter swimming and forgot to complain. I filled my lungs deep with sustenance and glided into the push and pull of my old aquatic friend. Though it had been too long for my cells to remember the feel of indoor gym chlorine, my body had a visceral memory lodged in muscle and breath.

And slowly, I made new currents with my older, wiser self and strode to a long-lost meditation of renewal.

*   *   *

Over the years I built on that moment—gym memberships I used only once a month, and brief courtships with crowded, tree-lined city pools—until I worked up to swimming in a large, beautiful outdoor pool a few times a week. I loved the grandiose size of the shimmering pool and the rich variety of bodies: large, curvy women in colorful bikinis and buff old men who looked like teenagers underwater. I was tentative at first, venturing into the women's locker room with the same trepidation I had when I navigated any women's bathroom, even though gender nonconformity was not an anomaly at this particular pool. Still, when I arrived, I quickly stripped down to reveal female parts, in an effort to gain my membership in the intimate, private space of the women's locker room.

It was 2007, but the pool was crawling with dykes I knew in the 1980s, like a flashback parade of readings, meetings, parties, and woo-woo beach rituals from a bygone era. I didn't know how to be a trans person masquerading as a woman in a gendered space where skintight strips of cloth left little to the imagination. I was no longer that dyke who rocked the '80s in a flash of hot turquoise, bad hair, and MC Hammer pants, thank God. But neither were they. Well, maybe there were some vestiges of bad hair, but they were living in this new century, too. Still, I didn't know how to navigate the assumption that my coming-out process was long over when I came out as a lesbian like them, with them. My story had taken a lot of twists and turns since that time.

At closing time, I'd head to the locker room with the chatty group who had lingered in the hot tub until the whistle blew. Conversations went from politics to shampoo to "I love that blouse! Where'd you get it?" But I was there for utilitarian purposes only. I worked with the same "get in and get out" speed I used in any gender-specific environment. It wasn't comfortable; I didn't belong; I was moving too fast for conversation. When people talked to me, I was surprised they saw me, caught off-guard in my hurried, distant stance.

While the women I entered the locker room with were still slathering themselves in the shower, I was already dressed and moving toward the mirror, where I'd style my hair in seconds with a dollop of gel. "I like your hair," the women at the mirror would tell me, as they worked a comb through their long, wet manes. "I wish that was all *I* had to do." The others emerged from the shower and called out, "See ya later." "Willy's gone already" trailed off as the door slammed behind me.

Occasionally women would startle at my presence or children would ask me if I was a boy or a girl, but not nearly as often as I imagined they would. Still, I maintained my sense of myself as a distant bystander in a space I didn't belong in. Women would interrupt my contemplative reverie to ask me a question, draw me into the conversation. I'd respond when spoken to, but it was a few years before I started to really engage, which was very out of character for me. In other situations I had no trouble jumping into shit-shooting banter. I was usually the one to start it.

One cold, blustery evening, I found myself alone in the locker room with a young woman I'd never seen before, who asked me for assistance with her swim cap. She bent her head forward and asked me to pull it to the back of her head. My first thought was, *Really? You're asking me? And you want me to do something that might pull your hair? Okay, then*, and I helped her and she thanked me like it was no big deal, an everyday occurrence in the women's locker room, where collaboration and cooperation are givens.

* * *

Over time, I became friendlier with the women I saw on a regular basis. We'd find ourselves in the hot tub, chitchatting about random topics or the powerful mental health boost of swimming. Over the years, despite my awkward stance as "other" in a world of like-minded, barely clad swim junkies, I became part of the scene.

On the eve of my 2012 top surgery, I found myself alone in the locker room with one such friend from years past. I said, "I want to tell you something. I'm finally transitioning to male. I'm getting top surgery tomorrow."

"Wow, so fast!" she responded, as if it hadn't required decades of contemplation. Then she congratulated me. I told her that she could tell anyone she wanted and that I wouldn't be back for six weeks.

Though I was supposed to wait six weeks before working out, I could wait only five. I went back to the pool and walked right into the men's locker room. At that point I had been on a low dose of testosterone for only three months. My voice had changed a little, and I was developing some musculature, but not enough to seem significant. One guy looked at me, a little startled, but when I responded with a little swagger and tough-guy attitude without being threatening, he went back to his business. Another man, who had "noticed" me in my sports bikini, seemed to notice me again as a guy. But he just left me alone. Otherwise, no one looked my way.

I had already scoped out the men's locker room, noting that there were a couple of urinals, one functioning stall, and a small, open shower with four showerheads. Compared with the ginormous pool, the locker room had the bite-size intimacy of a restroom.

I changed into my junk-packed, tight, black Durafast swim trunks and white swim shirt, to protect my scars from the sun, and got into the shallow end of the pool. From a distance, I saw the friend I had told about my transition. She and another woman broke out into applause and cheered my return. I had not seen that coming. As I immersed myself again into the gentle embrace of clear water on a sun-drenched day, I felt a congruent balance of being welcomed and seen, despite the care I took to be inconspicuously invisible. It wasn't long before I was swimming shirtless and free.

*   *   *

As it turned out, women who knew me casually—not those who knew me by name, but women with whom I had exchanged brief pleasantries in the hot tub or even discussed politics or parenthood in the locker room—no longer registered a connection. Even though we had spoken to each other many times before, once I presented as male they looked right through me as if they had never seen or known me. I was just a few months into medical transition, and already I was beginning to experience my life in an alternate universe.

I discovered that the men's locker room is not nearly as chatty as the women's locker room. Sure, there's some playful banter and intelligent discussion of issues, but most of the time it's dead quiet. And whereas I was quick on the women's side, plenty of guys groom in a sprint, much faster than I do. That's because some don't even shower. I'd look at them and think, *Really? Don't you want to wash that stuff off?*

One time I was showering in the locker room of a local city pool when my regular pool was closed. An Asian guy with long, unkempt hair tapped my shoulder vigorously from behind. He held out his cupped hands and motioned repeatedly in front of me. It was a cross between a universal Oliver Twist begging posture and *chung chung*, the Chinese gesture of respect that we were trained to do when receiving *li-see*, like bowing with clasped hands motioning up and down repeatedly. I looked at him quizzically. "Huh?" He repeated the gesture, then practically grabbed my shampoo out of my hands.

"I need some shampoo."

"Uh, okay, sure." I gave him the bottle.

"Do you know how long it's been since I washed my hair?"

I was thinking, *No, and do I care?*

"I can't remember. It's been so long, I don't even know," he shared with pride.

If my people neglect to groom, I really don't need to know about it.

Then I went to get dressed on the benches. Off to my side was an older white guy whose large paunch hung low enough to completely obscure his junk, which I found fascinating. Something smelled very bad, and I thought that since he was the closest person to me, it must be him. Then I realized that something didn't just smell nasty; it smelled like shit. I looked over at the guy. He was drying himself off from the pool and shower. I thought, *Now, why would he smell so bad if he just got out of the pool?* I looked down and saw a caramel-colored smear on the bench, with a mottled yet symmetrical design, much like a textured Rorschach test. *Maybe it's rust,* I thought. But no. It was the shit smear of an ass crack.

It was amusing to experience these choice moments but even more fun to recount them in all their glorious detail to fellow swimmers, all of them female, who grossed out and swore they could never swim at that pool again.

*   *   *

One afternoon at my usual pool, I was getting dressed in the locker room after a vigorous workout. A wiry white guy, the only other person in the locker room, turned to me and said, "Can I ask you a question?"

"Sure," I replied, turning away from him to put on my pants.

"Did I take care of you at Davies? With Dr. Brownstein?" he asked.

I thought he looked a little familiar. "Are you the anesthesiologist? I remember you telling me what was going to happen, and that it was all very pleasant and friendly, and then nothing."

"Good," he responded. "It's supposed to be pleasant. I've seen you around and thought, *I know this person.*"

We talked about Dr. Brownstein, the skilled surgeon who'd performed chest reconstruction for three decades, perfecting a flawless technique that served me well as a swim junkie. We talked about Dr. Crane, who took over Dr. Brownstein's practice. He said he'd heard good things about what Dr. Crane was capable of doing. I told him that people had been very happy. Then someone entered the locker room. We coded our conversation in universal terms, and I wondered if it was weird to see people in the world whom you've watched in slumber, people you've kept alive in some manufactured, unconscious state. For the first time in two years, I felt like I had a friend in the locker room, but really I just felt relieved to be my whole self in this naked, male setting.

*   *   *

The guys in the locker room are generally harmless—the regulars, any-way. I've heard guys mention hanging out with their lesbian friends or attending lectures on the politics of race in America. They probably wouldn't hurt me for having the audacity of not disclosing my trans sta-tus, or having been born female.

Yet the legacy of male violence is all around me, in the whispers of our mothers, who transmitted their fears at the cellular level, and in the grow-ing list of trans people who have been murdered for being their true selves.

What about the teenage boys who are twice my size, adult in stature but immature in thought as they mock others, too inconsiderate to care that they entered my lane and blocked my path? What about the guys who are posturing and challenging each other's manhood? What about the guys whom I don't see coming?

It's not that I live in fear, exactly. It's that I don't want to suffer hu-miliation. I live with the burden of ensuring that my trans status is not discovered, because I don't know what people would do with this infor-mation, the same way I don't want to risk people's knowing my girl name because experience has shown that they may not handle this information responsibly. It's that I need to be seen for who I am, male, without the static of anyone else's opinion, in the precious intimacy of my drug of choice, swimming.

One morning my schlong was especially adventurous in my trunks, moving this way and that. As I clung to the edge of the deep end of the pool, I reached in to adjust my junk so it would stay put in the crudely sewn internal pouch I had created. I didn't want to be that guy who got the attention of the lifeguard because I kept adjusting my junk. But its position wasn't right, so I dove underwater to use both hands, hoping she wouldn't worry that I might be a distressed swimmer. If I was going to have to dive down thirteen feet to chase after the dislodged troublemaker, then yes, I was going to be one hell of a distressed swimmer.

*   *   *

I began to contemplate genital surgery after I had been on testosterone for a year and was consistently perceived as male. It became a daily thought, this ongoing desire to claim my body as male and to feel the liberation of congruence. I wondered what it could be like to have a body that would go unnoticed among men in the locker room; I fantasized about one day going for a swim without concern for my emotional and physical safety.

In a timely confluence of the changing landscape of access to care for trans people in California, cutting-edge technology, and new medical expertise, I was able to get phalloplasty (surgery to create a penis) in July 2014. I knew that most trans people did not have access to transition-related surgery that was covered by their health insurance, and I was grateful for the opportunity to be part of this first wave. In 2014 it was a new day for trans access to care in California.

That was two years after my January 2012 top surgery. As preparation for phalloplasty, I needed to have a complete hysterectomy three months prior. When I went to the initial consultation with the surgeon who would perform my April 2014 hysterectomy, she asked me if I exercised. I told her I was an avid swimmer, that I swam three or four times a week. She studied my chest and shoulders and said, "Let me guess your stroke." I thought to myself that this friendly assessment was way better than people trying to guess my racial heritage or my gender. She said, "Fly? Crawl?" and I responded, "Freestyle and breaststroke."

A couple of weeks later, I was staying at a conference hotel in Southern California, splashing in the pool at midnight with a colleague who was teaching me this new stroke. We laughed as I floundered, until I managed to stretch my arms wide over my head, pulling back awkwardly but determinedly as I swam across the pool. It was time I learned the butterfly, because the pool is the center and soul of my transformation.

After eight weeks of recovery from my July 2014 phalloplasty, I returned to the pool, just in time for my birthday. As I changed in the locker room before my swim, I felt at peace, relieved that I didn't have to worry about exposing my body or constantly determining my proximity to danger. I could let it all hang out and be much more relaxed and friendly now in my new birthday suit. I joked around without timing my movements against others', looking over my shoulder, or chasing my wayward schlong across the funky, wet floor.

And when I exited the locker room in my tight, black Durafast swim trunks, with no carefully placed accessory to manage or worry about, I felt elated to dive right in and feel the cool embrace of my old friend. This time it was just me, all of me.

Locker Room Access Denied

When Bryan Ellicott went to change in a men's locker room at a New York City pool in July 2013, three Parks Department employees kicked him out. Ellicott was asked to use the women's locker room and told, "If you don't like it, you can leave." He left feeling "upset, embarrassed, and stigmatized" and afraid to use pools and locker rooms. What's more, to add to his trauma, he had previously been assaulted in a men's room in 2012, and the perpetrators were never found.

When I heard this story, my heart sank. Bryan Ellicott is a trans man.

In June 2014, the Transgender Legal Defense and Education Fund filed a lawsuit on his behalf, claiming that the treatment he experienced at the hands of city employees is in violation of the New York City Human Rights Law. If the New York Supreme Court rules in his favor, it would be the first decision in the state to affirm that human rights law protects against discrimination based on gender identity and expression.

But the mistreatment didn't end in the locker room. All the news outlets described what he was wearing; the Associated Press made a point of describing his testosterone experience and his genital status.[85] While these exact details may be relevant to the lawsuit, his basic human right to use the facility that corresponds with his gender identity does not hinge on what he wore, or on his hormonal or surgical status. These statements about his body say nothing about how he himself characterizes his experience with medical transition, nor do they acknowledge what has historically been a glaring lack of access to care in New York State for people who want to pursue transition-related surgery.

Details about Ellicott's appearance and body sting with the legacy of trans subjugation and imply that his humiliation was deserved. They are reminiscent of rape culture, which blames female-bodied people for their victimization because of what they wore.

Yet Bryan Ellicott has been courageously fighting while being forced to undress in front of the media and to endure vitriolic comments from readers who state that all trans people are "sick" and "confused," that endless drivel of Internet hate speech that accompanies news coverage about trans people. I hope he wins this impact discrimination lawsuit and that the day when all New Yorkers can participate equally in society comes soon.

Sadly, Ellicott is not alone. In January 2015, A. T. Furuya, an Asian American transmasculine individual, was allegedly removed from the men's locker room at San Diego State University by a staff person at the campus recreation facility after another gym patron harassed them[86] about their trans status. The patron allegedly yelled, "Get your titties and go across to the other locker room. That's where the other women are. And if you don't go, I'll remove you myself." Compounding the harassment, the campus staff person allegedly apologized to the patron for Furuya's presence in the locker room, before asking Furuya to leave.[87]

Furuya is represented by Transgender Law Center, which also represents Seamus Johnston, a Caucasian trans man and former honor student who was denied access to men's restrooms and locker rooms at the University of Pittsburgh in the fall of 2011. According to Ilona Turner, Transgender Law Center's legal director, the university "engaged in a campaign of persecution" against Johnston by having him arrested, criminally prosecuted, and expelled, which led to his losing his full scholarship.[88] He was followed around, barred from using any restroom or locker room on campus, ordered into counseling, given disciplinary probation for a year, and charged with disorderly conduct, criminal trespass, and indecent exposure simply for using the restroom and locker room.[89]

Both Furuya's and Johnston's cases are in violation of state law and Title IX. In April 2014, the US Department of Education clarified that Title IX's sex discrimination prohibition in educational settings "extends to claims of discrimination based on gender identity or failure to conform to stereotypical notions of masculinity or femininity."[90]

Yet in April 2015 a federal judge dismissed Johnston's case by claiming that he had not provided the university with enough documentation of his gender transition—namely, a birth certificate that reflected his male gender.[91] Pennsylvania law requires transition-related surgery in order to change a birth certificate,[92] an impossible and outdated standard. Surgery is not universally desired by all trans people and is out of reach for many who want it, because it is cost-prohibitive and often not covered by health insurance. Even though Johnston attended college as a man, had changed his driver's license, had registered with the Selective Service, and later changed his passport and Social Security record,[93] both the university and the judge felt that Johnston was *not male enough* to urinate or change in campus facilities in accordance with his gender identity. The judge also asserted that other students had the right to "sex-segregated spaces based on biological or birth sex."[94]

Trans people are frequently harassed in restrooms and locker rooms all over the United States and are not always explicitly legally protected. In recent years, a number of states have proposed "bathroom harassment" bills[95] designed to prevent trans people from using restroom facilities like everyone else. These instances of dehumanization of trans people are reminders that we need comprehensive, federal civil rights protections based on sexual orientation and gender identity. They also point to the compelling need for comprehensive health care access for trans people nationwide, as well as the need to remove surgery requirements in order to obtain identity documents that reflect one's gender identity. Moreover, these cases on American campuses highlight a universal systemic problem at colleges nationwide—the bureaucratic hurdles that make it difficult for trans students to update student records to reflect their gender identities.

WALKING IN PRIVILEGE

Snapshot: March 2015

At the end of the day, after the kids are bathed, the dishes are done, the laundry is sorted, and the first load is in the machine, Georgia and I breathe a sigh of relief. We have finally quieted the mayhem of raucous children avoiding bedtime and collected the detritus of scattered toys in some temporary order. Our kids, no longer in perpetual motion, are sleeping soundly and softly in their beds.

I venture into the dark night. Like the soundless buoyancy of water, the tree-lined streets beckon as I walk in meditative bliss swiftly up the Oakland hills. The air is still, the sounds have quieted to a muffle, and all the chaos is behind me. I have become that multicolored set of vertical bars that signify a TV station that has gone off the air for the night. I stop to tighten my shoelaces. I feel my feet grip the crooked tar. I walk with a broad stance now, my hips turned outward, rather than inward, as if becoming male automatically shifted my center of gravity forward, made me take up that much more space, orient my junk like an outie, no longer an innie.

I pass an older white man with gray hair and a medium build, walking his little cockapoo. The man is light on his feet yet heavy in the way he owns the road. In his day, the ground was made for him, and he has always expected it to be that way. As I greet him, the sound of my deep voice announces me with confidence in my right to walk the street at night. I have been given a guest pass, and no one has asked to verify my ID. I have taken it on with a sense of relief, however transitory this new privilege may be. I pretend I have always known that I was meant to walk the dark streets at night.

*   *   *

I pass a short Jewish woman walking her German shepherd, a lesbian I knew briefly in the '80s and see at the pool from time to time, but now she doesn't know me anymore. I know the drill: keep a safe distance and appear as nonthreatening as possible. I recognize the responsibility of not doing anything to negatively impact women's sense of safety at night.

I've heard a lot of trans guys who have lived as men for ten, fifteen, twenty years talk about never getting used to the distance that being male puts between them and women, which sometimes manifests in women's guarded suspicion or steely coldness. I have experienced asking a simple question and being dismissed by a pretty woman who has clearly had far too many men harass and try to hustle her. But I've also experienced that women are much more open to me now than when I was a butch. Women who might have scowled at me in the past smile and talk to me now.

As I walk past a red house with a long path to the front entryway, on a very dark section of the street, the door swings wide open and a woman walks out and gestures a broad wave. "Hi, Manny," she says, in a melodic, singsong voice, like she's had a crush on this guy for years.

I lower my voice and respond, "Hi," as friendly as possible. I'm not about to correct her. I think, *Is Manny that small brown guy I say hello to at the school?* Maybe I'm wrong, but I figure it's better just to keep on stepping and be gone, rather than stop to explain that I'm not who she thinks I am. I never stopped to explain my gender to people who were confused when my gender presentation was ambiguous. Why turn this friendly moment into something awkward? And yet now I have become an unknown man walking by in the obscure night, a man who has chosen not to disclose at least one thing about himself.

*   *   *

I walk down the middle of these quiet residential streets like my mother once did, avoiding lonely, drunk soldiers on dark, dirt roads in rural Hawaii during World War II. I walk nimbly, my legs reaching long for each step, fast-paced, up a canopy-covered hill. I breathe in the crisp air and listen intently for the crunch of leaves, the jingle of car keys, the howl of dogs. My sense of hearing is heightened and finely tuned, simply because I've lived as a woman, and as a parent who is always monitoring child safety and drama. I am the newly awakened, amnesiac assassin Jason Bourne, keenly aware of and continually assessing my surroundings. I have been bathed in the undercurrent of the threat of violence passed to us from our mamas through the waters of amniotic wisdom, a collective warning shared among the knowers and delivered to us before birth. Our childhood innocence was stained early on with the glare from frequent images of girls and women mutilated, raped, and murdered for being female. The war on women is multiplied by the war on trans people, brutally killed for the audacity of being ourselves, fueled by the perceived incongruity of our bodies and spirits.

*   *   *

I started walking these hills at night following my hysterectomy in April 2014 because I wasn't supposed to swim during the healing process. I felt this mix of archetypal female fear, male privilege, and the intersecting danger of having genitals that were not congruent with my gender presentation. My demographic blur included the vulnerability of being a small Asian guy in a racially mixed, middle-class neighborhood rattled by burglaries and car break-ins.

Yet as a child, I walked the streets with ease. When Bay Area Rapid Transit (BART) was new in the early '70s, it broke down on a regular basis, leaving passengers stuck for hours. One time, when I was twelve, I rode BART from my home on the Peninsula to the East Bay to visit my grandparents. On the way back, I got stranded at MacArthur Station in Oakland for seven hours. I called my grandma on the pay phone to inform her, then enjoyed the spontaneous opportunity to socialize with other passengers. When I finally arrived across the bay in Daly City, I caught a bus down the Peninsula, disembarked on the freeway in San

Mateo, and walked two miles until I arrived home after midnight. My parents were totally freaked out, but I casually told them that I knew how to hide from cars and walk like a dude.

I learned a long time ago that the streets were owned by dudes who never had to think about the war on women or trans people. I wanted to be one of them. As I blaze through residential Oakland tonight, my stride is wide and confident. I am brilliantly cast to play the character of a man who has never questioned the certainty of his male privilege or been spoon-fed the graphic warnings.

In a neighborhood exhausted by crime and hypersensitive to the imagined threat from people perceived as outsiders, I'm working hard to make sure it's clear that I'm out for an athletic experience. With my arm sweatband and track pants, I'm hoofing it up those hills at a clip, pushing till my legs and glutes stretch past the boundaries of what my body thinks it can do. I'm friendly, moving fast, and demonstrably *not* interested in snooping in anyone's car or garage.

And I think, *This is privilege.* How many black trans men do I know who would feel comfortable walking in a middle-class neighborhood at night, even if it is somewhat racially mixed? Would they wear a big white sweatband across their forehead to emphasize how nonthreatening they are, or would they skip it altogether? I've seen the neighborhood e-mail list. Neighbors try to act like they're not extra suspicious of people based on race, but it comes across. I know that my skin tone affords me great privilege to have the freedom to walk these streets at night.

* * *

My friend Charles said, "As a black woman, I could take people on, be very aggressive, get out of the car, and argue with a big guy about how he parked, and in fifty-nine years, no one ever punched me out. But now, as a black man, I can't do that. I have entered a group that is targeted. It's no longer 'I push you, you push me back.' They will take out a gun and *kill* you."

When I travel to the South or the Midwest, I feel like such a small person. I look up at big, tall white people, and I'm like Jack and the fricking beanstalk, trying to sneak past the giant. When I go to Hawaii, with its large Asian population, I feel medium-size, not small, or at least I did as a female-bodied person. And in California, I'm right at home with the rich beauty of so many short Asian and Latino people. As a small person, I didn't think I would be perceived as male so consistently. I thought I was destined to be pissed off on a regular basis when someone misgendered me. But, as it turns out, I'm just another short guy in a world with guys of all sizes.

Now that I'm perceived as male, men who may not have seen me in the past approach me in a spirit of camaraderie and treat me like an equal. Black and brown guys address me as "brother" or "bro." Guys of all races address me as "boss" and "my man." I have been welcomed into the circle. But men also push me around, big white or black guys who cut in front of me in line and act like I'm not there. As a butch, I would not have hesitated to take that on, get up in their faces, and demand justice. But for a small guy, well, that's okay—I'm not in a hurry anyway. I am not about to get my ass kicked over nothing. Now that I'm male, the threat of violence is different.

But, as my brothers remind me, we never stop being trans.

Once I had genital surgery, I felt a huge burden lift: the fear of having my trans status revealed, and the threat of violence, ridicule, and harassment associated with that discovery. No longer could my would-be attackers "pants" me, pull down my pants in an effort to reveal female genitalia—the perceived incongruence of my body—with the same outcome: to present evidence of my lack of humanity to make me a justifiable target of transphobic and misogynistic hate violence.

But transphobic violence targets us no matter what our bodies look like underneath our clothes, especially if we're black or brown. In the case of Juan Evans, an African American trans man who lived in a suburb of Atlanta, Georgia, the local police arrested him in October 2014 because they wanted to perform a "gender search." Fortunately, they did not go through with the threat of a genital search, but they repeatedly called him "it" and "thing." Such humiliations are far too common for trans people, especially trans people of color.

*   *   *

As I walk these hills, I contemplate my privilege: my skin tone, the able-bodied act of walking itself, the neighborhood, my journey from female to male. The free education that helped my parents rise from the stark hardships of the Great Depression to the middle class. The quality public school education I received and the class privilege that has helped me navigate the world as a professional person. The love and support I now have from both my family of origin and the family I created. The open-minded, progressive people that surround me in the Bay Area, home to so many who push the boundaries. I feel grateful to be alive at this particular time and place, and to have lived to bear witness to my liberation.

And yet my struggle continues. Though I am long past the desperation of disabling chronic illness, my financial woes are much deeper and more dangerous now. Keeping a family of five fed, clothed, housed, educated, and cared for is no easy task in the high-priced Bay Area; I am not making ends meet. But here we are, living in a big house in a nice neighborhood with an excellent school.

I walk along, pretending I have always known the right to walk these streets at night, and that I have the currency to live in this neighborhood. I walk in privilege.

EMBODYING A CHANGING LANDSCAPE

My three little kids entered my hospital room excitedly, inquisitively searching and scanning the equipment, fascinated with the buttons and all the dangling wires of the hospital setting. It was my fourth day in the hospital following phalloplasty, a surgery that had previously seemed out of reach. Everyone in my family had had their own meltdowns in my absence, and they needed to know that I was okay. They pointed excitedly to the photos of each of them that were taped to the wall. We hugged gingerly, as Georgia had prepped them very well on how to avoid sensitive parts of my body. Fortunately, I no longer had an oxygen line to my nose or monitors on my chest, and intravenous drips were intermittent, though the hookup still hung from my wrist. I wanted to be sure I didn't look too scary, and that I was rested and looked my best; I had even forgone pain medication so I would be as lucid and awake as possible.

From the hospital's food-service department, I ordered a bunch of comfort food, which we divided into kiddie portions. They settled into closely arranged chairs and carefully chosen spots on my bed, and we delighted in being together as a family again, enjoying a meal, the five of us calmed by the sharing of a mundane and homey activity.

Like other kids with a parent who is having surgery, my kids needed to be prepped in age-appropriate ways on what to expect: why I was having surgery, how long I'd be in the hospital, and how to be careful around me once I returned. My eight-year-old son and five-year-old daughter understood my surgery within the context of an ongoing conversation about my trans status that is a normalized part of our daily lives, just as we talk about being mixed and multicultural. My two-year-old son may not have fully understood why I needed surgery, but he knew exactly where my boo-boos were and that I couldn't pick him up for a while.

My older son was so happy for me, glad that we would both be able to stand to pee. He came to an understanding about my gender as a toddler and understood my trans status both before and after my medical transition. He was excited that I was going to align my body with the person I always believed I was inside.

Several nurses said that though they saw many phalloplasty patients, they hadn't seen many guys with kids. I'm proud to be a trans father whose kids understand, embrace, and celebrate my trans identity as part of the unique fabric of our lives.

*   *   *

I was supposed to be at the White House that day. Over the years, a growing number of my friends, colleagues, and community members have received invitations to the White House to address LGBTQ issues in some form, so maybe it's becoming old hat. But it was my first and, thus far, only invitation, and I was pretty thrilled. I was supposed to attend a briefing on LGBTQ issues and the Affordable Care Act (ACA) with my colleagues at Out2Enroll, a national project with which I was training insurance navigators on how to create equal access for LGBTQ people enrolling for health insurance under the ACA. I briefly considered postponing my surgery so I could attend, but it wasn't like President Obama was going to be there to take a selfie with me. There wasn't much that could stand between my surgery and me.

I loved the irony that instead of discussing LGBTQ issues and the ACA at the White House, I was kicking back in the hospital in San Francisco with a handsome new schlong, thanks in part to the ACA.

I am an early member of the new wave of trans people who are finally—after decades of having our health care needs excluded from the vast majority of health insurance plans—accessing medically necessary, insurance-covered, transition-related surgery in California. The physical appearance and well-being of trans communities are quietly transforming in this new era of technological advances, nondiscriminatory insurance options, and culturally competent providers. As we move forward, we will be seeing more and more of our trans community members going through this experience.

I'm grateful for the changing landscape of trans health care access and recognize that we still have far to go. While many in the general public believe that all trans people have surgery, even equating transgender status with a mythical idea of "the surgery," as if there were just one, the reality is that the vast majority of trans people do not have any surgery at all. Historically, and to a great extent currently, most trans people who desire it are unable to access gender confirmation surgery, because it's not covered by their health insurance if they have it, because it's cost-prohibitive, and/or because they have been advised not to pursue surgery because of their health status.

Of course, not every trans person wants surgery; many trans people on the transfeminine and transmasculine spectrums are happy with the bodies they have. Certainly, a penis does not make a man and a vagina does not make a woman. I know many trans men who feel tremendous satisfaction with the genitalia they were born with and have no interest in trading them in. Given the way society celebrates the phallus, and all the patriarchal domination its reverence implies, it's important to challenge the notion that one needs a penis in order to be male. These types of societal messages are profoundly hurtful to trans people, not just psychically and socially but legally, as many jurisdictions worldwide have historically relied on outdated and impossible notions of genital surgery as an ultimate determination of one's legal gender. On a global level, civil rights advocates have worked tirelessly to ensure that laws that protect people based on gender identity and expression do not have a provision requiring surgery or, in some cases, explicit sterilization in order for those people to obtain a legal gender change or to have their gender recognized under the law. As a trans person who for many years actively chose *not* to medically transition, I stand in full support of the many trans people who choose not to pursue genital surgery, or any surgery, for that matter.

When I began my medical transition, I had no interest in genital surgery. I did not desire it, nor did I think I ever would. When a colleague asked me if I was going to "get a dick," I responded, "I don't need a penis to be a man!" At the time, I also did not see it as a viable option. I believed that there was no surgery to create a fully functioning penis. In 2012, few people on the female-to-male (FTM) spectrum in the United States had pursued genital surgery. In the FTM community in the San Francisco Bay Area, the widespread belief was that even if one had $100,000 lying around, FTM genital surgeries were risky and had far too many complications. Apart from the legendary "show-and-tell" by Belgian trans men at an FTM International meeting in San Francisco, and my own jaw-dropping experience of seeing an African American guy's well-formed phalloplasty at Jamison Green's house back in the '90s, I drank the Kool-Aid like everybody else. I listened to the rumors about guys who had multiple surgeries to achieve mixed results, getting penises that would not allow them to comfortably navigate the locker room, pee standing up, or make love the way they wanted to, as well as guys who endured painful surgeries only to lose the graft altogether. Few American trans men had accessed genital surgery, and for those who did, rumors described limited satisfaction.

In the foreword to *Hung Jury: Testimonies of Genital Surgery by Transsexual Men*, Shannon Minter eloquently describes how he relied on negative portrayals of genital surgery as inadequate, cost-prohibitive, and risky in order to defend the legal gender of transgender men who had not had genital surgery and were fighting for recognition as legal fathers to their children or needed access to the appropriate restroom. He expressed remorse as he acknowledged the pain these arguments caused by portraying trans men as "freakish" or "tragic."[96] His words resonated with me, as I thought back to my early work as an LGBTQ cultural competency trainer. I also feel remorse as I recall how, in the process of describing the health care access hurdles for trans people, I portrayed the genitalia of trans men as inadequate.

In addition to highlighting the trappings of legal efforts to win the rights of trans men to be recognized for their legal gender without having had genital surgery, Shannon acknowledges the daunting health care access obstacles that are the contextual framework for understanding why surgeries have been financially out of reach for the vast majority of American trans men. He also recognizes a "troubling aspect . . . which speaks to more deeply rooted issues in our psyches and communities. . . Many transgender men suffer from an inordinate amount of misplaced guilt about seeking out medical modification of our bodies—and in particular genital surgery—and many others are quick to judge those who do." He recognizes that many trans men have devalued genital surgeries because they have not been accessible, that we've been "conditioned to deny our deepest needs," and that we may "even unconsciously fear that we will be punished if we dare to seek it out." Thus, the idea that trans men in the United States largely don't want genital surgery, whereas trans men in countries that provide coverage for these surgeries do, speaks to our coping strategies and resilience: we don't want what we believe we cannot have.

*   *   *

Apart from concerns about the state of the art and level of medical expertise available in the United States, genital surgeries have been out of reach for most trans people in the United States because of economic and health care access issues. Without insurance coverage, a population that experiences pervasive employment discrimination, and is vastly underemployed and underpaid, has not had access to these lifesaving surgeries.

American health insurance companies have historically discriminated against trans people in several ways, largely because of bias that is endemic to the larger society. Many in the general public assume that transition-related surgery is "cosmetic" or "experimental," equating medically necessary trans care to elective procedures such as nose jobs or breast augmentation for cisgender women. The American Medical Association, American Psychological Association, American Psychiatric Association, and American Academy of Family Physicians have all deemed transition-related care medically necessary for transgender people.

In 2001, the City and County of San Francisco made the landmark decision to prohibit gender-based insurance discrimination for employees and their dependents, while the opposition used the argument that others shouldn't have to pay for what was akin to a "nose job." We often hear that argument today in relation to access to transition-related care, especially genital surgery, for trans prisoners, for example. In actuality, the cost of providing transition-related care is insignificant and can greatly improve mental health status, counteract the high trans suicide rate, and augment one's ability to fully participate in society.

Yet insurance companies have considered being transgender a preexisting condition and have denied or canceled insurance policies on the basis of gender identity. They have used gender identity as a basis for determining premiums and denied coverage for claims for health care services for trans people when coverage is provided for nontransgender people for the same services. Most insurance policies have had specific language excluding "transgender care and services"; many still do. That meant that not only was transition-related care (hormones, surgeries, mental health therapy, and other procedures) excluded, but these policies also excluded any other procedures that the insurance company deemed related to one's trans status. For example, coverage for a liver issue, and even a broken bone, has been denied for trans people because these conditions were considered related to hormone therapy. In addition, gender-specific procedures, such as gynecological care for trans men and prostate screening for trans women, have been dinged as not congruent with people's gender on their medical record and thus not covered, again because of transgender exclusions.

In 2012, the California Department of Insurance conducted an Economic Impact Assessment that found that removing transgender exclusions has "a positive impact on the health, welfare, and worker safety of the transgender population, which is a very small subset of California residents, [and that] the aggregate cost to the state population as a whole [is] very insignificant. . . . Analysis of the potential increase in claim costs from the proposed regulation [clarifying the prohibition against discrimination on the basis of gender or sex] shows that any such costs are immaterial and insignificant."[97] Department staff made these conclusions after conducting a thorough literature review, as well as analysis of actuarial and utilization data, and cost and premium data from employers. For example, the City and County of San Francisco had only thirty-seven claims in the first five years (0.0325 to 0.104 claimants per thousand employees per year), which ultimately removed any additional premium cost per employee.[98]

Estimates of the transgender population are difficult to obtain because of the significant disenfranchisement and discrimination that trans people face. Department of Insurance staff concluded that of California's 37.3 million residents, trans people make up between 0.0065 and 0.0173 percent of the total California population, and when the rate of uninsured Californians (19 percent) is factored in, only 0.0052 to 0.014 percent would be impacted by the removal of transgender exclusions, between 1,955 and 5,214 people.[99]

It should also be noted that, from a public health perspective, the costs of *not* removing transgender exclusions are more significant than providing nondiscriminatory coverage. When trans people are covered, there are cost savings associated with overall improvement in mental health status, lower rates of substance use disorders, reduction of suicide attempts and suicide completion, and improved health and well-being. Many studies have documented the correlation between difficulty accessing culturally competent health care and suicide attempts among trans people. In the first large-scale study of the transgender population, which we (trans people and concerned public health professionals) conducted in San Francisco in the late '90s with over five hundred participants (and which I documented in the Lambda Literary Award finalist *Transgender Rights*),[100] we found that the strongest predictor associated with suicide risk was gender-based discrimination in health care.[101]

*   *   *

On October 2, 2014, I was honored to receive the Vanguard Award from Transgender Law Center (TLC) at its annual gala. Few people present that night were involved in the trans community in 2004, when I started the Health Care Access Project at TLC, the first program in the nation to provide transgender cultural competency training for health care providers, educate community members about their rights in health care settings, and advocate for comprehensive access to care. I felt like Grandpa on the mic when I broke it down during my acceptance speech. I shared that when I started the Health Care Access Project, there weren't a lot of health care providers banging on the door for free training. What I didn't say was that I'll never forget the training coordinator at an East Bay hospital who went apeshit on me when I called to offer free training because "a transgender patient had had difficulty accessing services." When she went off on me very unprofessionally, I learned that calling from a law center offering free training, and the suggestion that a trans patient had experienced discrimination, made people highly emotionally reactive.

I also shared in my speech that the educational workshops with community members were a "downer" because "they were all about the multiple ways that we were getting screwed by health insurance." Honestly, it felt disempowering to emphasize how we weren't getting our health care needs met. So I developed patient advocacy materials, tools, and resources so that *hopefully* we wouldn't get treated like dirt in the doctor's office. These materials included suggestions, like contacting a provider ahead of time to see if they were *willing* to treat a trans person, and if they had had *any* experience with trans people. People were encouraged to bring someone with them to the doctor's visit to help advocate for them so they would have backup when a provider started asking invasive questions about their genital status, for example. An advocate or friend could not only help them remember their questions and take notes but also help them set boundaries when the provider wanted to use them as a training opportunity with a group of interns, or when eight people all of a sudden needed to come in to look for something in a drawer as soon as the trans person got undressed.

In reference to the multiple forms of discrimination that we experience in the doctor's office, with insurance companies, and systemically, I said in my speech, "Now, I recognize that this is still the case for so many people across the country and around the world, but in California the landscape has changed!" My voice escalated as the crowd cheered. "Who knew that ten years later I'd be educating community members about how to get their surgery covered, and that *I* would access *medically necessary, transition-related surgery paid for by my health insurance*. I got new junk this summer! Thank you, Transgender Law Center!" The audience went wild. I'm amused that the video of my speech captures Kortney Ryan Ziegler, one of the MCs, standing behind me, snapping and cracking up.

I had just had a medical procedure under anesthesia the day before.

I had a catheter, and my pain level was eight on a scale of one to ten. I was functioning without pain medication, because it doesn't agree with me and I never take pain medication before speaking engagements. But as I spoke my naked truth on the mic, as I acknowledged this incredibly historic moment in our health care access journey, my elation and its resonance with the community enveloped the physical pain.

*   *   *

The landscape changed in California because of the tireless work of many activists. In 2006, the Insurance Gender Nondiscrimination Act went into effect. It clarified that "state law prohibited insurance companies and health care service plans from discriminating on the basis of gender in the creation or maintenance of service contracts or the provision of benefits or coverage."[102] In September 2012, the California Department of Insurance issued regulations requiring that PPOs issued in California remove exclusions that discriminated against transgender individuals. The Department of Managed Health Care followed suit in April 2013, when it required that HMOs based in California (except self-insured plans, which the federal government regulates) remove transgender exclusions and cover care on the bases of parity and medical necessity. In September 2013, Medi-Cal, California's Medicaid program, issued a memo to all Medi-Cal-managed care plans explicitly stating that transition-related care is a covered benefit. Finally, Section 1557 of the Affordable Care Act, which was implemented in January 2014, requires that insurance companies not discriminate on the basis of sexual orientation or gender identity, though it does not dictate what services should be covered.[103] In addition, the ACA prohibits insurers from denying coverage based on a preexisting condition, such as being transgender.

Make no mistake: there are still many trans people in California who are not getting their health care needs met—people without coverage, people with self-insured plans (health insurance specific to their employer's plan), students whose health insurance falls short, and veterans, to name a few.

Given the changes in health insurance options, we had a sudden demand in California for qualified surgeons. In San Francisco, the most renowned surgeon was Dr. Michael Brownstein, who provided chest reconstruction for the FTM community for thirty-five years. I was fortunate to access his skills during his last year prior to retirement. In July 2012, when I went in for a six-month follow-up, his assistant confided that a surgeon who knew "how to do everything" was coming to town. She shared that he was skilled in all surgeries for trans men and women. I was intrigued.

In January 2013, Dr. Curtis Crane took over Dr. Michael Brownstein's business and began conducting phalloplasty procedures within a few months. Amid the high demand, he has been doing a brisk business ever since, frequently performing two phalloplasties a week. Insurance providers such as Kaiser Permanente and the University of California, San Francisco (UCSF), for example, have scrambled to get new surgeons trained.[104]

* * *

There are two types of genital surgery for trans men: metoidioplasty and phalloplasty. With testosterone therapy, the clitoris gradually enlarges to approximately 1.5 to 2 inches. In metoidioplasty, the surgeon separates the enlarged clitoris from the labia minora, severing the suspensory ligament to approximate the position of a penis. Tissue from the labia minora can be used to add girth. A urethral extension can be done to allow for urination through the penis, using mucosal tissue from either the vagina or mouth tissues. The neopenis can achieve erection with the erectile tissue from the clitoris and does not require an implant. Scrotoplasty (creation of a scrotum) can be done from the labia majora. If the person desires, vaginectomy (removal of the vagina), hysterectomy, and oophorectomy (removal of the ovaries) can be done at the same time as metoidioplasty.

As a two- to three-hour surgery with fewer complications, metoidioplasty is a much less invasive procedure than phalloplasty, which generally requires eight to ten hours of surgery. The goal of phalloplasty is to create a penis that is aesthetically appealing, with erotic and tactile sensation, and that allows the person to urinate while standing and engage in penetrative sex.[105] Free flap phalloplasty involves construction of a phallus with a skin graft from one of three locations in the body: the radial forearm, anterolateral thigh (ALT), or musculocutaneous latissimus dorsi (MLD, or upper back). Alternatively, a pedicle flap can be constructed from the abdomen or a number of other donor sites on the body. The radial forearm, ALT, and MLD procedures develop a phallus with both touch and erotic sensation. The pedicle flap does not have blood flow or nerve connections and is not sensate.

Ideally, a hysterectomy (hysto) has been done at least three months prior to phalloplasty, unless the patient has chosen to forgo vaginectomy; one cannot have a vaginectomy without a hysterectomy, since a vaginectomy removes the avenue for discharge to exit the body. Moreover, it is not advisable to complete a hysto during phalloplasty because it adds time to an already-lengthy surgery. If a skilled urologist performs radial forearm phalloplasty, they can in most cases complete a urethral extension, vaginectomy, and scrotoplasty in the first stage (though it can take two stages to complete the urethra in the ALT and MLD procedures).[106] Once tactile sensation has grown down the phallus, penile and testicular implants can be inserted.

The radial forearm procedure is universally considered the gold standard among surgeons in the field, though there are differences of opinion within the FTM community. Certainly, many people have been happy with phallo from all the free flap donor sites. The radial forearm procedure is said to have the best sensation and cosmetic appearance, though, again, opinions in the community differ. With technical advances and the best postsurgical results, the radial forearm procedure ideally requires two surgeries, though often additional surgeries are required in order to address complications.

Radial forearm uses the skin, artery, vein, and nerve from the non-dominant forearm to create a penis, which functions as a tube within a tube in order to accommodate a new urethra, as well as an erectile implant. A very thin layer of skin from the thigh is used to cover up the arm. The radial artery maintains blood flow of the phallus graft by connecting to the femoral artery in the leg.

A nerve from the forearm is microsurgically connected to the clitoral nerve at the base of the penis, with the goal of achieving erotic sensation throughout the penile shaft. When a nerve is cut, its food supply dies but its casing remains. The living pelvic nerve is connected to the axon sheath of the arm nerve (now in the phallus), which acts as a highway. The nerve grows down the highway and connects to the nerve receptors in the flap (neophallus) at a rate of one millimeter per day, ideally achieving erotic sensation down the shaft to the tip of the penis in approximately nine months after phalloplasty.[107] It can take two to two and a half years to achieve full nerve regeneration.

Two types of penile implants are used to achieve erection: the semirigid rod and the three-piece pump. Doctors and health insurance carriers have a strong preference for the semirigid rod because it has far fewer complications than the pump. Developed for the elder man with erectile dysfunction, the pump, with its many moving parts, may not be best suited to the young, horny trans man who has a penis for the first time. Yet, anecdotally, there are trans guys who are very happy with it nonetheless and have not had to haul themselves into surgery for a replacement pump after five years, as feared. Whereas the pump requires working a mechanism to bring fluid into the shaft, the semirigid rod works like a gooseneck lamp or Gumby: the individual simply manipulates the phallus into its desired position.

*   *   *

During the first radial forearm surgery, a vaginectomy is performed, the urethra is extended, the phallus is created, including glansplasty (creation of a head), scrotoplasty is done, and a very thin layer of skin is harvested from the thigh to cover up the donor site. The first twenty-four hours following surgery are critical; medical personnel monitor a Doppler hourly to ensure that there is continued blood flow and no loss of the graft. No one wants the phallus to fall off.

The downside to radial forearm surgery is the significant scarring on the forearm, though a high percentage of trans guys who opt for this surgery are willing to have an arm scar in exchange for a functional, sensate, and aesthetically appealing penis. Trans guys opt for the other donor sites if they don't want an arm scar and/or prefer a penis with more girth, which can approximate five to seven inches in circumference. In addition, a radial forearm–based phallus is generally shorter than phalluses from the other donor sites. The exact penis length is unknown prior to surgery, dependent on the position of the vein that is revealed surgically, whereas patients who opt for the other donor sites can request a longer penis. When the thigh or back is used as a donor site, the glansplasty (creation of the head) doesn't occur until the second stage, at which point reduction of girth can take place, if desired. The ALT and MLD procedures require three stages, whereas the radial forearm requires two, unless there are complications; the last stage involves insertion of the penile and testicular implants.

The functionality of the donor sites used in free flap phalloplasty has been excellent in many cases. With hand therapy, people usually regain full strength, flexibility, and mobility following radial forearm phalloplasty.

*   *   *

Ultimately, my initial perspective about genital surgery changed as I began to experience life as a man. Honestly, I didn't want to get killed in the locker room; safety is an ongoing concern for trans men, especially guys of color. I know far too many trans brothers of color who have experienced extremely stressful, frightening experiences when they were targeted as men of color in airports, at border crossings, and on the streets. One Chicano friend was strip-searched at a border crossing in Mexico when his wife packed a few joints without his knowledge. He was forced to disclose that he was transgender, which was confusing to the guard, who wondered if he liked to dress as a woman. As my friend stood naked, exposed, and completely alone, it was the guard's confusion that saved him, but my friend was so stressed about crossing the border again, he couldn't sleep and had to call off his vacation in Mexico. He wondered whether, by the time he passed through again, the guard would have told all his coworkers, and whether they would be waiting to victimize him as a female-to-male trans person.

As Cinque wrote in *Hung Jury: Testimonies of Genital Surgery by Transsexual Men*:

"Since transitioning, I notice that people treat me a lot differently now, especially cops, customs officers, and border patrol. Depending on the context and person(s), I get pegged as a thug, criminal, undocumented worker, or terrorist. To make matters worse, three of my friends had horrible experiences of being strip-searched by TSA [Transportation Security Administration] officers and border patrolmen. All of them described their fear and humiliation in vivid detail. They felt like they had been singled out because of their race and ethnicity. The same thing was beginning to happen to me when I traveled out of the country. Being so vulnerable and exposed all the time became unbearable. I had to find a solution."[108]

The National Transgender Discrimination Survey found that female-to-male transgender individuals and visually gender-nonconforming people report higher incidents of police harassment than male-to-female transgender individuals, a statistic I found surprising.[109] We often hear about the horrible mistreatment that trans women, especially trans women of color, experience at the hands of police, immigration officials, customs officials, and airport personnel, yet the experience of trans men of color mirrors the police harassment experienced by cisgender men of color. We need to look at the war on black and brown men and boys with a trans lens; part of that equation involves recognition of the impact of limited access to care.

Though I have experienced privilege as a light-skinned Asian brother, I have also experienced many incidences of people treating me with great suspicion in stores, at airports, in restrooms and hotels, and on the streets. Whether it's related to my racial incongruity, gender-outlaw vibe, or life in the disability underworld, I don't know. I just know that I needed to feel secure that I would not be targeted for having the appearance of a gender-incongruent body. Most of all, I wanted to feel fully myself in body, mind, and spirit. Phalloplasty was a journey to align my body with my soul.

With phalloplasty, there is the dream and then there is the reality. As a member of the first vanguard of trans men accessing genital surgery through health insurance during this new era in California, I learned the reality the hard way. I found that providers who were wonderfully culturally competent lacked the medical competency to keep up with the quickly changing health care needs of trans patients postphalloplasty. One prescribed antibiotics for a month, even though my urine cultures were negative, because my symptoms looked like a urinary tract infection but actually indicated a postsurgical urethral stricture. When I did actually have a urinary tract infection, one insisted on having me go to the lab to be tested for sexually transmitted infection because she saw pus coming out of my penis. It was only four weeks after my phalloplasty; it wasn't like I was running around town. No amount of my speaking my truth would change her insistence that I get into my car and drive, stand in line, which hurt like hell, and spend too much money for an unnecessary lab test.

I also experienced many providers who were truly offensive in their cultural incompetence during my hospital stay. There was the nursing professor who peppered me with questions about my trans status while I tried to eat my meal. "Now I never know if a man is really a man!" She asked me invasive questions about my race while washing my naked backside. There was the intern who said, with no awareness of her condescension, "This must really be a dream come true for you." Or the nurse I dealt with upon waking from surgery, who loudly described me as "the transgender patient" while other patients lay next to me, separated only by a thin curtain. And the horribly insensitive graveyard nurse that first night who couldn't have cared less if I felt nauseated or hurled and refused to answer my questions, saying, "You don't need to know."

Yet when I went to medical appointments, I was treated respectfully by everyone from the receptionist to the person who took my vitals to the doctor. I was thoroughly surprised. No one treated me like a dirtball or a freeloader. As a gender-transgressive person who had been living with chronic illness for decades, I felt *confused* every time I was treated like a human being. I still do.

There were systems and data management issues that concerned me, too, like when I looked over at my physical therapist's screen and saw my name with the word "transgender" next to it. That's not cool. It made me wonder how many people in the system had this confidential information.

I feel profound gratitude for the opportunity to take advantage of this new era of health care access. I don't take for granted that I have health insurance that covers my health needs as a trans person. It is indeed a great privilege that many others in California, across the country, and around the world do not have. There are amazing advocates who are down with trans issues, who are working tirelessly to help coordinate our care and ensure that we are treated with respect. Still, there is work that needs to be done on an institutional level—everything from staff training to appropriate aftercare, support groups, pre- and postsurgical health education programs, data management, data collection, and reasonable accommodations at the pharmacy for people who can't stand.

Despite my health care institution's large, comprehensive health education department, there was no health education component available for us, so we as a community organized three forums to educate ourselves about FTM genital surgery, and I provided information on insurance options. There was no in-home aftercare, no educational workshops for caregivers. My health care institution did not provide postsurgical support groups, and, most of all, there was no education about the realities of complications during the first year after phalloplasty.

In a postsurgery support group, organized from within the community, I commented that getting phalloplasty was like getting hit by a truck. They say it can take as many months as hours you were under anesthesia to feel like yourself again. I certainly felt scrambled in mind and body for a good eight months. One guy, who was bandaged and using a cane, said, "I actually did get hit by a truck, and I can attest to the fact that phalloplasty is worse." He was referring to an accident that happened five months after phallo, in which he was thrown a hundred feet from his motorcycle after impact, if you can imagine that.

*   *   *

Most of the people I know had a team who helped them recover. Partners worked around the clock with emotional and practical support. Some guys rented hospital beds so that it would be easier to get in and out of bed. One guy had a friend who was a nurse stay with him. People needed help with showering, going to the pharmacy, keeping track of their meds, and getting fed. Most took two to three months off from work.

Georgia worked overtime, running to the pharmacy, making food, and caring for the kids. We had only enough child care that she could visit me for a few hours a day for the five days when I was in the hospital. Once I got home, I found myself watching my kids for hours the next day, getting up gingerly to fetch my daughter snacks while Georgia ran to the pharmacy and the grocery store. During recovery, my main concern was being fed and having the time to rest. That and minimizing painful moments, like when a hardback book was thrown into my lap: "Read this book, Dada!" The kids were their adorable selves, making me cards and snuggling with me in bed while I read to them.

A few days after I got home, I was back in my office, working a full day. At three weeks, I was on a plane to Orange County to do a workshop on providing equal access for trans people at a statewide substance-use-disorder conference. It still hurt like hell to stand for any length of time, but I needed the work. I stood in line at airport security, and I stood for an hour and a half as a trainer. I conducted my workshop in diapers, necessary for a good month postsurgically to catch the ongoing drainage of blood and interstitial fluid, with a catheter bag strapped to my leg, with a pain level of nine and no pain meds, and no one knew any different.

I was sporting an arm splint, the only visible sign of my medical experience. When I ran into two colleagues at the conference, wonderful African American women who work in the cultural competency field and have been thoroughly supportive of trans issues, they asked me what happened to my arm. I told them, "Gender confirmation surgery, actually." One looked at me quizzically. "You gotta get something from somewhere," I replied. She bugged in a freeze frame while she did the math, much to my amusement.

At the workshop, I spoke of the historic difficulty of getting health insurance without arbitrary exclusions, the presumption of criminality of trans women of color, and the particular stresses trans men of color experience when they are profiled and targeted. One of the participants, a colleague who leads workshops on how to provide culturally sophisticated substance use disorder treatment services for African Americans, said that in the recovery field, the questions they ask people are "How can you come into the person you're meant to be, and how can you get out of the way of yourself?" He continued, "I don't think there's any experience comparable to being transgender that the rest of us can imagine. I admire the courage it takes to be true to yourself in the face of a lack of acceptance within the family and larger society, and all the discrimination and violence."

It does take a leap of faith to jump off this particular cliff. I knew I couldn't rest until I could be completely who I was meant to be. Is that courage or necessity?

*   *   *

Individual bodies react to phalloplasty in different ways. Everyone I know has had a complication that needed some sort of resolution during the first year after phallo. The one guy I know who didn't have a medical complication got fired from his job a week after returning to work from phalloplasty, in what appeared to be a clear case of discrimination based on trans and disability status. Guys I know have experienced various complications, such as large fistulas (holes), strictures (narrowing, especially in the urethra), partial necrosis (in which part of the phallus fails), urethral failure, sutures in the phallus opening up, serious infections, and bladder perforation. A number have experienced disabling complications, such as the firefighter who has been homebound with chronic pain, infection, and bladder perforation for a year, with no resolution in sight. I also know many people who have gotten past the first year of complications and are happily functioning very well.

It's important to note that experiences with phalloplasty vary greatly, depending on when the surgery is performed, which surgeon performs it, and the particular health parameters of the individual. At the time of this book's publication, there are limited or no available data about complications and outcomes. Indeed, a number of phallo patients have taken to e-mail lists and social media to express anger about their outcomes, the care they have received, and the tremendous difficulties they have experienced communicating with their surgeon's office staff. Phallo patients are seeking out other surgeons, providers, and advocates to find solutions for their complications. Moreover, there is ongoing concern that those who experience complications, working with a variety of surgeons, have difficulty getting support on listservs designed for patient support; any mention of complications has been systematically silenced in these groups. I stand in full support of trans guys who have experienced lengthy health crises in the aftermath of phalloplasty, which in some cases have gone on for many years.

In my case, my arm healed beautifully; its appearance is apparently better than that of anyone's my surgeon has seen in fifteen years. The push and pull of swimming strengthened it and helped me develop flexibility. Working out on my TRX suspension bands also helped. My complication has been what one urologist described as the Achilles' heel of phalloplasty: urethral stricture.

A month after phalloplasty, I began to urinate out of the new urethra in my penis, which of course was exciting, but soon afterward, urination became more and more painful. After a month of ingesting antibiotics I didn't need for a urinary tract infection that didn't exist, I discovered that I had a urethral stricture. Dr. Crane told me that it was a people-of-color thing, that since I'm Chinese I make more collagen, and that's why there was a narrowing in my urethra that made urination painful. He told me that the reason my arm healed so well—my ability to make a lot of scar tissue—was the same reason why I had a urethral stricture so quickly after surgery. I learned that urethral stricture is a very common complication from this surgery. Dr. Sanders, a seasoned urologist who has repaired urethral stricture in patients with phalloplasties from Belgium, Thailand, and the United States, made it clear to me that folks should expect to have a complication, such as urethral stricture, rather than to assume that it's an anomaly.

He said that patients from the Brussels team, as well as patients from Dr. Crane, have excellent results with tissue survival. The difficulties arise in the new urethra. Scar tissue contracts by nature, which is good except when something is round, such as a urethra, and you're forced to pee out of a pinhole, which is very painful. As time goes on, the increased pressure can blow out a fistula, an opening through the skin. These complications are the reason some surgeons do not do a urethral hookup, and why some wait until the second stage to complete it.

My urethra started to close up completely, so I had to wield what looked like a huge knitting needle, an endotracheal tube, to dilate the urethra in order to pee. It was extremely painful and had to be done every time I needed to urinate. I had a lot of travel scheduled to the East Coast and was worried about having to get the knitting needle through security and being able to use it on the plane. It would be life-threatening if I couldn't urinate. So I had a catheter placed, and that was painful as well.

The catheter came with its own adventure. Five days after its placement, I caught an early flight. Since I was still in pain, I was using a catheter leg bag. I was halfway through the long airport security line before it occurred to me that the X-ray machine was going to get a nice picture of the liquid on my leg, which was surely more than three ounces. But if I exited the line, emptied the urine in the restroom, and got back in at the end of the line, I'd miss my flight. Just as I was about to go through the X-ray machine, by some divine intervention, a new TSA agent opened a new line and ushered me through, bypassing the X-ray machine.

Instead of a catheter bag, I began to use a plug, a small piece of plastic that I inserted into the catheter tube. That's when things got really exciting. Over time the rubber in the tube would expand and the plug would dislodge at inopportune moments, such as while I drove a rental car late at night, trying to find a hotel in an obscure location. Next thing I knew, I was bathed in a warm liquid. I was supposed to pick up my very important, serious colleagues the next day, and I didn't want to show up with funky-smelling wheels or sitting on a towel. I was washing down that car seat in the parking lot at midnight, grateful for the drying power of the morning sun.

There was the time I was about to perform at a university; fortunately, it happened while I was still near my accommodations and could wash off and change. But one time the plug opened up to splash my legs and the sidewalk just as I stepped out of my car to speak at another university. I was running late and had no change of clothes. Good thing I had learned to wear black pants. I did the whole speaking engagement urine-soaked, but I kept my wits about me and delivered it with a smile. Good thing I had stopped eating asparagus!

One afternoon, my toilet-training two-year-old was sitting on my lap, his booty naked so he could use the potty chair with ease. "Oh, no, baby, you have to go to the *yio-yio*," I said, using the Greek word for "potty chair." Then I realized that the urine dripping down my legs wasn't actually his. The darn plug had dislodged again.

After six weeks of catheter excitement, I was in too much pain and had it removed. I had to dilate again, but since dilation was excruciating each time I had to urinate, I kept the tube in place. That left me in a different kind of constant pain because its rough edge tore up my urethra and bladder. It was bad enough that I had to take out the tube and wash it every other day. Getting it back in hurt like hell.

Then I fell through the cracks for several months, in the absence of provider observation. As a man who supported a family of five, I could no longer afford the pricey, $700-per-month Covered California plan. Since I had Medicare, I was ineligible for financial assistance. Recovery from phalloplasty had kicked up my chronic illness, and my ability to work had become more limited. The state contracts that had paid me handsomely to provide LGBTQ cultural competency training and technical assistance had all dried up, and my national contract ended.

After I got onto a less costly, Medicare-managed care plan, I spent many hours over several months wrestling with insurance drama. Despite the supposed victory in May 2014 when the Centers for Medicare & Medicaid Services (CMS) announced that it would remove trans exclusions, it actually became more difficult for trans Medicare recipients to get coverage for care.[110] I couldn't access Dr. Crane's services because he didn't take Medicare.

In the aftermath of this supposed victory, Medicare has not described or defined what transition-related services it covers; surgeons bill for several services, then discover after performing the procedures that only one service is covered, for example. In addition, Medicare's reimbursement rates are so abysmally low that providers can't possibly cover their costs. For instance, it has reimbursed less than $1,000 for genital surgeries, including 180 days of follow-up care. Dr. Marci Bowers, a highly experienced surgeon in the Bay Area, was reimbursed literally *$1* by Medicare for performing a vaginoplasty surgery.[111] Trans people with Medi-Medi (Medicare and Medi-Cal) are especially screwed because Medicare is considered the primary insurance, gets billed first, and either won't cover transition-related care or won't provide adequate reimbursement. Individuals who have Medi-Cal coverage alone, however, can get covered for transition-related care, although this is not the case for people with Medicaid in the vast majority of the country.[112]

One cannot disenroll from Medicare without a huge financial penalty, and even if Medicare is not associated with a recipient's current health plan, it will always be considered the primary insurance, which means that transition-related services will not likely be covered. I learned the hard way that there was nothing I could do to combat the Medicare discrimination I experienced. I couldn't disenroll from Medicare, and no matter how hard I worked to disassociate my Medicare from my other health insurance, I couldn't get my plan to ignore my Medicare coverage. Without a system of implementation or realistic reimbursement rates, Medicare is an albatross around the necks of trans seniors and people with disabilities.

Dr. Crane's office had scheduled a surgical revision, but since my Medicare prevented me from being covered for his services, I endured several more months of pain before I could get relief from my complication. I finally discovered Dr. Sanders, the urologist with many years experience treating urethral stricture in phallo patients. His approach involved a series of excruciating diagnostic procedures with the edict "measure twice, cut once." The first procedure was a cystoscopy, which involved running a long scope into the urethra to get a good look. For whatever reason, there were difficulties getting the data he needed, and the excruciating procedure went on for an hour. I knew it wasn't going to be fun, but since I was by myself and had to drive back from San Francisco to Oakland, I was unmedicated. I yelled out at level-ten pain for an hour on that table. Dr. Sanders couldn't believe that I had been dealing with this situation on my own, and that my bladder and urethra were so torn up.

The procedure was so invasive that afterward I could no longer pee with the tube and had to have a catheter placed again. I got out of there, stumbled to the pharmacy, unable to stand, and pulled up a hefty chair in order to maintain my place in line. When I finally got to the parking lot, I began to heave. The pain was so intense, I sobbed in my car before I could pull myself together to drive home for an hour and a half in Friday afternoon rush-hour traffic.

A week and a half later, I returned to San Francisco for a urethro-gram, an X-ray that involved shooting liquid into my urethra and pulling the catheter out slowly, which also hurt like hell. Afterward, I walked blocks to my car and drove a mile and a half to Dr. Sanders's office, where he conducted another painful cystoscopy and reinserted the catheter. Two weeks later, I went to another urologist, who inserted a suprapubic catheter (in the groin, rather than the penis) in order to give my urethra a rest. This way they could determine exactly where the scar tissue was, without interference from a catheter or tube in my urethra. When she told me, "My goal is to keep you as comfortable as possible," I should have known that was code for *the pain will be so intense, you will go to the primal scream.* I thought I knew what level-ten pain was, but this was off the charts. The experience amounted to having unexpected mi-nor surgery while awake and feeling everything. The procedure took an hour because I tensed up when they cut into my bladder; the anesthesia reached only the upper layers of skin. As much as I try to be a tough guy, as much as I think I can handle pain, I scream-sobbed for an hour on that table and woke the dead.

I've become one of the gentlemen in the urology department wait-ing area, seated next to decent old guys in their sixties and seventies with walking sticks and wheelchairs. These are my people now, seasoned elders who probably know all about navigating life with a catheter bag attached to your leg. I nod and say hello to the weathered sixtysomething African American man seated in a wheelchair draped in a red and black check-ered bathrobe. He looks like a straight-up guy who probably doesn't have enough joy in his life. And no matter how friendly the thirtysomething female doctor is with me, I'm always Mr. Wilkinson, never Willy. After several e-mails back and forth, she started signing off by her first name but never deviated from addressing me as Mr. Wilkinson. It's urology department culture, apparently. It's a funny thing, what my name has become because of my urethra.

*   *   *

On May 11, 2015, the US Department of Labor, the Department of Health and Human Services, and the Treasury jointly issued guidelines clarifying that under the ACA, the plan or issuer must provide coverage for "sex-specific recommended preventive services . . . without cost sharing, regardless of sex assigned at birth, gender identity, or gender of the individual otherwise recorded by the plan or issuer." That means that trans men should be covered for gynecological screening and trans women should be covered for prostate screening, for example.[113]

As of August 2015, ten states and the District of Columbia prohibit transgender exclusions in health insurance coverage issued in their respective states.[114] On September 3, 2015, the US Department of Health and Human Services announced a proposed rule that would make it illegal for insurance plans to deny, cancel, or limit coverage; categorically exclude transition-related care and sex-specific care; or deny access to restrooms and room assignments in accordance with one's gender identity. This proposed rule would apply to all health insurance plans sold on state and federal exchanges, as well as all plans sold to companies with a federal contract or that receive federal funds.[115] This is tremendous progress, and I long for the day when we have comprehensive, nondiscriminatory health insurance nationwide (and internationally).

Despite having lived in pain for a year, and with a catheter for half that time, I have never for a minute regretted my decision to have phalloplasty. I like how my penis looks, and at nine months I did indeed gain full sensation down the phallus to the tip, which seems to be a common outcome with radial forearm but not guaranteed.[116] I have achieved my goal of being passable in the locker room and feel safer in the world.

During my excruciatingly difficult suprapubic catheter placement, a seasoned urologist was called in to help. At the risk of sounding like a braggadocious asshole, I want to share that this urologist, who had thirty-five years' experience with looking at dicks all day, had no idea that my penis was surgically crafted from my flesh. It's a testament to the worldwide technological advances of genital surgery for trans men, which in 2015 are still unknown to many trans people and most of the general public.

A year after my initial phalloplasty surgery, I finally had the revision

I had been waiting for: a repair to my urethral stricture. It was a long-awaited celebration when I finally stood to pee, without pain, through my new urethra. I was advised to wait a year after surgical revision to get my penile and testicular implants—longer than other patients, to ensure that my propensity for building collagen doesn't create another painful stricture. Like my lifelong gender journey, phalloplasty is a process that requires patience, endurance, and faith.

I've lived through a challenging, painful health crisis and temporarily have erectile dysfunction, but I'm very happy that I was able to access phalloplasty. It has helped me relax into my masculinity and confidence. I can expand into my full psychic, spiritual, physical, and emotional self.

When we gather, sporting blue sweatbands and pink Lycra rash guards, silicone sleeves and black leather wrist cuffs, intricate blue tattoos, and, mostly, naked exposure, we are a people who bear the same markings. Straight, queer, and of every color, we are each on a quest for something that is highly individual and deeply personal and yet resonates with all of us. Though the expectations and desires for this archetypal symbol of manhood vary, the thread of transmasculinity in this changing landscape connects us. These are my phallo brothers, brave warriors all of them.

Increasing Access to Surgery in a County Health Department

In 2013, as a result of the unwavering advocacy of Transgender Law Center and the San Francisco Health Council, the San Francisco Department of Public Health (SFDPH) launched the first program in the nation to provide transition-related surgery access for low-income city residents. Run by a small, underfunded staff, the program demonstrates a solid commitment to the complex, multiple needs of a historically underserved public health population in a diverse urban setting. Other county health departments and health care institutions can aspire to the SFDPH's comprehensive model of care.

The SFDPH recognized back in the '90s that transgender people were not receiving appropriate, respectful care. As I documented in *Transgender Rights*,[117] we conducted a large-scale participatory action research project in the late '90s with the goal of getting solid health data about the transgender community. The data showed very high HIV seroprevalance among trans women of color, an astounding 63 percent rate of infection among African American trans women respondents.[118]

Though San Francisco had a legacy of strong community advocacy, an early commitment to the informed-consent model, and recognition of the particular mental health needs of trans people who have experienced tremendous discrimination and trauma, transition-related surgery was considered out of reach. For many years, mental health providers counseled people on acceptance that their lifelong dream of surgery would not likely come to be.

In 2012, the San Francisco Health Commission approved a surgery program for Healthy San Francisco recipients, the city's health plan for low-income, uninsured residents. In 2013, I had the privilege of providing consultation services for the SFDPH as it embarked on the grandiose effort to train fourteen thousand employees on transgender issues, including staff at San Francisco General Hospital. One of the goals was to ensure that providers developed competency to provide culturally responsive services throughout the city so that trans people weren't relegated to two clinics but could seek services in their neighborhood, in their appropriate language.

In August 2013, Transgender Health Services (THS) was launched. The program has coordinated surgery referrals for Healthy San Francisco and Medi-Cal managed-care recipients in San Francisco, trained providers on assessment and referral for surgery, and provided multisession health education programs for patients and caregivers. THS seeks to bridge the assumptions of the World Professional Association for Transgender Health (WPATH) Standards of Care 7, that a patient will be well resourced by education, English-language capability, money, and family support. Rather than expecting that trans people and their caregivers be responsible for educating themselves on all aspects of care, which has tradi-tionally been the case for much of trans care, THS utilizes a peer model to foster education about trans surgeries and postsurgical care, help with patient preparation, and provide peer support. There is emphasis on continuous care management from referral to the postoperative period, including mental health support. What I espe-cially appreciate about the THS model is the way it creates a sup-port structure that delivers positive health outcomes while not dis-criminating against patients who might otherwise not be considered good candidates for surgery, based on mental health, substance use disorder, or housing status.

In the program's first year and a half, there were referrals to 237 surgeries and 62 surgeries completed. THS has secured insurance approval for a range of surgeries and procedures, such as facial electrolysis, and advocated for coverage of procedures not usually covered, such as presurgical electrolysis, facial feminization sur-gery, tracheal shave, and penile implants. In addition, it has support-ed homeless individuals to stay in medical respite following surgery.

This comprehensive program has come together because of the heart and brilliance of a few dedicated individuals, whom I'm proud to call my colleagues.[19] This model is replicable and conducive to positive health outcomes.

SHOW-AND-TELL

In September 2015, I had the privilege of attending Transmission, the first-ever retreat in the Sonoma County woods north of San Francisco, where a beautifully diverse group of transmasculine individuals connected in community, shared intimate vulnerabilities, and built their self-acceptance and self-confidence. After spontaneously joining the six-person panel at the well-attended Lower Surgery workshop, I educated community members about the medical details and got real about my phallo journey. When I was researching the subject, guys who had been through the experience educated me and showed me their surgeries, so I've been happy to reveal my dong at genital surgery forums, behind bedroom doors at house parties, and in awkwardly intimate moments in bathrooms with giggling partners of trans guys. As one appreciative participant remarked, seeing pictures online is not the same as seeing a surgery outcome in person.

When it came time for the show-and-tell portion of the session, I dropped trou and entertained six revolving groups of ten guys each with stories about my dick. They asked questions about sex, orgasm, masturbation, implants, surgical stages, and how I felt in terms of my safety. As the small group session came to a close, I quipped, "Okay, now you need to either buy me a drink or show me your junk!" One guy, who had never shown his meta to anyone before, complied.

At next year's retreat, I'm sure there will be an enhanced entertainment factor. We'll put on some *Magic Mike* music, rip off our stripper pants, do some circus tricks, and circulate a tip jar. No dollar, no show.

BEAUTIFUL SYMMETRY

The movement for transgender equality has two key messages: 1) As trans people, we have the need and the right to live our lives authentically, and 2) despite navigating ongoing challenges in multiple spheres of life, we have tremendous resilience. These ideas are not unique to trans experience; we can all absorb and find our agency in these fundamental truths. My story took an unexpected turn that taught me the power of harnessing my inner strength to rise above life's challenges so that Georgia and I could be true to ourselves.

It was early April 2015, the night after the first cystoscopy, my first foray into the excruciatingly painful series of diagnostic tests in which tubes and wires were jammed repeatedly into my urethra and bladder. I had had no pain medication, screamed on the table for an hour with level-ten pain, and broken down in the parking lot afterward. The procedure was so invasive that I was unexpectedly left with a catheter.

Still in agonizing pain, I helped host a kiddie slumber party. After food, rowdy times, and a meltdown, the kids finally knocked off after eleven o'clock. I got connected to my nighttime catheter bag, which hooked onto the side of the bed frame, and got into bed. Georgia had seemed distant at the party and in recent weeks. I decided to go look for her to check in. There, in my underwear, with a pain level of eight, holding my nighttime catheter bag, I learned the intricate details of my next major life decision, made for me without my consent.

We sat down on the couch and had a conversation that was surprisingly calm. It felt surreal watching words that I hadn't seen coming tumble out of her mouth. She had come to understand that, in order to be her authentic self, she needed to be in a butch-femme relationship, rather than a heterosexual relationship, and that she needed to end our romantic relationship.

I was surprised, but honestly, my first feeling was a deep sense of relief. It had been exhausting holding myself tight in a little ball, pretending that everything was okay. We had been emotionally disconnected from each other for a long time. We had both tried to be someone we weren't for the sake of the relationship and for the kids.

Georgia suggested that I live downstairs and she live upstairs so the kids wouldn't be displaced. She said that she wanted us both to be happy and that she would always be my family. She wanted me to be with someone with whom I could enjoy my new body, and she knew she couldn't give me that.

She had received wide acclaim when she'd published an article nine months earlier about her process of accepting my gender transition. I was proud of her for bravely and honestly describing how difficult it was for her to be with a man when she had worked so hard to claim her lesbian identity. But there was more to the story. We both knew in our hearts that as much as we celebrated my choice to live *my* life authentically, we weren't actually living *our* lives authentically, not in our marriage. At the same time, I believed that we would survive transition. We had worked through so many other things. We took on major life challenges and came out the other end. We built beautiful things from *nothing*. I believed that we would work this out, too.

I was in the middle of a manuscript deadline, a long, painful health crisis, and a deep financial crisis. I had multiple high-profile events scheduled. My urethra and bladder were torn up, my pain level was excruciating, and my chronic illness had flared up. My ass was buck naked in the wind.

I can catch a curveball. I've had a lot of practice. I quickly rose to the challenge. I knew she had made the right decision for us.

*   *   *

Every night that first week, we told each other hard truths, hashing out the past and where we went wrong. Sure, there were other reasons it took me so long to medically transition, but I had stayed in a female body in large part because I didn't want to lose her or our kids. But I had reached the point where I was suffocating; I could no longer prioritize anyone else's needs. When I medically transitioned, I got to experience the profound psychic relief that I had craved for so many years but that had been prohibited. And Georgia rose to the occasion. She supported me and championed my bravery. She saw how my decision made me phenomenally happy, and she loved me for it, even when it hurt her.

Now it was my turn to do the same for her—to give her the space to be the lesbian she is. As the youngest girl children in our families, neither of us was raised to take care of ourselves. We were not raised to honor the inner voice that told us we were dying inside. When we could no longer ignore that voice, we knew we had no option. Our survival depended on it. Georgia spent all day every day taking care of other people. It was her turn to prioritize herself. I could support her as she stretched her wings and flew. I could champion her bravery as she took steps to live her life authentically. I could mourn her and cheer her on, just as she did for me.

As we grieved together, I began to feel elevated. I now had permission to really, truly come into myself. I hadn't even begun to live my life authentically, and now I was going to find out what liberation felt like.

A week after the breakup, in a moment of confusion, she wondered whether she'd made a mistake. But I had already had a taste of a life where my male gender expression and body were not a defect I had to overcome, but rather a positive, congruent representation of who I was. She had let me go so I could be me, and I had already started to come into myself as a polyamorous, pansexual man with a new body. I couldn't go back.

Three weeks into our breakup, the Asian Pacific Islander Queer Women & Transgender Community (APIQWTC) presented me with the Phoenix Award at its annual Lunar New Year Banquet. There were three hundred people in attendance. Georgia and I felt surrounded by so much love from the community that we became nostalgic about our past. The next day, we went our separate ways to contemplate. When we came back together that night, we found that we had both come to the same conclusion: we had made the right choice in ending our relationship.

Even if we could resolve everything else that wasn't working, the penis was the line in the sand.

The next day, I was "divorced dad doing IKEA," buying beautiful dark-wood furniture and kitchen basics. I thought I got clocked at Bed Bath & Beyond for my home-decorating flair, developed over years of watching HGTV with Georgia. When the seasoned, sassy saleswoman eyed my color-coordinated satiny curtains and silky sheets, she asked, "You having company, girlfriend?" Only later, when I recounted the story to a trans male friend, did I realize that the saleswoman assumed that I was a gay man, not that I had once been female.

At four weeks, when the timing felt right, we told our kids in an age-appropriate way that we had broken up, which meant balancing vagueness with enough information to help them understand. We wanted them to feel confident that we would always be there for them—a promise we demonstrated every day. A short time later, my son told me, "I feel fine about the divorce because I know it's not because you and Mama are mad at each other. It's because Mama's a lesbian and you're trans."

It was my highest priority to ensure that the kids' lives weren't disrupted. It was very fortunate that we had the capacity to create separate homes in the same dwelling. I always knew that I would never leave my kids; I wasn't going to live in some tacky, overpriced apartment somewhere, missing everyone. It hadn't occurred to me that we could turn our home into a duplex. The space that had been my office during the day and man cave at night became "Dada's house." The kids helped me arrange my stuff, and I stocked my kitchen with all the right kiddie snacks. Excited to help me decorate my place, the kids embarked on an art project to produce lots of colorful, smiley drawings, which they lovingly taped to the walls.

*   *   *

Partners of trans people often get the message that in order to support us, they aren't supposed to discuss what's difficult about medical transition, which may include the addition of new body parts and the loss of the sexual markers that attracted them to their partners in the beginning of the relationship. For some, the shift is not congruent with their social identity or sexuality. Fifty-five percent of relationships end when one partner medically transitions. The older the person is at the time of transition, the more likely the relationship is to end; 64 percent of relationships end when transition takes place between ages forty-five and fifty-four. The incidence is much higher for trans women (67 percent between the ages of forty-five and fifty-four) than for trans men (39 percent between the ages of forty-five and fifty-four).[120] I didn't expect to be part of that statistic, but I also couldn't imagine how powerful the experience of opening the door to new possibilities would be.

Through bouts of sadness, doubt, hope, and fear, Georgia and I both began to glow. We mellowed out. We each hummed at a new vibration. We became more gentle and patient with the kids and each other.

Over time, we developed clear boundaries for our houses and maintained a flexible coparenting schedule so our kids could run freely between our homes. Every evening they ran excitedly downstairs to spend time at Dada's house, bouncing off the walls, creating a fort in my bed, and playing enthusiastically with me in the backyard.

Sure, there were bumps in the road, some messy moments, but Georgia and I worked through them with the foundation we had developed over the past twenty years.

I felt myself expanding into my masculinity without reservation. I was a tough guy, a sensitive poet, a jaded old fart, and a bright-eyed virgin, decidedly queer. I imagined myself being single for some extended period so I could take my time to get to know myself. I felt calm in the quiet of my alone space.

But I couldn't help but feel the tracks of Georgia's turned heels across the disabled landscape of my mixed, trans body, crooked, burnt, and scarred. The trans body that had a catheter running through it, was oozing funk from the open wound, and had been in gnawing physical pain for nine long months. The trans body that reeked of apparent rejection but also radiated with new beginnings. Like a puzzled deer caught in headlights, I tried to make sense of all the mixed messages, the sorrows of what didn't work, and the beautiful memories of what did.

I had begun the process of adopting my third child the week we broke up, a task I hadn't gotten around to since his birth two and a half years prior. Even though I got the paperwork in quickly, it took two months to get a home visit from the social worker. We were eager to announce our amicable divorce, but since I was engaged in a legal process that required us to be in a domestic partnership, I didn't think it was strategic or safe for us to make any written statements about it. Disclosure to friends about my divorce was a slow process, and even so, I was overwhelmed by their reactions. People were sympathetic about the multiple challenges I faced, yet I still felt their pity. I was being perceived as a "tragic trans person." There was no escape from the subjugation I experienced as a result of the assumptions people made about my story, and I hated it.

Mine is not a tragic trans tale. I am not a pitiable, victimized trans person, marked, once again, by defect and rejection. Georgia isn't a villainous, transphobic lesbian. This divorce was a mutual decision made with love, the courage to let go, and elation as we changed our marriage into a family relationship and celebrated the latest evolution of our authentic selves.

After I told my parents, they sent me a sweet note about how I was a "person of strength," listing challenging moments in my life from which I had emerged with resilience. Georgia's mom told me, "You'll always be the father of my grandchildren. I love you, Willymou."

*   *   *

In mid-June, two months after the breakup, I went to the Mixed Remixed Festival in Los Angeles to perform spoken word about the intersection between mixed and trans experience. Before the event, Emily, an APIQWTC member who had been an acquaintance for the past decade, contacted me to tell me that she planned to go, and to ask if I needed any assistance at the performance. I was happy that there would be at least one other queer person in what appeared to be a predominantly straight, cisgender scene.

After the performance, I hung out with Emily and a few other women over dinner and lively discussion about the complexities of our mixed lives. Korean and Jewish, racially nonconforming, and gorgeous, Emily captivated me when she articulated in brilliant detail the racially charged nuances of one of the performances. It was LA Pride weekend, so, after dinner, a few of us drove all over, looking for parties, which in each instance had ended hours before we arrived. But the party was in the adventure, not the destination. After the others headed back to their hotels, Emily and I hit a twenty-four-hour diner for breakfast at four in the morning. I asked her how she identified, and she replied, "Like you, I'm pansexual and polyamorous." I was intrigued.

A couple days later, when she arrived in Oakland after I had already returned, I picked her up from the bus station. I just wanted to see her again, carry her bag, and give her a ride home. It was the last two weeks of Pride Month in San Francisco, and we kept hitting each other up to attend various events. Both compact in size and compatible in many ways, we found that we had much in common besides being hapa. A Pilates instructor, personal trainer, trapeze artist, and circus performer, Emily shared my love for swimming, hiking, writing, and performance. One night, over Spanish tortilla and sangria, I asked her if she would help me with my performance at the upcoming Trans March. After I read her my piece, she made astute suggestions, which I thought were spot-on. I found myself gazing at her beautiful features as the words fell from her lips, thinking, *Oh, shit, I'm gonna fall in love with her.* By the time I performed on the Trans March stage a few days later and we marched in celebration of trans pride, we were radiant with the buzz of our newfound connection.

Whether we were staying up late at my place or laughing at live performances, we had so much fun together. We found ourselves surprisingly in sync on multiple levels: in our racial nonconformity, our strong queer identities, and our sexual compatibility. I loved that she was both queer and attracted to men, and that she had been down with trans issues for years. Emily embraced my maleness as an inherent part of who I was, without the need for explanation, modification, or justification. She said that she appreciated my ability to recognize her queerness in a way that no cisgender, straight man ever had, and without the prejudice and rejection that she had experienced from some lesbians for being attracted to both women and men.

I never thought I would get laid while I had a catheter. It was unexpectedly exquisite to find someone with whom I could celebrate my trans journey. Psyche and body became one as I integrated my new body part, connecting my brain and lifelong imagination with the mind-blowing sensations of my virgin flesh. As my nerve endings lit up like a Christmas tree, I felt the electricity of our heteroqueer connection.

When Emily went to a presurgical doctor's appointment with me at the crack of dawn, Georgia was impressed with her kind heart and remarked, "That's all I need to know about her." Since Emily was going to be caring for me after surgery, Georgia and I decided to introduce her to the kids. Emily brought Georgia jam that she had made from apricots she grew in her garden, and Georgia gave her a big, welcoming hug. The next day, when Georgia went to Southern California to spend time with her new butch, Amy, Emily and I and the kids splashed, played, and giggled in a beautiful lake. Emily knew exactly how to engage each one of them in age-appropriate ways. I basked in the warmth and effervescent smiles that surrounded me.

*   *   *

Four months after Georgia and I broke up, we had our first double date, Georgia and Amy, Emily and I. We ate, shared stories, laughed, cared for the kids, and celebrated our newfound love.

Over the summer, it was beautiful to see the kids playing with such levity. Georgia and I were no longer transmitting our stress to them; there was happiness all around. When the kids went back to school in late August, the new principal pulled Georgia aside and said, "I want to give you a hug. Your kids are so happy and well adjusted." She didn't even know we had divorced.

When Georgia published her article about accepting my transition, I enjoyed the five minutes during which we were the poster children for long-term trans love. But our relationship shifted, and, rather than being a devastating experience, it has been an opportunity for growth. As we move forward, I'm going to work hard to ensure that we continue to prioritize our kids' best interests, support each other to live as our true selves, and be family to each other in new and different ways. I hope that as a community we always remember that we have resilience, and that love can multiply when we live our lives authentically.

GETTING FED

At one point on our cross-country bike trip so many years ago, after a long, grueling ride, my friend Checka and I arrived in a small Kansas town in the early evening and were disappointed to discover that there was no lodging for rent. We knocked on the door of a house with clucking chickens and a vibrant vegetable garden and asked the small family if we could camp in their backyard, though we knew the temperature was expected to drop to thirty degrees that night. The woman who answered exclaimed, "No, but you can camp inside!" She had had a vision that someone was coming and had been cooking all day. I ate a hearty steak for dinner, slept in a warm bed, and in the morning enjoyed the best grits of the trip.

The journey is long, but sometimes you get fed along the way.

DIVINE

Revel in your authenticity
Bring the reveal
Showcase it
Strut it
Dress how you feel
Gimme your swagger
your skin ink sleeve
that high hair
or care bear
or long-ass weave
boy girl or girl boy
brown skin with pink swirls
queer Asian eyes
short skirt twinkle twirl
big hips and small hands
white t-shirts and chains
people of size
black leather and canes

Trans beauty is us
It's you and it's they
Let's celebrate our fierceness
And this awesome new day
You're handsome

and beautiful
and studly
and fine
Keep being yourself
You are the divine

Stomp it tone it
Thick black boots own it
Smooth it hone it
shout it condone it
pluck it paint it
shine and delight
smile in the morning
groove in the night
salsa merengue
hip hop the ghetto
swish skin to skin in
red-hot stilettos

Trans beauty is us
It's you and it's they
Let's celebrate our fierceness
And this awesome new day
You're handsome
and beautiful
and studly
and fine
Keep being yourself
You are the divine

When you can't leave the house
And it's hard to be out
Just know that the mirror
Applauds you, no doubt
Mixed signals, high fashion

Just gives you more clout
Uniqueness is treasured
So give this a shout

Trans beauty is us
It's you and it's they
Let's celebrate our fierceness
And this awesome new day
You're handsome
and beautiful
and studly
and fine
Keep being yourself
Cuz *you are the divine*

THE
CUTTING
EDGE

ORGANIZATIONAL ASSESSMENT TOOLS

Culture is defined as "the integrated pattern of thoughts, communications, actions, customs, beliefs, values, and institutions associated, wholly or partially, with racial, ethnic, or linguistic groups, as well as with religious, spiritual, biological, geographical, or sociological characteristics."[121] Cultural competency refers to the ability to understand, communicate with, and effectively interact with diverse populations. It can be measured by awareness, attitude, knowledge, skills, behaviors, policies, procedures, and organizational systems. The goal of cultural competency work is to treat everyone as an individual and to develop a better understanding of population groups (racial/ethnic, disability, or LGBTQ, for example) while providing equal access to those who have been historically marginalized. It is fundamentally about holding another human being's cultural framework as authentic to them and accepting their perspective without question, judgment, or revision. Cultural competency involves seeking out knowledge, harnessing tools, speaking the appropriate language, and developing practical skills and systems that honor these truths on a large scale.

Critiques of the concept of cultural competency highlight concerns that people sometimes view the work as short term, or that power imbalances are not addressed. The term "cultural humility," which emerged in a 1998 article, emphasizes self-evaluation and nonpaternalistic approaches.[122] Though both concepts recognize the need to develop an understanding of and respect for diverse cultures and experiences, I prefer the term "cultural competency." In my work in health service settings, I don't ask providers to be humble, meek, or submissive, or to have a modest opinion of their importance (humility by definition). While a humble attitude may be helpful for those who exhibit unexamined entitlement, I prefer to emphasize skills development, respectful practice, and systemic tools. If people are to be expected to subjugate themselves in order to demonstrate cultural humility, I find the concept potentially disempowering for both the provider and the client.

To be sure, cultural competency is not something you learn in an afternoon workshop, in a training series, or in one book or class. It's a lifelong process of engagement. It's a travelogue of infinite destinations, a commitment to exploration with an open mind, a journey that traverses the landscape of the heart. Cultural competency involves the concrete integration of practical skills and the ingenuity and dedication to develop and implement systems that ensure fairness, consistency, and a nondiscriminatory environment.

The CLAS Standards

Health inequities in the United States and around the world are well documented. The provision of services that are respectful of and responsive to the health beliefs, practices, and needs of diverse patients, tailored to an individual's cultural framework and linguistic preferences, can help close the gap in health disparities. Dignity and quality of care are the rights of all, not the privileges of a few.

With these ideals in mind, in 2013 the US Office of Minority Health released enhanced Culturally and Linguistically Appropriate Services (CLAS) Standards, which updated the original standards, first released in 2000. The enhanced CLAS Standards are fifteen guidelines for improving quality of care and advancing health equity through effective governance, training, culturally and linguistically appropriate communication, community engagement, and accountability. The new standards expand the concept of culture well beyond the domain of racial and ethnic groups (though certainly key cultural competency areas) to include a total of twenty-five categories for culture. In addition to immigration status, age, disability, geographic location, and other cultural groups, sexual orientation and gender identity are included for the first time. Though the CLAS Standards originated in reference to health care settings, they also recognize the broad audience that can benefit from a cultural competency approach, moving beyond a limited scope of health care providers to include educators and anyone working in community health in some capacity. I believe that the need for cultural competency and the relevance of the CLAS Standards extends much further, throughout all of society.

Over the past three decades, I have worked with community health organizations, educational institutions, businesses, governmental agencies, county health departments, social justice organizations, faith-based institutions, prisons, and other groups to help develop staff and organizational cultural competency on LGBTQ, Asian American, and disability issues. In my work creating equal access for LGBTQ populations, with an emphasis on trans and gender-nonconforming individuals and families, I've observed that many entities share similar areas of concern. Based on these experiences providing training and consultation services, I've developed cultural competency organizational assessment tools for three key entities: community health organizations, educational institutions, and businesses. I've chosen to focus on transgender cultural competency issues, since that is an area that especially poses challenges for many organizations, institutions, and companies.

A Note on Pronouns

Appropriate pronoun use is an essential part of building rapport with trans and gender-nonconforming people. Examples of pronouns include "she"/"her"/"hers," "he"/"him"/"his," and "they"/"them"/"theirs." Inappropriate pronoun use creates a barrier to access; it can be interpreted as disrespect, bias, and discrimination and can lead to distrust. When people are not referred to appropriately, they may delay or avoid interacting with those who they perceive as not respecting their gender identity, and thus may not access the care or services they need.

What do you do when you are unsure about how to address a person with regard to pronouns or gendered terms? I encourage training groups to ask politely and privately for clarification. You can ask, "What pronoun is appropriate?" "How would you like to be addressed?" "I'd like to show you respect. How would you like me to refer to you?" While there is no perfect handbook on how to navigate these interactions, generally people would rather that you ascertain the appropriate language than get it wrong or dance around the issue. One approach is to use gender-neutral language, such as the person's last name in clinic waiting rooms, and skip "ma'am" and "sir" altogether. Though it's sometimes necessary, it can be linguistically tedious and awkward to avoid pronouns or repeat the person's name. Awkward language use can come across as discomfort with the individual and can be interpreted as bias.

Find out what's appropriate, and document this information systemically so the person doesn't get asked repeatedly. When you're aware that you have made a mistake, recover gracefully. Apologize briefly and move on. Appropriate name and pronoun use is a respectful practice and demonstrates a commitment to equity for trans and gender-nonconforming people.

Reexamining How We Talk About Pronouns

Though many people in trans and gender-nonconforming communities, and our allies, use the term "preferred gender pronoun," or "PGP," I do not subscribe to the concept. Over the years, I have educated training groups that the '70s term "sexual preference" was outdated, inaccurate, and offensive because one's inherent sexual orientation did not play out like a flippant choice on a sandwich menu ("I'll take one of those, or maybe I prefer one of those"). Similarly, the concept of preference in relation to one's appropriate pronouns is also inaccurate and offensive. Just as sexual orientation is an innate part of a person, one's appropriate pronouns are intrinsic and true—not a whim or passing fancy to be cast aside at a later time. Indeed, some people who are exploring their gender identity or are flexible with regard to their pronouns may feel that the concept of preference is accurate for them. Yet, given the multiple ways in which trans and gender-nonconforming people are dismissed and disrespected as inauthentic, I have always found it problematic and surprising that the trans community has adopted a concept that suggests that our gender identities are insubstantial rather than profoundly necessary, superficial rather than inherent. When we perpetuate the idea that the very essence of a trans person's deeply felt, gendered soul is nothing but a *preference*, and that we just *prefer* to be recognized as our true selves, we are setting ourselves up to be disbelieved, disregarded, and dehumanized. We deserve better than that.

Some years ago, and to some extent currently, the general public thought that gay people had a sexual preference—just gay people, of course, not straight people. As trans people, we use pronouns like everyone else; they're *appropriate* pronouns, not *preferred* pronouns. When we use the language of PGPs, what we are literally saying is that we are giving people permission to opt out of recognizing who we are and referring to us appropriately. Though we are accustomed to being treated as if our gender expressions are inconvenient for others, we do not need to perpetuate our own subjugation. I encourage the transgender community to reexamine a practice that I believe is in direct opposition to the key messaging of the movement for transgender equality.

The Tools

In each category that follows, a series of fifteen question blocks will assess your community health organization, educational institution, or business based on transgender cultural competency issues. This is not a comprehensive list, and the questions may not apply to all entities that share these broad categories. These tools help identify training needs and shine a light on systems that may need updating.

Community Health Organizations

Community health organizations—broadly defined to include medical, mental health, substance use disorder, public health, and other entities that provide health-related services—face varied challenges in providing trans-affirming care and services. Many are recognizing the need to develop clear policies and procedures, provide regular staff training on how to navigate interactions and procedures respectfully, conduct data collection, and manage the data appropriately. Substance use disorder treatment organizations, shelters, and others that provide residential accommodations often have questions about how best to educate their client populations.

Trans people have the right to receive services in accordance with their gender identity, regardless of the name and gender on their identification or medical record, and their hormonal or surgical status. This includes all gender-specific settings, such as support groups, restrooms, residential treatment, bed placement, urinalysis, etc. It's important to have a clear policy that staff at all levels understand, and skilled staff who can handle complexities on a case-by-case basis.

Electronic health records in large health care institutions present an ongoing challenge. The goal is to create a concise, feasible method for identifying a person's sex and gender that enables transgender people to see and identify themselves, minimizes confusion by the general cisgender population, and obtains answers readily and accurately from all populations in all programs. While it's important that the data are available throughout the system so that trans people don't repeatedly get asked about their name and pronoun, and so providers have identity and medical information that is relevant to care, this information exchange must be balanced with client/patient/consumer concerns about confidentiality.

The Center of Excellence for Transgender Health, a program of UC San Francisco, recommends a two-part gender question in health care settings.[123] For example, one approach is as follows:

1) What is your current gender identity? (Check all that apply.)
- ❑ Male
- ❑ Female
- ❑ Transgender male
- ❑ Transgender female
- ❑ Genderqueer
- ❑ Additional cwategory, (please specify): _____
- ❑ Decline to state

2) What was your assigned sex at birth? (Check one.)
- ❑ Male
- ❑ Female
- ❑ Decline to state

PART I: IDENTIFYING AREAS THAT NEED IMPROVEMENT

1) Does your community health organization exemplify a demonstrated commitment to the CLAS Standards, with the recognition of the importance of developing cultural competency on the issue of gender identity?

2) Are there visible signs on your organization's website and in your facilities (waiting room, counseling or treatment rooms, staff offices, etc.) that you are welcoming to trans and gender-nonconforming people? Are there posters, brochures, health education materials, flyers, resources, and/or media about transgender issues?

3) Do you provide regular transgender cultural competency training for staff at all levels of your organization?

4) Do your staff have a thorough understanding of the spectrum of gender identity and demonstrate respectful practice when engaging with transgender clients/patients/consumers?

5) Do you collect data on gender identity? Do you collect data on appropriate pronouns? Is there an "additional name" field to capture a chosen name, which may be different from the name on the client's/patient's/consumer's identification or medical record?

6) Do trans people access services in accordance with their gender identity? This includes all gender-specific settings, such as support groups, restrooms, residential accommodations, bed placement, urinalysis, etc.

7) Are there staff, board members, members of your advisory committees, and/or volunteers who openly identify as trans? Do they have decision-making power and/or leadership opportunities?

8) Do your referral sources include programs that provide culturally competent services for transgender individuals?

9) Do you provide client education on transgender issues in a manner that does not breach the confidentiality of trans clients or require them to educate?

10) Has your community health organization built effective partnerships with organizations that serve transgender individuals and families? Does your agency have a visible presence at transgender events?

11) Does your organization partner with trans community members to design, implement, and evaluate policies, practices, and services to ensure transgender cultural competency?

12) Does your organization conduct regular assessments of transgender community assets and needs and use the data to determine, plan, and implement services for the community?

13) Does your organization's nondiscrimination policy include explicit language that states that you do not discriminate on the basis of gender identity?

14) Does your organization have a system for addressing grievances that can identify, prevent, and resolve conflicts or complaints?

15) Do you communicate the organization's progress in implementing trans-affirming care and services to all stakeholders, constituents, and the general public?

PART II: ASSESSING YOUR ORGANIZATION'S CULTURAL COMPETENCY

Does your organization or institution provide equal access for trans and gender-nonconforming populations? How does it rate?

Hostile: Trans and gender-nonconforming individuals feel as if the organization is antagonistic to them. Staff and administrators make disparaging remarks and/or make inappropriate assumptions about trans people.

Don't Ask, Don't Tell: There is no acknowledgment of transgender issues. It is assumed that everyone is not transgender or gender-nonconforming.

Naive: There is some realization of the presence of trans people, but the organization has not explicitly addressed trans issues.

Tolerant: Some staff may support transgender issues, but such discussions are limited to these individuals, rather than occurring within the organization as a whole. There are no programs that specifically serve trans and gender-nonconforming individuals.

Sensitive: There are programs serving trans and gender-nonconforming individuals, but transgender issues are addressed only in transgender groups, not in other groups that serve the larger community.

Welcoming: Transgender and gender-nonconforming individuals receive ample cues that the organization welcomes them. Policies, forms, and staff behavior demonstrate a thorough commitment to trans access. Transgender issues are addressed in all programs.

PART III: NEXT STEPS

What can you do to make your organization more trans-affirming, increase feelings of trust and safety, and improve care and services for trans people? What changes would you make to your organization's policies, practices, and programs to ensure a nondiscriminatory service environment?

Educational Institutions

Educational institutions, including colleges, universities, vocational schools, K–12 schools, and preschools, are responding to the needs of a growing population of transgender, gender-nonconforming, and gender-expansive students. Administrators may experience challenges with creating a welcoming environment for these students, out of uncertainty about how to proceed, fear of reaction from the larger community, and/or personal bias. Since discussion about the needs of children of trans parents has been limited, these institutions may not be prepared to support students whose parent or caregiver has a trans identity and/or transitions. In addition, trans and gender-nonconforming faculty and staff need systemic support.

Some of the key issues that arise in college and university settings include a lack of culturally competent faculty; problems with student identification systems; a need for culturally competent mental health and medical providers on campus; and access to gender-specific settings, such as housing, restrooms, locker rooms, athletics, and sororities/fraternities.

Many institutions find it challenging to get faculty to attend professional development workshops on transgender issues. While personal bias and disinterest are factors, time constraints play a role. For example, faculty members who have limited time on campus, such as at community colleges, may have difficulty making time for these vital learning opportunities.

Perhaps the most challenging systemic issues in campus settings are the tremendous hurdles that students generally experience when they want to change their name and gender on their student record and identification card. Whereas difficulties updating electronic health records can lead to instances of cultural incompetency in health care settings, difficulties updating student records can create situations that are upsetting and feel unsafe for trans and gender-nonconforming students. For instance, when a trans student's appropriate name is not reflected on the student roster and the faculty member calls out the old name in class, the student may be outed as trans. Moreover, a student ID that does not reflect trans students' current name and appearance can make it difficult for them to participate fully in campus life, and can potentially put these students at risk for ridicule, harassment, and violence.

K–12 schools also benefit from trans-affirming faculty, staff, and administrators; restroom, locker room, and athletics access; and the ability to change student records. Challenges in schools involve understanding the needs of trans and gender-expansive kids at varying age levels, working with parents and caregivers who have different ideas about how to respond to their child's gender expression, and navigating reactions from the larger community of parents and caregivers. (For more ideas about creating LGBTQ- and trans-affirming schools, see the chapter entitled "Celebrating a Parent's Transition in an Elementary School Setting.")

PART I: IDENTIFYING AREAS THAT NEED IMPROVEMENT

1) Are there visible signs on your website; in flyers, brochures, posters, educational materials, and resource referrals; and in counseling rooms, staff offices, etc., that your campus or school is welcoming to queer, trans, gender-nonconforming, and gender-expansive people?

2) Do faculty, staff, and administrators receive regular training on transgender issues? Do they have a thorough understanding of the spectrum of gender identity and the needs of trans, gender-nonconforming, and gender-expansive students?

3) Are there academic departments that address transgender issues? If so, do they extend beyond queer studies, transgender studies, and gender and women's studies departments?

4) Are there clear policies for changing name and gender on student records and identity documents? Is there an "additional name" option on registration forms?

5) Are there faculty, staff members, and administrators who openly identify as trans? Do they have leadership roles and/or decision-making power? Are institutional policies and the campus climate supportive of trans and gender-nonconforming faculty and staff?

6) Are jokes and pejorative comments about trans and gender-nonconforming individuals that are made in class or in administrative offices challenged as inappropriate and disrespectful to this population?

7) Are transgender students welcome to participate in gender-specific activities, such as restrooms, locker rooms, sports teams, sororities/fraternities, and support groups?

8) Does your educational institution have a clear policy for appropriately accommodating transgender students in student housing?

9) Are there on-campus resources for trans and gender-nonconforming students, such as support groups, a resource center, discussions, events, and other activities? Do you empower students to build leadership skills in the development and implementation of these programs?

10) Do counselors, mental health providers, and other campus health providers ask students if they are exploring or questioning their gender identity? Do students feel comfortable discussing their gender identity and experience? Are mental health provid-

ers equipped to assess readiness for medical transition, including hormones, surgeries, and other procedures?

11) Does your campus health plan provide a transition-related care benefit, including mental health services, hormones, surgery, and other transition-related procedures?

12) Are medical providers at the student health center equipped to treat transgender medical concerns? Do they have medical competency to address postsurgical complications?

13) Do you provide referrals to community resources that meet the needs of and are welcoming to transgender individuals and families?

14) Does your campus have a number of gender-neutral restrooms? Have you conducted an educational process to help the larger campus community understand why gender-neutral restrooms are vitally important?

15) Are campus religious and spiritual organizations welcoming to transgender and gender-nonconforming individuals?

PART II: ASSESSING YOUR EDUCATIONAL INSTITUTION'S CULTURAL COMPETENCY

Does your educational institution provide equal access for trans and gender-nonconforming populations? How does it rate?

Hostile: Transgender individuals feel as if the educational institution is antagonistic toward them.

Don't Ask, Don't Tell: There is no acknowledgment of transgender issues. It is assumed that everyone is not transgender or gender-nonconforming.

Naive: There is some realization of the presence of trans and gender-nonconforming people, but the campus or school has not explicitly addressed transgender issues.

Tolerant: Some faculty and staff may support trans issues, but such discussions are limited to these individuals, rather than occurring within the educational institution as a whole. There are few or no academic support programs or policies that specifically serve trans individuals.

Sensitive: There are programs serving trans individuals, but trans issues are addressed only in transgender groups and programs, not in other groups that serve the larger community.

Welcoming: Transgender and gender-nonconforming individuals receive ample cues that the campus welcomes them. Policies, programs, and faculty and staff behavior demonstrate a thorough commitment to creating a nondiscriminatory environment for transgender, gender-nonconforming, and gender-expansive individuals.

PART III: NEXT STEPS

What can you do to make your educational institution more trans-affirming, increase feelings of trust and safety, and improve the school or campus climate for trans, gender-nonconforming, and gender-expansive individuals? What changes would you make to your campus or school policies, procedures, and programs to create a nondiscriminatory educational setting?

Businesses

As previously stated, Title VII of the Civil Rights Act of 1964 is a federal law that prohibits employment discrimination based on sex, race, color, national origin, and religion. Title VII applies to employers with fifteen or more employees, including federal, state, and local governments; private and public colleges or universities; employer agencies; and labor organizations. Almost all public- and private-sector employees and job applicants are covered under Title VII.

In the landmark April 2012 *Macy v. Holder* decision, a case brought by Transgender Law Center, the Equal Employment Opportunity Commission (EEOC) ruled that antitrans bias is sex discrimination under Title VII. It is unlawful to discriminate with respect to compensation, terms, conditions, or privileges of employment based on sex, which includes gender identity and expression.[124]

Some of the ways in which businesses create a trans-affirming workplace include working with a transitioning employee to develop an individualized transition plan; providing equal access to restrooms and changing rooms; removing gendered expectations associated with dress codes; changing official records and providing identity documents in a timely manner, regardless of legal gender change or appearance; providing regular staff training; and providing health insurance that covers transition-related care.

Perhaps the most challenging issue in business settings is respectfully navigating an employee's gender transition, including having management provide leadership and helping staff at all levels to understand and respond appropriately. Transitioning employees should make their transition known to a manager, such as the human resources (HR) manager, who can serve as a point person to help facilitate the process. If the HR manager is not the point person, they should refer the employee to the appropriate person, such as another manager. The employee should meet with all staff (such as the employee's supervisor and HR manager) involved in the workplace transition in order to create a customized transition plan. All people involved should familiarize themselves with company policies and have a clear sense of the transition timeline.

The workplace transition plan should address the date of official transition (which may include changes to name and pronouns, restrooms and locker rooms, ID badge, e-mail address, and other factors). There should be a plan for communicating with all staff about the employee's transition. The plan can address staff training, updates to records, changes in e-mail address, and medical leave for transition-related care. Staff training should occur before the official date of transition. It's best for management to announce the transition in an in-person meeting, if possible, and by respectfully modeling appropriate name and pronoun use. Emphasize the employee's importance at the company, provide concrete information about how to refer to the employee appropriately, discuss any other relevant changes, ensure that business will go on as usual, and respond effectively to questions.[125]

PART I: IDENTIFYING AREAS THAT NEED IMPROVEMENT

1) Does your business have a clear written policy that states that you will not discriminate on the basis of sex, gender identity, and gender expression?

2) Does your business have a clear policy that provides access to gender-specific settings and workplace assignments in accordance with people's gender identity and expression?

3) Do employees have access to the restroom that is congruent with their gender identity and expression? Are unisex, single-stall restrooms an option for those who desire privacy?

4) Do employees have access to the locker room that aligns with their gender identity? Is a private, alternative changing area made available?

5) Are employees allowed to comply with company dress codes in a manner that is consistent with their gender identity and expression?

6) Does your business provide a health insurance plan for its employees and access to transition-related care, including hormone replacement therapy, transition-related surgery, mental health counseling, and other transition-related procedures?

7) Does your business have a clear written policy that specifies the right to privacy for transgender and gender-nonconforming employees?

8) Does your business have a clear written policy that specifies what is required in order to change one's name and gender on official records? Can employees change their name on official records without proof of a legal name change? Can photos on identification documents be changed in a timely manner?

9) Do you have a written policy that states that employees have the right to be referred to by the appropriate name and pronoun, regardless of the name and gender on their ID or whether or not they've gone through a legal name and gender change?

10) Do management and the human resources department support transitioning employees? Can transitioning employees expect that management will help them develop an individualized transition plan, including which staff persons will be available to assist the employee, a plan for communicating with other staff about the transition, adjustments to personnel and administrative records, and changes to procedures?

11) Is your business prepared to schedule transgender cultural competency training in order to improve job performance, work more effectively with the community, and/or support a transitioning employee?

12) Does your business extend itself to transgender organizations with in-kind donations of goods and services, in an effort to build community networks and develop its transgender cultural competency?

13) Does your company have an LGBTQ employee affinity group that helps ensure support for transgender employees? LGBTQ

employee groups can partner with management to develop and implement LGBTQ-affirming policies and practices; develop LGBTQ-affirming programming and visibility; and help with recruitment, business strategies, and leadership development.[126]

14) Does your business contact LGBTQ campus and professional organizations to ensure LGBTQ recruitment? Do you specifically recruit trans employees by attending transgender job fairs and submitting job announcements though transgender community networks?

15) Does your business have a clear policy on and response to discrimination, harassment, or violence based on actual or perceived gender identity? Does your business investigate all allegations; determine suitable corrective action; and access relevant resources, including staff training on transgender issues?

PART II: ASSESSING YOUR BUSINESS'S CULTURAL COMPETENCY

Is your business a trans-affirming workplace? How does it rate?

Hostile: Transgender employees feel as if the workplace is antagonistic toward them.

Don't Ask, Don't Tell: There is no acknowledgment of transgender issues. It is assumed that no employees are transgender or gender-nonconforming.

Naive: There is some realization of the presence of trans and gender-nonconforming employees, but the company has not explicitly addressed transgender issues.

Tolerant: Some company staff may support trans issues, but such discussions are limited to these individuals, rather than occurring within the company as a whole. There are few or no company policies or programs that specifically support trans individuals.

Sensitive: There are programs serving trans individuals, but transgender issues are addressed only by the LGBTQ employee group, not company-wide.

Welcoming: Transgender and gender-nonconforming employees receive ample cues that the company welcomes them. Policies, programs, and management and staff behavior demonstrate a thorough commitment to creating a nondiscriminatory workplace for transgender and gender-nonconforming employees.

PART III: NEXT STEPS

What can you do to make your business more trans-affirming, increase employee satisfaction, and improve the workplace for trans and gender-nonconforming employees? What changes would you make to your business policies, procedures, and programs to create a nondiscriminatory workplace?

You Know What Time It Is

1. The word "dyke" is used affectionately to describe a lesbian of any gender expression. When Dykes on Bikes wanted to patent their name, the US Patent and Trademark Office rejected their application, on the grounds that the term "dyke" was disparaging. With assistance from the National Center for Lesbian Rights, they appealed twice, with hundreds of pages of testimony about how the word "dyke" was a positive, empowering, and affirming term. The Trademark Office granted the application in December 2005.

2. My coeditor was Kitty Tsui, author of *The Words of a Woman Who Breathes Fire* (San Francisco: Spinsters Ink, 1983), the first book published by an out Chinese American lesbian.

3. The Dragon Club, which ran between 1995 and 2000, was a support group for Asian and Pacific Islander butches and female-to-male- (FTM)-identified people, in partnership with Asian & Pacific Islander Wellness Center in San Francisco. The support group for FTMs of color was held monthly at the Pacific Center in Berkeley between 2000 and 2003. I started the Trannyfags Project, an HIV prevention program for transmasculine people who were exploring sex with other men, at STOP AIDS Project in San Francisco in 1999. With 523 participants, the groundbreaking research project on the transgender community, which began in 1997, was the largest-scale study of the transgender community in the world at the time. I documented this participatory action research project, conducted by the San Francisco Department of Public Health, in *Transgender Rights*.

4. See the chapter "Swim Junkie" for a discussion of restroom and locker room access. "Naming My Destiny" and "Celebrating a Parent's Transition in an Elementary School Setting" address improving access for LGBTQ students and families in K–12 schools.

5. See the chapter "Embodying a Changing Landscape."

6. Ann P. Haas, Philip L. Rogers, and Jody L. Herman, "Suicide Attempts Among Transgender and Gender Nonconforming Adults," the Williams Institute, 2014.

7. Mitch Kellaway, "Trans Teen Activist, Former Homecoming King, Dies in Charlotte, N.C," *The Advocate*, March 24, 2015. "Following the reported death of Alcorn, as well as three young trans men, 23-year-old Jay Ralko, 24-year-old Andi Woodhouse, and 17-year-old Riley Moscatel, last year, the first quarter of 2015 saw the reported suicides of Taylor Wells, 18, March 15 in Springfield, Ill.; Aubrey Mariko Shine, 22, February 24 in San Francisco; Zander Mahaffey, 15, February 15 in Austell, Ga.; Melonie Rose, 19, February 11 in Laurel, Md.; and Ash Haffner, 16, February 26 in the same town as Blake Brockington—Charlotte, N.C."

8. Nillin Dennison, "Two More Communities Mourn Trans Deaths by Suicide; Both Reported in 24 Hour Period," *Planet Transgender*, September 30, 2015. These numbers are lower than the actual statistics. Anecdotally, there are many more trans suicides than get reported or counted.

9. Advancement Project, Equality Federation Institute, and Gay Straight Alliance Network. "Power in Partnerships: Building Connections at the Intersections of Racial Justice and LGBTQ Movements to End the School-to-Prison Pipeline," 2015.

10. Trans* Activists for Justice and Accountability (TAJA) Coalition, www.tajascoalition.org.

11. Mitch Kellaway and Sunnivie Brydum, "These are the U.S. Trans Women Killed in 2015," *The Advocate,* updated October 21, 2015. There is an additional victim, whose gender identity has been disputed by the media, family members, and activists: http://www.advocate.com/transgender/2015/07/27/these-are-trans-women-killed-so-far-us-2015.

12. Jen Richards, "Op-Ed: It's Time for Trans Lives to Truly Matter to Us All," *The Advocate*, February 18, 2015.

13. Garrett Epps, "What makes Indiana's Religious Freedom Law Different?" The *Atlantic*, accessed March 31, 2015, http://www.theatlantic.com/politics/archive/2015/03/what-makes-indianas-religious-freedom-law-different/388997/.

Scorched

14. "Scorched" was reprinted from Sharon Lim-Hing, ed., *The Very Inside: An Anthology of Writing by Asian and Pacific Islander Lesbian and Bisexual Women* (Toronto, Canada: Sister Vision Press, 1994).

Four Minutes to Midnight

15. Wikipedia, "Foot Binding," accessed May 14, 2015, http://en.wikipedia.org/wiki/Foot_binding.

16. Ibid.

17. Wikipedia, "Mormon Pioneers," accessed May 14, 2015, http://en.wikipedia.org/wiki/Mormon_pioneers.

Naming My Destiny

18. With an appreciative nod to the legendary June Jordan for the apropos title of this chapter.

Finding My Voice

19. E! Online, Star Boards, July 1998.

Professional Traveler

20. Though technically Lois is *mi hermana de nacimiento*, my birth sister, I still think of her fondly as *mi hermana de la concepción*, my conception sister. It has a ring to it.

21. Audre Lorde, *Sister Outsider* (Trumansburg, New York: The Crossing Press, 1984), 112.

Family Privilege

22. Caitlin Ryan, "Supportive Families, Healthy Children. Helping Families with Lesbian, Gay, Bisexual, and Transgender Children" (San Francisco: San Francisco State University, 2009), accessed May 12, 2015, http://familyproject.sfsu.edu/publications.

Reveling in Our Authenticity

23. The letter "T" is commonly used as an abbreviation for "testosterone."

24. "Transfeminism" describes the integration of transgender and feminist discourses, including the concepts that "biology is not destiny" and that people should not be confined by sex and gender norms.

So Far

25. Director Jules Rosskam, *Against a Trans Narrative*, 2009.

Turn of the Head

26. Ibid.

The Queering of CFIDS

27. Centers for Disease Control and Prevention, chronic fatigue syndrome case definition, accessed September 15, 2015, http://www.cdc.gov/cfs/case-definition/index.html.

28. Ananya Mandal, "Chronic Fatigue Syndrome History," *News Medical*, accessed September 15, 2015, http://www.news-medical.net/health/Chronic-Fatigue-Syndrome-History.aspx.

29. Two hundred of the town's twenty thousand residents came down with an extremely debilitating, flu-like illness. *Newsweek*, "Chronic Fatigue Syndrome," accessed September 15, 2015, http://www.newsweek.com/chronic-fatigue-syndrome-205712.

30. Wikipedia, "Alternative Names for Chronic Fatigue Syndrome," accessed September 16, 2015, https://en.wikipedia.org/wiki/Alternative_names_for_chronic_fatigue_syndrome.

31. Miriam E. Tucker, "Panel Says Chronic Fatigue Syndrome Is a Disease, and Renames It," National Public Radio, accessed September 15, 2015, http://www.npr.org/sections/health-shots/2015/02/11/385465667/panel-says-chronic-fatigue-syndrome-is-a-disease-and-renames-it.

32. Centers for Disease Control and Prevention, "Chronic Fatigue Syndrome: The 1994 Case Definition," accessed September 15, 2015, http://www.cdc.gov/cfs/case-definition/1994.html.

33. Hillary Johnson, *Osler's Web: Inside the Labyrinth of the Chronic Fatigue Syndrome Epidemic* (New York: Crown, 1996). Paul Cheney (96, 142); Dan Peterson (96); Robert Gallo (150); Anthony Komaroff (655–6); Nancy Klimas (158–9); Michael Holmes (660–1); Jay Levy (484); Carol Jessop (484); and Alan Landay (484) are some of the CFIDS researchers who have drawn connections between CFIDS and AIDS.

34. Charles W. Lapp, "Chronic Fatigue Syndrome Is a Real Disease," *North Carolina Family Physician* (winter 1992): 6–11.

35. Molly Holzschlag, "Congressional Testimony Smashes CFS Myths," *CFIDS Healthwatch* (summer 1995): 1.

36. Ibid., 4.

37. S. Dinos et al., "A systematic review of chronic fatigue, its syndromes and ethnicity: prevalence, severity, co-morbidity and coping," *International Journal of Epidemiology* 38, no. 6 (2009): 1554–70. The article indicated higher incidence among African Americans and Native Americans than among Caucasians.

38. Centers for Disease Control and Prevention, "Chronic Fatigue Syndrome: Who's at Risk?," accessed September 15, 2015, http://www.cdc.gov/cfs/causes/risk-groups.html; National Health Service, "Chronic Fatigue Syndrome," accessed September 15, 2015, http://www.nhs.uk/conditions/Chronic-fatigue-syndrome/Pages/Introduction.aspx.

39. Wikipedia, "Controversies Related to Chronic Fatigue Syndrome," accessed September 16, 2015, https://en.wikipedia.org/wiki/Controversies_related_to_chronic_fatigue_syndrome.

40. Wikipedia, "Xenotropic Murine Leukemia Virus-Related Virus," accessed September 16, 2015, https://en.wikipedia.org/wiki/Xenotropic_murine_leukemia_virus-related_virus.

41. Centers for Disease Control and Prevention, "Chronic Fatigue Syndrome: General," accessed September 16, 2015, http://www.cdc.gov/cfs/general/index.html.

42. Ibid. Countless researchers and medical providers agree that CFIDS does not appear to be contagious.

43. "Be your worst day" was an expression used among people I knew who were living with chronic illness, to remind us to embody how we felt on our sickest days so that authorities would believe that we were ill.

44. A number of doctors and researchers have received death threats. In one incident, Dr. Myra McClure, department head of Infectious Diseases at Imperial College in London, was threatened with being shot for publishing a study that showed no association between the retrovirus XMRV and CFIDS.

45. Patty Berne radio interview, KPOO *Reality Sandwich*, January 6, 2011.

46. Sins Invalid website, accessed September 13, 2015, http://www.sinsinvalid.org/mission.html.

47. As quoted in Annie Pentilla, "Embodying Our Humanity: Performance Project 'Sins Invalid' Promotes Disability Justice Through Live Performance Art," *Tikkun Daily*, December 31, 2014, http://www.truth-out.org/news/item/28301-embodying-our-humanity-sins-invalid-promotes-disability-justice-through-live-performance-arts.

48. As quoted in Nomy Lamm, "This Is Disability Justice," *The Body Is Not an Apology*, accessed September 13, 2015, http://thebodyisnotanapology.com/magazine/this-is-disability-justice/.

49. Queer Women of Color Media Arts Project, "About Us," accessed September 15, 2015, http://www.qwocmap.org/aboutus.html.

50. Project Open Hand, an organization that was originally founded in order to provide hot meals for people with AIDS, now serves people who are disabled by chronic diseases: www.projectopenhand.org.

Christopher, Badass Dragon

51. Christopher's chosen family includes Chino Scott-Chung, Maya Scott-Chung, Shivaun Nestor, Elise Hurwitz, Isa Abrahams, Trystan Cotten, Jae Carranza, Leeroy Joyce, Vega Darling, and Spencer F.

52. Jaime Grant, Lisa Mottet, and Justin Tanis, "Injustice at Every Turn: A Report of the National Transgender Discrimination Survey" (Washington, DC: National Center for Transgender Equality and the National Gay and Lesbian Task Force, 2011), accessed September 24, 2015, http://www.thetaskforce.org/downloads/reports/reports/ntds_full.pdf.

53. Haas et al.

54. Grant et al.

55. Haas et al.

56. Ibid.

57. T. E. Joiner, *Why People Die by Suicide* (Cambridge, MA: Harvard University Press, 2005).

58. Ronald W. Pies, MD, "Is Suicide Immoral?" *Psychiatric Times*, February 17, 2014.

Becoming Dada

59. The expression *gyro gyro* is Greek for "spinning around and around." We also use the expression *huli huli*, which means the same thing in Hawaiian, e.g., "*huli huli* chicken" for rotisserie chicken.

60. In October 2015, Baby Buds Generation #6 was beginning to form.

61. The film *A Womb of Their Own*, by Cyn Lubow, of Serious Play Films (to be released in 2016), features masculine female-bodied individuals who choose pregnancy. The film depicts me performing "The Poetry of Scars" at the 2015 San Francisco Trans March.

Winter of Love

62. Same-sex marriage became legal nationwide on June 26, 2015.

63. Fred Karger, "Mormongate—The Church's Cover-up of Its Prop 8 Funding," *Huffington Post*, accessed December 16, 2014, http://www.huffingtonpost.com/fred-karger/mormongate——the-churchs_b_163016.html.

64. The Church of Jesus Christ of Latter-Day Saints, "Same-Sex Marriage and Proposition 8," accessed December 16, 2014, http://www.mormonnewsroom.org/article/same-sex-marriage-and-proposition-8.

65. US Supreme Court opinion, *Obergefell v. Hodges*, accessed September 9, 2015, http://www.supremecourt.gov/opinions/14pdf/14-556_3204.pdf.

66. Sarah McBride et al., "We the People: Why Congress and U.S. States Must Pass Comprehensive LGBT Nondiscrimination Protections," Center for American Progress, December 2014.

67. "Beyond Marriage Equality: A Blueprint for Federal Non-Discrimination Protections" (Washington, DC: Human Rights Campaign, 2014), accessed December 16, 2014, http://www.hrc.org/campaigns/beyond-marriage-equality-a-blueprint-for-federal-non-discrimination-protect.

68. Americans with Disabilities Act of 1990, as amended, Section 12211, accessed December 16, 2014, http://www.ada.gov/pubs/adastatute08. htm#12211.

69. Chris Johnson, "More Pressure on Obama to Bar Workplace Discrimination," *Washington Blade*, accessed December 16, 2014, http://www.washingtonblade.com/2012/03/30/more-pressure-on-obama-to-bar-workplace-discrimination/.

70. Dana Beyer, Jillian T. Weiss, and Riki Wilchins, "New Title VII and EEOC Rulings Protect Transgender Employees," Transgender Law Center, accessed March 31, 2015, http://transgenderlawcenter.org/wp-content/uploads/2014/01/TitleVII-Report-Final012414.pdf.

71. András Tilcsik, "Pride and Prejudice: Employment Discrimination Against Openly Gay Men in the United States," *American Journal of Sociology*, accessed December 16, 2014, http://www.jstor.org/stable/10.1086/661653.

72. M. V. Badgett et al., "Bias in the Workplace: Consistent Evidence of Sexual Orienta-

tion and Gender Identity Discrimination," the Williams Institute, accessed January 27, 2015, http://web.stanford.edu/group/scspi/_media/pdf/key_issues/sexual_policy.pdf.

73. Sophia Kerby, "How Pay Inequity Hurts Women of Color," Center for American Progress, accessed December 16, 2014, http://www.americanprogress.org/issues/labor/report/2013/04/09/59731/how-payinequity-hurts-women-of-color/.

74. "When Health Care Isn't Caring: Lambda Legal's Survey of Discrimination Against LGBT People and People with HIV," accessed December 16, 2014, www.lambdalegal.org/health-care-report.

75. Grant et al.

76. Luke Brinker and Carlos Maza, "15 Experts Debunk Right-Wing Transgender Bathroom Myth," *Media Matters*, accessed December 16, 2014, http://mediamatters.org/research/2014/03/20/15-experts-debunk-rightwing-transgender-bathro/198533.

Celebrating a Parent's Transition in an Elementary School Setting

77. Visit www.welcomingschools.org for more information.

78. Visit www.collaborativeclassroom.org for more information.

79. "Schools in Transition: A Guide for Supporting Transgender Students in K-12 Schools," accessed September 9, 2015, https://www.genderspectrum.org/staging/wp-content/uploads/2015/08/Schools-in-Transition-2015.pdf.

80. Gay, Lesbian, and Straight Education Network and National Center for Transgender Equality, "Model District Policy on Transgender and Gender Nonconforming Students," accessed May 25, 2015, www.transequality.org.

81. "Toronto District School Board Guidelines for the Accommodation of Transgender and Gender Nonconforming Students and Staff," accessed May 25, 2015, www.ncgs.org.

82. Our Family Coalition website, accessed May 25, 2015, www.ourfamily.org.

83. COLAGE website, accessed May 25, 2015, www.colage.org.

84. Gender Spectrum website, accessed May 25, 2015, www.genderspectrum.org.

Swim Junkie

85. V. Dobnik, "Transgender man sues NYC over locker room access," *Yahoo! News* (Associated Press), June 3, 2014, http://news.yahoo.com/transgender-man-sues-nyc-over-locker-room-access-213404643.html.

86. A. T. Furuya uses gender-neutral "they"/"them"/"their" pronouns.

87. A. Sandeen, "Trans student allegedly told by SDSU staff person to get out of men's locker room," *LGBT Weekly,* January 22, 2015, http://lgbtweekly.com/2015/01/22/trans-student-allegedly-told-by-sdsu-staff-to-get-out-of-mens-locker-room/.

88. Transgender Law Center, "Big News! DOE guidance says transgender students protected under federal law," April 29, 2014, http://transgenderlawcenter.org/archives/10249.

89. Z. Ford, "Look at how this university responded after winning case against transgender student it expelled," *ThinkProgress*, April 2, 2015, http://thinkprogress.org/lgbt/2015/04/02/3642054/university-of-pittsburg-transgender-suit/.

90. United States Department of Education, Office for Civil Rights, "Questions and Answers on Title IX and Sexual Violence," April 29, 2014, http://www2.ed.gov/about/offices/list/ocr/docs/qa-201404-title-ix.pdf.

91. Ford.

92. Lambda Legal, "Changing birth certificate sex designations: state-by-state guidelines," February 23, 2015, http://www.lambdalegal.org/know-your-rights/transgender/changing-birth-certificate-sex-designations.

93. "Opinion, *Seamus Johnston v. University of Pittsburgh*," March 31, 2015, http://www.utimes.pitt.edu/documents/johnstonOpinion.pdf.

94. Ibid.

95. C. Charles, "Why I Am Afraid of the Bathroom." American Civil Liberties Union of Northern California, April 24, 2015, https://www.aclunc.org/blog/why-i-am-afraid-bathroom. States that have attempted to legalize discrimination, impose fines, and criminalize trans people for using restrooms include California, Massachusetts, Florida, Texas, Kentucky, Missouri, Arizona, and Nevada.

Embodying a Changing Landscape

96. Shannon Minter, "Foreword," in Trystan T. Cotten, ed., *Hung Jury: Testimonies of Genital Surgery by Transsexual Men* (Oakland, CA: Transgress Press, 2012).

97. State of California Department of Insurance, "Economic Impact Assessment: Gender Nondiscrimination Regulations," April 13, 2012.

98. Ibid.

99. Ibid.

100. W. Wilkinson, "Public health gains of the transgender community in San Francisco: Grassroots organizing and community-based research," in P. Currah, R. Juang, and S. Minter, eds., *Transgender Rights* (Minneapolis: University of Minnesota Press, 2006), 192–214.

101. K. Clements-Nolle, R. Marx, and M. Katz, "Attempted suicide among transgender persons: The influence of gender-based discrimination and victimization," *Journal of Homosexuality* 53, no. 3 (2006), 53–69.

102. Equality California, "AB 1586 Fact Sheet: Insurance Gender Non-discrimination Act," accessed May 18, 2015, http://www.eqca.org/site/apps/nlnet/content2.aspx?c=kuLRJ9MRKrH&b=4025609&ct=5195061.

103. The US Department of Labor, the Department of Health and Human Services, and the Treasury jointly issued guidelines in May 2015 clarifying that preventive screenings should be covered, without cost sharing, for trans people. See end of chapter.

104. This chapter should not be construed as a recommendation for any specific medical provider. Competencies, attitudes, and bedside manner vary among providers.

105. Stan J. Monstrey, Peter Ceulemans, and Piet Hoebeke, "Sex reassignment surgery in the female-to-male transsexual," *Seminars in Plastic Surgery* 25, no. 3 (2011): 229–44.

106. In some instances, lean ALT patients may get urethral lengthening in the first stage, but generally the full urethra is not complete until a later stage.

107. "The Nerve Hook-Up: Creating Sensation in a Free Flap Phalloplasty," accessed May 20, 2015, http://brownsteincrane.com/videos/.

108. Cinque, "Before and After," in Trystan T. Cotten, ed., *Hung Jury: Testimonies of Genital Surgery by Transsexual Men* (Oakland, CA: Transgress Press, 2012).

109. Grant et al. By gender, including people of all races, 26 percent of female-to-male transgender individuals and 29 percent of visually gender-nonconforming people report higher incidents of police harassment than male-to-female transgender individuals (20 percent).

110. Before Medicare claimed to cover transition-related care, it flat-out denied coverage, which allowed individuals to get coverage from Medi-Cal or another insurance plan that had removed trans exclusions.

111. E-mail communication from Dr. Marci Bowers, September 14, 2015.

112. Movement Advancement Project, "Healthcare Laws and Policies," accessed August 23, 2015, http://www.lgbtmap.org/equality-maps/healthcare_laws_and_policies. As of August 2015, Medicaid in eight states (California, Oregon, Colorado, Illinois, New York, Vermont, Massachusetts, and Connecticut) and the District of Columbia covered transition-related care. Sixteen states had Medicaid policies that specifically excluded transgender health coverage and care, and twenty-six states had no explicit policies on transgender health coverage and care.

113. Centers for Medicare & Medicaid Services, "FAQs About Affordable Care Act Implementation (Part XXVI)," accessed May 22, 2015, http://www.cms.gov/CCIIO/Resources/Fact-Sheets-and-FAQs/Downloads/aca_implementation_faqs26.pdf.

114. Movement Advancement Project, "Healthcare Laws and Policies," accessed August 23, 2015, http://www.lgbtmap.org/equality-maps/healthcare_laws_and_policies. As of August 2015, California, Oregon, Washington, Nevada, Colorado, Illinois, Vermont, Massachusetts, Connecticut, New York, and the District of Columbia prohibited health insurance issuers to deny or limit coverage based on gender identity and required the removal of transgender exclusions from health plans.

115. US Department of Health and Human Services, "Nondiscrimination in Health Programs and Activities Proposed Rule, Section 1557 of the Affordable Care Act," accessed September 3, 2015, http://www.hhs.gov/ocr/civilrights/understanding/section1557/nprmsummary.html. (This victory is a result of years of advocacy by the National Center for Transgender Equality and others.)

116. Without specific data on complications and outcomes, I am making an anecdotal assessment based on a small sample size of phallo patients with whom I have connected in person and online. Outcomes vary widely depending on when one had surgery, which surgeon performed the procedure, one's health status, and chance sensation.

117. Wilkinson.

118. K. Clements-Nolle et al., "HIV prevalence, risk behaviors, health care use, and mental health status of transgender persons: implications for public health intervention," *American Journal of Public Health* 81, no. 6 (2001): 915–21.

119. J. Graham et al., "Transgender Health Services: 1.5 Years of Surgery Access in SF," workshop presentation at the National Transgender Health Summit, Oakland, CA, April 18, 2015.

Beautiful Symmetry

120. Grant et al.

Organizational Assessment Tools

121. Office of Minority Health, "National Standards for Culturally and Linguistically Appropriate Services in Health and Health Care: A Blueprint for Advancing and Sustaining CLAS Policies and Practice" (Washington, D.C: US Department of Health and Human Services, 2013).

122. Melanie Tervalon and Jann Murray-Garcia, "Cultural Humility vs. Cultural Competence: A Critical Distinction in Defining Physician Training Outcomes in Multicultural Education," *Journal of Health Care for the Poor and Underserved* 9, no. 2 (1998): 117–25.

123. See "Recommendations for Inclusive Data Collection of Trans People in HIV Prevention, Care, and Services," Center of Excellence for Transgender Health, http://transhealth.ucsf.edu/trans?page=lib-data-collection.

124. Dana Beyer, Jillian T. Weiss, and Riki Wilchins, "New Title VII and EEOC Rulings Protect Transgender Employees," Transgender Law Center and Freedom to Work, 2014.

125. Transgender Law Center, "Model Transgender Employment Policy: Ensuring Inclusive Workplaces," 2014.

126. "Employee Groups," Human Rights Campaign, accessed October 31, 2015, http://www.hrc.org/resources/entry/employee-groups.

ACKNOWLEDGMENTS

I want to thank all the gender outlaws, racially nonconforming folks, queer rebels, and people with disabilities everywhere who daringly push the edges.

Thank you to my parents, Bob and May-Blossom Wilkinson, and my siblings, Su-Lin Wilkinson, Sunya Hutchison, and Steve Wilkinson, for believing in me as a writer.

Thank you to my editor, Brooke Warner, for her editorial and publishing expertise, and for giving me the tools to become an author. Much appreciation to her publishing team Annie Tucker, copyeditor, and Tabitha Lahr, designer.

Thank you, Georgia Kolias, for enduring years of inspiring conversations about this book, and for being a phenomenal editor.

Thank you, Emily Park, for her dedication, wisdom, and keen eye for details.

Thank you to my colleagues and friends Shannon Price Minter, Masen Davis, Chino and Maya Scott-Chung, Julia Serano, Kylar Broadus, Mitch Kellaway, Zander Keig, Jamison Green, Kris Hayashi, Tracy Nguyen, Mark Snyder, Susan Stryker, Janet Mock, julie graham, Judy Appel, Alberto Lammers, Kate Kendell, Patty Berne, Shivaun Nestor, Prado Gomez, Jai and Nela De Lotto, Charles Bennett, A. Scott Duane, Bobby Cheung, Fresh! White, Madalynn Rucker, Lilyane Glamben, Cecilia Chung, Jenna Rapues, and Alix Sabin for supporting this project.

Thank you, Red Envelope Giving Circle, An Goldbauer, and my parents, Bob and May-Blossom Wilkinson, for their financial support, and Our Family Coalition for its fiscal sponsorship.

Thank you to all the organizations featured in this book for supporting queer and trans people, and others on the margins. Please give to them generously.

Finally, I want to thank all the rabble-rousers, storytellers, artists, lawyers, providers, educators, students, business professionals, and others who demand dignity and respect for all.